MODERN
SURVIVAL

MODERN SURVIVAL

SURVIVAL

HOW TO COPE WHEN EVERYTHING FALLS APART

Barry Davies

Skyhorse Publishing

Skyhorse Publishing books may be purchased in bulk at special discounts for
sales promotion, corporate gifts, fund-raising, or educational purposes. Special
editions can also be created to specifications. For details, contact the Special
Sales Department, Skyhorse Publishing, 307 West 36th Street, 11th Floor,
New York, NY 10018 or info@skyhorsepublishing.com.

Skyhorse® and Skyhorse Publishing® are registered trademarks of Skyhorse
Publishing, Inc.®, a Delaware corporation.

Visit our website at www.skyhorsepublishing.com.

10 9 8 7 6 5 4 3 2 1

Library of Congress Cataloging-in-Publication Data

Davies, Barry, 1944-
  Modern survival : how to cope when everything falls apart / Barry Davies.
    p. cm.
  ISBN 978-1-61608-552-0 (pbk. : alk. paper)
1. Survival—Handbooks, manuals, etc. 2. Survival and emergency
equipment—Handbooks, manuals, etc. I. Title.
  GF86.D378 2011
  613.6′9—dc23
                        2011043764

ISBN: 978-1-61608-552-0

Printed in China

Disclaimer

The Author and the Publishers offer in good faith the information regarding the survival skills and techniques described in this book. They point out that some of these may be dangerous in certain circumstances. Therefore, they disclaim any liability for any injury which may result from employing these skills and techniques.

Readers should also note that these skills and techniques are for use in the context of emergency survival situations only. When practicing any of these skills and techniques, the relevant laws of the State, as well as all individual rights, must be strictly observed. The Author and the publisher are unable to accept any responsibility for proceedings of use, correct or otherwise, of these skills and techniques.

Before I undertook this project, I took serious legal advice regarding the reproduction of the photographs in this book. I have complied with the law and the various regulations required by other bodies. Where I do not hold the rights to the original, I have the owner's consent, or this consent has been published within their website. Where there has been doubt as to ownership, every reasonable effort has been made to locate the true owner of each picture.

Finally, the pictures in this book will hopefully help save the lives of many people, and for all those who have contributed, knowingly or unknowingly, I thank you.

CONTENTS

Chapter 4 — Forest & Wild Fires

Chapter 11 — Water and Food   213

Chapter 12 — Disaster First Aid and Emergency Care   237

DISASTER

It strikes anytime, anywhere. It takes many forms—a hurricane, an earthquake, a tornado, a flood, a fire, or a hazardous spill, an act of nature or an act of terrorism. It builds over days or weeks, or hits suddenly without warning. Every year, millions of Americans face disaster and its terrifying consequences. (FEMA)

INTRODUCTION AND OUTLINE CONCEPT

I was commissioned to write a modern survival book relating to disasters by Skyhorse Publishing at the start of February 2011. Most of my previous 'survival' books have been written along military lines, designed for those that challenged the great wild open spaces of our planet. You may ask yourself, "why the change of direction?" It's simple. The date is March 15, 2011, and there are earthquakes, tsunamis, floods, hurricanes, tornados, volcanic eruptions, wildfires, landsides, famine, unstable nuclear reactors, and wars killing or threatening millions of people around the world at this very moment. So, the purpose of this new book is to make 'survival' constructive and allow those that do endure a disaster to live on.

A month into the book, on Friday, March 11, 2011, at 2:46 in the afternoon, the largest recorded earthquake hit eighty miles off the Northeast coast of Japan. The resulting tsunami swept inland, causing unimaginable loss of life and damage. As it happened, television channels beamed the devastation around the world, flooding our homes with visual images of disaster. Sitting in my living room in the beautiful country of Spain, it was hard to comprehend the scale of the catastrophe, imagining the personal torment that would follow: the loss of loved ones, homes crushed under waves of sludge, and all the pain and agony that these people were going through. So great is the devastation, this book will be long finished before the Japanese people have recovered to anywhere near normal.

Japan, a nation known for being prepared for earthquakes, was caught off guard, and the resulting tsunami swept away entire villages under a sea of matchwood which drove inland. Unlike the flood that happened in Indonesia in December of 2004, which cost an estimated 150,000 lives, Japan had an early warning system in place—unfortunately, it still was not enough. As the alarm sounded, many took to their cars and headed inland for higher ground. The roads became blocked, and people simply drowned in their cars. To avoid further danger, and within minutes, most of Japan's nuclear reactors were shut down—unfortunately, it still was not enough. Some of the nuclear reactor plants were damaged and quickly became unstable; backup generators designed to cut-in should a five meter tsunami hit, were overwhelmed by the seven meter waves that swamped the generators. With no electrical power to pump the water that was needed to cool the reactors, and with back-up batteries that only had a life span of nine hours, Japan was in serious trouble.

I have spent a lifetime first learning, and then teaching survival skills. By serving for many years in Britain's Elite Special Forces, the SAS, I have learned to face death and the fear of death. I have traveled and operated in almost every part of the world where I have seen people survive on less than nothing in the most adverse conditions; I have battled in many small wars, and seen the devastation thrust upon innocent civilians. For the past twenty-seven years, I have worked as a consultant for the world's largest supplier of 'survival equipment,' BCB International Ltd. Almost every aircraft, ship or Special Forces soldier in the Western Hemisphere and beyond, holds a survival kit supplied by BCB International Ltd. So it is with these skills that I write a modern survival book. Even if it helps save the life of just one person in the future, it will be worth it.

Disasters, both natural and man-made, happen on a regular basis. When we witness the destructive power produced by a combination of an earthquake and tsunami, it simple highlights how vulnerable we are to Mother Nature and the folly of the human race. After each disaster or war, we always say the same thing, "this can never be allowed to happen again!"' But it does, and on a regular basis, showing that we rarely learn from history.

In January 2010, more than 230,000 people were killed when a 7.0 magnitude earthquake struck Haiti. Soon after that, there was an outbreak of cholera which produced another 3,333 deaths. Two years before, about 70,000 people were killed and 18,000 people were reported missing after a 7.9 magnitude earthquake struck Sichuan, China; while in December 2004, an earthquake with a magnitude of 9.0 triggered a tsunami that swept through the coastal regions of a dozen countries bordering the Indian Ocean. The death toll has been estimated at between 225,000 and 275,000. Of the half-million dead in just six years, over 28,000 were known to have been tourists or travelers. While these disasters account for many deaths, suffering has many faces; in January 2011, some 77,000 were trapped in Queensland, Australia, by the worst flooding in over 100 years. There was little or no warning for any of the above, little preparation, and for many, little chance of survival.

Apart from natural disasters, many men and women have found themselves in danger from a 'War Zone,' which in itself is a man-made disaster. Each year, thousands of brave young men and women in our armed forces risk their lives in Afghanistan, Iraq, Sudan, India, and Yemen, just a few of the countries currently suffering from war. As of the first of January 2011, the war in Afghanistan alone has taken the lives of 2,284 men and women; of these, 1,797 were either American or British, and many died or were severely injured from Improvised Explosive Devices (IEDs). Unfortunately, these war zones are not fought on battle-fields, but in cities where the population cowers as their homes and families are destroyed. In the aftermath, the survivors bury their dead, look for water and a safe place to shelter; disease and famine swiftly follow. Most of these people are innocent of any crime or misdoing, and are simply considered 'collateral damage.'

Strangely enough, the civil war in Libya started in February 2011, the same time as I started this book. The book is finished as is the war, with a death toll in excess of 10,000. So let us forget about survival books that are written for those who brave the great outdoors, and concentrate on what can be done should you find yourself in a disaster zone.

Survival is a basic instinct and generally means that something, usually unplanned, has happened that is a threat to your life. In such a case, we find ourselves in a totally unknown and unexpected situation or environment from which there is no immediate solution. The first day I walked into the barracks of the British Special Air Service (SAS) Regiment, I saw a sign that stated 'Knowledge Dispels Fear.' In this book, you will find why disasters happen, how to prepare for them, and how to survive. You will learn many new survival techniques, and hopefully, you will never have to use them; but always remember the words: 'Knowledge Dispels Fear.'

The advice in this book has been gleaned from many sources, all of which are relevant to the possible danger. For example, advice on how to survive a tsunami came from the people of Japan, and the survivors from Haiti explain how they escaped the devestating earthquake. From the soldiers operating in Afghanistan and Iraq, the advice on Improvised Explosive Devices (IEDs) came from the British or American military. For the rest, BCB International Ltd., of Cardiff, UK, whose knowledge base of survival is second to none, supplied all the relevant technical detail on equipment and techniques. To Professor Stephen Prior of Middlesex University, a fellow military observer, for his prodigious support. I thank each and every person that has contributed to this book.

FEDERAL EMERGENCY MANAGEMENT AGENCY (FEMA)

Having called on many agencies and organizations for advice or information, the one I found most useful was the Federal Emergency Management Agency (FEMA). FEMA can trace its origins back to the Congressional Act of 1803; an Act considered to be the first piece of disaster legislation. Since then, various legislations have been passed in response to earthquakes, hurricanes, floods, tornadoes, and other natural disasters. There were massive disasters in the late 1960s and early '70s which required a federal response to recovery operations. Yet, the responses remained fragmented with more than 100 agencies becoming involved in various disasters. President Carter's 1979 Executive Order #12127 merged many of the separate disaster-related responsibilities into the Federal Emergency Management Agency. In March 2003, FEMA became part of the American Department of Homeland Security (DHS), and billions of dollars of funding were provided to encompass an 'all-hazards approach' for FEMA.

FEMA'S MISSION STATEMENT

FEMA's mission is to support our citizens and first responders to ensure that as a nation we work together to build, sustain, and improve our capability to prepare for, protect against, respond to, recover from, and mitigate all hazards.

MODERN SURVIVAL

Chapter 1

PERSONAL REQUIREMENTS FOR DISASTER SURVIVAL

The earth is changing—while it could be nature, man is still making a mess.

When a major disaster happens and you are caught in the middle of it, you quickly realize that you're nothing more than a speck of dust at the mercy of nature. The aim of writing this book is to provide some clear guidelines which, in the worst case scenario, will act as a catalyst, should the reader find themselves in a disaster situation, either natural or man-made. In the past, I have written several survival books, and while I am proud of these, they are more formal in their structure towards survival techniques. With *Modern Survival*, I want to go beyond this structure and offer genuine advice that will help and assist anyone who is caught up in an unforeseen situation.

So what situations are we talking about? Well, you could have been a tourist on the beaches of Thailand in 2004. You may have been an aid worker in Haiti during the massive earthquake of 2010; likewise, you may have been a fisherman on the Northeast coast of Japan on March 11, 2011. Conversely, you could simply be a soldier doing your patriotic duty in Afghanistan, Iraq, or any of the many countries currently in conflict. It is not just the soldiers that are in danger, as each year, thousands of families and ordinary people become ensnared in various 'War Zones.' In all of these cases, you would have experienced a disaster first-hand.

WHY ARE WE IN DANGER?

Make no mistake, we are in danger because natural and man-made disasters (including wars), seem to be escalating and affecting an increasingly large number of people throughout the world. Major efforts have been made to make sure we are better prepared for, and are able to prevent serious deaths from, such disasters. While the cause of many natural disasters has not been accurately established, the role of humans in climate change is starting to come to the forefront.

The world's climate varies naturally as a result of three main attributes:

1. The way the ocean and the atmosphere interact with each other.
2. Changes in the earth's orbit.
3. Changes in energy received from the sun.

Now there is strong evidence that global warming is not due just to natural causes, but as a result of human behavior.

In 1966 I would fly to Asia, and, to alleviate the boredom of such a long flight, I would often look out the aircraft window. On occasion, I could see a small cluster of lights indicating a small village or town. By comparison, in 2011, if you took the same flight to Asia, all you would see are billions of burning lights from homes and floodlit streets. Have you ever felt the amount of heat a single light bulb generates? Imagine the heat from several billion light bulbs. I am not saying light bulbs are responsible for global warming, I merely wish to point out the difference in the amount of heat being produced over the past forty-five years, from one single source. Thus, the concentration of CO_2 in the earth's atmosphere is now higher than at any time than in the past 800,000 years.

Additionally, since the 1960s, there has been a massive rise in population, especially in the developing nations, up to tenfold in the past 100 years. For example, in 1950, there were around two and one-half billion people on the planet. Today, we are touching seven billion, with almost a third living in India and China.

There is also some disparity in the amount of deaths caused by disasters. For example, between 1980 and 2002, India experienced fourteen earthquakes that killed a total of 32,117 people, while the United States

Author's Note: I am not a scientist, and I do not proclaim to be an alarmist on climate change, but one thing I do know is that people are producing too much heat. We are told that the planet is becoming hotter due to the so-called 'greenhouse gases,' which are necessary to sustain life on earth. Like the glass walls of a greenhouse, they let the sun's rays enter, but stop some of the heat from escaping, keeping the planet warm enough to sustain life. The problem is that the number of people is increasing, which causes more greenhouse gases to be released into the atmosphere thus encouraging the greenhouse effect to become stronger. More heat is trapped, and the earth's climate begins to change unnaturally.

Nuclear plant at
Prypait, Ukraine.
(Source: Russian
Government)

experienced eighteen earth-quakes that killed only 143 people. A disproportionate share of the deaths caused by such environmental disasters took place in nations whose incomes were below $760 per-capita (IPCC 2001). In 1999, Kofi Annan, Secretary General of the United Nations, made this statement:

"Ninety percent of the disas-ter victims worldwide live in developing countries where poverty and population pressures force growing numbers of poor people to live in harm's way on flood plains, in earthquake prone zones and on unstable hill-sides. Unsafe buildings compound the risks. The vulner-ability of those living in risk prone areas is perhaps the single most important cause of disaster casualties and damage."

As for man-made disasters, we have had the odd nuclear reactor meltdown, the odd chemical leak, and more than the odd war or two. The largest indus-trial disaster on record happened in Bhopal, India, when a faulty tank containing poisonous methyl isocyanate escaped at the American-owned Union Carbide plant. The death toll was estimated to be between 4,000 and 20,000. Those that have visited India will understand why these estimated figures are so wide, as there are people everywhere, and many so poor that they are not even counted. In April 1986, the Russians lost control of the Chernobyl nuclear plant in Prypait, Ukraine. Some fifty people were killed by a steam explosion, and an estimated 4,000 additional cancer deaths in the years that followed. While we have learned not to stage world wars, we still face many small and costly (in terms of lives) wars around the planet. Most are to depose a dictator, or what the Western nations would term as 'repressive regime,' or some invader looking for more territory or assets (such as oil). For whatever reason, wars, no matter how big or small, kill many innocent people and disrupt millions of lives.

So here we are, faced with a disaster, injury, or death, and an uncertain future. The question then lies, "What are we to do?" Remember the motto, 'Knowledge Dispels Fear.' If nothing else, this should be a catalyst to get you thinking.

THE REALITY OF A DISASTER

Thousands Killed
Millions Homeless
The Threat of Disease
Costs Running into the Billions

These are the headlines we read or watch daily on our television sets. What we don't get from the media is the feeling that these poor souls are actually suffering. For some people, such as those living in Mogadishu, war, famine, and death are an everyday nightmare. They are forced by circumstance to live and bear with it, as they have no other options.

When disasters hit people who live in an organized and serene society, the effect is one of amplified disbelief. Your mind goes into shock, you can't believe what just happened, and chaos continues to happen all around you. Your head clears only to be confronted by a mass of dead people swirling around you, and you feel like you should do something, but what can you do? Others join you and you don't feel so bad. You talk eagerly to each other, telling of your experiences; you relish in the fact that you're not the only one left alive.

Then the darkness falls. There is no power and no lights, except for an odd torch or lantern that someone has managed to get going. The darkness seems to be pitch black, and to make matters worse, there is no sound, no cars, no radios, or music blasting. There's near silence, and the only thing you can hear is the crying of a baby. The babies cry all the time. You stay with the others to be safe. Around 11:00 p.m. there is another aftershock, a warning that it's not over yet. In the dark, your mind plays tricks on you. It's cold and you want to sleep, to rid yourself of the nightmare; even for a few hours. You rest your head on the hard surface of the park, with nothing but the clothes you stand up in for protection. You are cold.

During the night, you hear someone crying. The reality is that their family and home are gone, and their emotions are overcome and they need comfort. You do not move, as you have your own problems to deal with. Thoughts of your mother and father suddenly fill your mind—did they survive, and if so, where are they? Now you want to cry. You get some sleep but it is restless and you awake early to the sound of a helicopter passing overhead. More have joined your group in the night; some are jumping and waving in order to attract the pilot's attention. It does not stop.

The man next to you has a small bottle of water from which he drinks; it suddenly dawns on you that you have no food or water. You convince yourself that you are neither hungry nor thirsty. Later on, your stomach lets you know that it's time to eat, and you search your pockets, finding nothing; you need to find food and water. Your group has now grown to almost thirty members, two of which are seriously injured. There is still no sign of the emergency services or the army. A few of your group are huddled together; you join them to see what is happening. They want to send a few people out to find water and food and possibly some medical supplies. You volunteer.

The 7/11 store is gone, but several self-service machines,  although damaged and lying on their side, look full. You make a grab for a brightly colored candy bar and instantly rip away the paper. It's like eating the most wonderful food on earth. One of the others offers you a bottle of water; you smile for the first time since the disaster struck. It does not cross your mind that you are looting. The weather is warmer today and the sun shines.

Survivors in Japan.

Later on, you find a café that is untouched and the owner is serving around a dozen people; your group rushes over to eat and drink. The owner is happy to serve you, but you have no money. Thankfully enough, he will give you what he has. Soon, a large number of people arrive and the café is over-whelmed. The owner shuts up shop to angry exchanges and cries from the people who are hungry.

You spend a second night in the open, made possible by the use of some blankets you found in the ruins of someone's abandoned home. You wake to the smell . . . it hits your sens-es like a steam train. The dead are starting to decay. The rotting animal and plant life smell is overpowering and the group decides it must move. While they are discussing where to move to, the flies start to thicken, and within minutes you just want to run. The thought that they feed on dead bodies and then crawl on your face nauseates you.

The steady thud of helicopter blades suddenly breaks the silence. It comes closer; they have seen you and are looking for a suitable place to land. Everyone runs towards the helicopter. You are rescued.

That is the reality you can expect.

PRE-DISASTER

If you live in a country or area prone to natural disasters, it makes sense to formulate a contingency plan. You would be surprised to know that less than 20% of people who live in a disaster prone area actually prepare for such an event. Less than 10% discuss the possibility with their family, and hardly anyone makes a 'Disaster Grab Bag.' It is estimated that 100 million people still live in an earthquake zone, and over 500 million are affected by war and civil strife. It is now July 2011 and more than 13,000 people have been killed in the civil conflict in Libya, but I am pleased to say that it looks like Gaddafi is beaten.

For those that live in an area prone to natural disaster, it is also essential to know and understand the warning sounds and systems that are in place within your country. Likewise, you should also learn how and when the emergency services provide announcements, in particular to the severity and impact that you can expect. You should know how to contact your emergency services, and know who the local coordi-nator is. But most importantly, you, your family, and your neighbors need to have a reunification plan. It is also prudent

Living in a war zone.

to train members of your family and neighbors in basic life saving techniques and first aid.

Equally, wars do not start without some warning, and while this warning may be just a few days' notice, you will know it's coming. When it starts, the basic principles that apply to a natural disaster will still be applicable. If you live in a major town or city, especially one close to a government or military installation, the chances are that you and your family will be unwillingly prompted to take some sort of safety measures. The build up to war is now becoming very clear; political rhetoric, troops deployed, finalizing with shock and awe bombardment. If you wait until the bombs fall, it's most certainly too late.

It does not matter if it's a natural or man-made disaster, as the following points (which will be discussed in detail later in this book) offer you the best solution to survival.

- Emergency Plan.
- Reunification Plan.
- Survival Kit.
- Disaster Grab Bag (for forced evacuation).

Author's note: When making an emergency plan, always take into consideration the following facts:

You generally sleep for eight hours in your bed.

You will generally spend eight hours in your place of employment.

You will spend at least four hours on average in transit, traveling to and from work, shopping in the supermarket, visiting the cinema, etc.

Keep this in mind when you build your emergency plan and base it on your own lifestyle. A reunification plan is needed to reconnect families and friends once the effects of the disaster have subsided or passed. Its main object is to bring together your loved ones, or to know that they are safe.

The survival kit is based on where you are, what type of disaster you are expecting, and how many people you are catering to. Your Disaster Grab Bag is a simple rucksack that contains necessary items, should you be forced out of your home by the authorities or other unforeseen circumstances.

BEHAVIOR

How we behave before, during, and particularly after a disaster is so important to our chances of survival. When a natural or man-made disaster occurs, many male (very few female) individuals turn into predatory animals, preying on those unable to defend themselves. Gangs or thugs, mainly from poor areas, see the disaster as an open license to steal, rape, and murder without consequence.

There was also a marked contrast in behavior between the survivors of the tsunami in Japan compared to those people suffering as a result of the Haiti earthquake or Hurricane Katrina in America. In Haiti and New Orleans, there was an almost immediate descent into barbarity; while after the tsunami in Japan, the Japanese people maintained excellent civil order.

After the flooding that followed Hurricane Katrina in August 2005, the situation in New Orleans became so bad that the National Guard had to carry weapons to enforce order. Evacuation centers became nightmares of violence and lawlessness, and televisions screened images of looters making off with shopping trolleys full of plasma televisions and other luxury items. In Haiti, tent cities set up for the quake victims became scenes of mass rape and murder. During my research, these are just a few of the personal eyewitness accounts.

"We drove around once and it was like the Wild West," she said. "There were looters everywhere. I went in a convenience store looking for hand wipes and there were these guys in there breaking down the walls trying to get to the safe."

Behavior during and after a major disaster is very important.

Looting is commonplace after a disaster; you need food, but what use is a television?

"It was during the return walk that I personally observed several hundred people engaged in the act of looting. They were all around us that afternoon, pushing grocery carts full of athletic shoes, clothing and electronics toward the Memorial Convention Center. One guy had a brand new football still in the box that he was so proud of it; he held it up for my camera. Throughout all of this, I personally observed New Orleans police officers standing by, doing nothing. "

No such scenes were seen in Japan, as public order prevailed. In evidence, many countries sent search and rescue teams to Japan, while others sent medical and food aid. In almost every case, those aid workers returning home told the same story; the Japanese people acted in a controlled, calm, and civilized manner. There was no looting,

Author's Note: It is not up to me to say if looting is good or bad, but during my research, I came across this written by a student on the internet who posed the same question, "The morality of an action can be determined only by the motives behind it and not by the action itself. We would like to think that stealing is always bad, but when we consider circumstances, everything changes. To steal food from collapsed shops when starving is nothing less than natural—would any of us honestly choose starvation as an alternative?"

no climbing over the mangled debris searching for valuables, none of that. Those that did return to the wreckage of their homes, simply sorted out what had been theirs, never taking something that did not belong to them. As one American rescue worker told his local newspaper:

"I came away with the same sense, plus a sense of awe at the civility of the Japanese people. There was no looting. No picking through what was not theirs. In the face of utter devastation they were always looking to help someone else."

How do you explain the behavior of people who use the aftermath of a disaster to go on an orgy of rape, murder and looting? Why do people assault the very people sent to rescue them, and abuse the doctors and nurses that are trying to save lives?

For the majority of people, they try to help rise to the occasion and work together to help those in need of immediate rescue or care. Natural leaders come to the forefront and spontaneously organize and restore order rather than wait for government agencies to arrive. So then the question arises, "Why are there people that do exactly the opposite?" Unfortunately, the answer is not simple. Many disasters happen in Third World countries, but here, we see the very poor helping each other. However, there is poverty in the Western countries and there is poverty in the Third World countries, and here lies some of the answers.

Society in the West has developed to the point where no one needs to be hungry, be without a home or shelter, and everyone has money in their pocket. It's called the 'Welfare State.' However, many of these people do have what the average working man has, earnings from their labor, self-respect, and a goal in life. Don't get me wrong, the Welfare State is a wonderful thing, providing for those in need, and I applaud it. But, like every institution, there are cracks in the fabric. Many people in the West live off the Welfare State. They do not work; many have never worked and some practice criminal activities, such as drug dealing, or work illegally for extra cash. It is this criminal element that sees the opportunity in a disaster; their moral fiber is weak, and the opportunity to take without paying is a natural part of their mental fabric. In a civilized society, would we let prisoners drown in a tsunami, or flooded waters? In New Orleans, some 7000 prisoners, many killers and rapists, were locked in their cells as the water reached chest height. This same prison also held many innocent people waiting for a court hearing, people whose only crime was to default on a $70 fine, be caught sleeping on the street, or have a minor traffic violation. The generation of anger is understandable, but was there an alternative?

In August 2007, two prisons collapsed after an earthquake in Pisco, Peru and some 600 prisoners escaped from one after the walls fell down. While some 200 gave themselves up voluntarily, more than half added to the incidents of assault, rape, and theft to the multiple sufferings of the earthquake's survivors.

As a final word on this subject, and having traveled to every corner of our planet, I have found that the majority of people are basically good. While no one can predict how any of us would behave during or after a disaster, we must equip ourselves to help others if at all possible. We all take for granted the thin veneer of civilization which exists only as long as society continues to function normally. When we feel that our lives are threatened, humans will resort to almost anything in order to survive. It is sad, but when law and order leave society, evil will quickly rise to the surface.

Children are hardy when it comes to living with pain and fear.

CHILDREN IN DISASTERS AND WAR CONFLICTS

A disaster such as an earthquake, hurricane, tornado, fire, flood, or violent act in war can be frightening to children and adults alike. Comfort your child, talk to them, and explain what is happening, as this will help calm their fears. When explaining, use words and examples the child can understand.

Children are also responsive to the way their parents act, so if they see you crying, they will know that something is wrong. Try to be strong for their sake; always admit your concerns, and explain why you intend to carry out the actions you are planning.

In both a disaster and a war zone, children will react to what they actually see and hear. They might see a loved one with a leg torn off, or see their mother raped, or hear an obliterating explosion close-by. The very young child will not heed this violation as much as an eight-year-old or teenager. Some teenagers may get angry wondering why their parents are helpless to change the situation—this is just fear raising its head. A child's age affects how the child will respond to a disaster.

- The very young may cling to their parents.
- Older children may become withdrawn, trying to hide from the situation.
- Teenagers will rebel.
- Create time for them, listen to what they say.
- Above all, while you are alive, reassure them.

Accept these feelings and offer comfort, ease their worries, and show them love and protection in any way possible. Once the disaster has past, seek professional advice for Post-Traumatic Stress Disorder (PTSD).

But war is not just about trauma and sight as it is about bombs and bullets. Last week, in Misrata, Libya, as NATO jets pounded the forces of Colonel Gaddafi's army, ten-year-old Mohammed sat with his family cowering. When the bombing had stopped he ran outside to play in his yard—seconds later a speeding bullet entered his skull.

Disaster, war, and terrorism are not easy for anyone to understand or accept. Many young children feel confused, upset, and anxious. Most children, even those exposed to trauma, are still quite resilient. It will take time, but they will get through it and hopefully get on with their lives.

DISASTERS ARE SUDDEN

Sometimes there will be a warning when disaster strikes, while other times it will just jump up and bite you. A disaster simply means that your circumstances or immediate environment has changed and you are in danger. In isolated cases, help and rescue could be immediately available, but in circumstances where the entire area is in danger, help and rescue may be a long ways away. In the latter case, you must identify the threats and deal with

This poor woman knows what fear really is.

them if you're going to survive. There are thousands of books and a myriad of items and equipment designed to help you survive in a disaster, but the one thing that really counts is YOU. Therefore, your first act is to control your own reactions to any disaster.

Disasters, especially unexpected ones, are the foundation for fear and stress. Injury causes pain and blood loss, and perhaps, the immediate threat of death. Seeing loved ones, family, or neighbors wounded or dead will all have a psychological effect. No matter what has happened, you must accept the reality of the disaster. Acceptance will bring the ability to choose an appropriate action. You will be thinking positively and your self-confidence will guide you on your way to becoming a survivor. Believe in YOURSELF!

When talking about the enemies of survival, we must also include pain, fatigue, loneliness, shelter, thirst, and hunger. The people of Haiti learned of these firsthand; some people were trapped for days beneath rubble, not knowing if they would be rescued. Many had broken bones, had no water or food, and were surrounded by darkness. These people experienced the full range of human emotions relating to survival, yet many were able to survive.

In the real world, your survival may depend upon your personality or character when facing a disaster situation. Fear is a two-sided weapon; it can produce panic, but it can also act as a spur to sharpen thought and action. The path you choose is more dependent on the person rather than the situation. The attributes important to survival are listed below. The more of these you have, or can aspire to, the greater your chance of success.

Author's Note: 'Knowledge Dispels Fear.' These words are hammered into every SAS soldier during their attempt to join Britain's elite force. Without doubt, fear is a major 'enemy of survival' and to survive you must first deal with fear, starting with your own.

- Accept the realities of your situation.
- Assess resources and alternative courses of action.
- Don't wait, improvise.
- Accept that isolation may be necessary.
- Rapidly adapt to your circumstances.
- Remain cool, calm, and collected.
- Make all possible preparations for the worst case.
- Extend your limits and bear the pain.
- Recognize your fear.
- Help those who cannot help themselves.

Be decisive and accept the reality of the situation, assess your resources, and consider alternative actions. Try to improve your immediate situation; this may mean moving just a few yards to shelter or higher ground—but it's a decisive action. If you are trapped under a collapsed building, be ready to accept isolation. Accept your surroundings, but adapt them if you can. This may only be putting your hand out to catch a few drops of water from a broken pipe—but it is a decisive action.

When there is nothing you can do, try to remain cool, calm, and collected—this in itself is a decisive action.

Few people really know their own limits, but deep down, there are reserves (a mother would offer her life for a child, men have died rescuing a friend), so extend your recognition of self-worth and be prepared for the worst. Dispel your own fears or worries by helping others, give others hope—this is a decisive action!

FEAR

There are two factors that mentally cause humans to think irrationally: fear and pain. These will raise their heads before, during, and after any disaster. In order to help yourself and others, you must face fear and learn to deal with pain.

The good thing about feeling afraid is that it means you are alive, and with life comes hope. Throughout our lives we will all experience fear, it is a natural emotion, a stimulus that recognizes the threat of danger. We can suddenly be confronted by fear or we can let it build within us. Fear controls our behavior and reactions are triggered by fear. We cannot avoid fear; therefore, the best thing to do is to accept it. Acceptance of fear will produce two immediate and positive benefits. You will recognize what it is that is making you afraid, and secondly, you will look for answers to dispel this fear.

Naturally, the depth of fear will depend on the immediate threat to the individual. For example, if you are confronted by an armed robber, you will be afraid they are going to harm you, or even shoot you. On the other hand, they may simply take your wallet and run. By comparison, people trapped in the debris of an earthquake may have no idea how long it will be before they are rescued. They will have time to worry about their family, the idea that no one may come to rescue them, that will they die, or how long can they bear the pain of the large slab of concrete crushing their legs. In both cases, fear must be recognized and controlled. If you are able to, take steps to assess your situation, as this will help in decreasing and controlling the fear that you're going through.

- You must be alive to know fear. Being alive is good.
- Is there anyone with you or close by? If so, talk to them.
- What just happened, and what is happening now?
- Is there any way you can reduce the reason for your fear; is there hope?

PAIN

Pain is a natural occurrence, and it normally means that there is something wrong with your body. Pain will not go away, but you can control pain. The best way is to concentrate and focus on the point where the pain is emitting. If you cannot see the damage, can you at least assess it in your mind?

- If you feel pain, you are alive. Being alive is good.
- Go through a quick body check; can you move your head, is your chest free when you breath, can you move your arms and legs? The answer to these questions will determine your physical state and also help remove fear (see Chapter 12).
- Are you trapped or pinned so that you cannot move or crawl? The answer to this will determine your next action.
- Is there anyone near you who can help? Reassurance from another voice is priceless.

- Do you have the means to address your pain, i.e., do you have a First Aid Manual on your mobile phone?

In dealing with pain and fear, we have established our condition. In some cases, your situation may be pre-ordained, and death seemingly inevitable. But you must look for the slightest optimism, and draw on the very fibers to stay alive. If you have children, think of their life without you. Dying is easy, so give yourself a reason to live and you will survive.

- Confront your fear.
- Bury your pain.
- Get on with the problem of surviving.

YOU'RE ALIVE

So you are breathing and alive–then there is hope, and with hope, comes survival. Let's go to the next step, which is assessing your situation. Here we need to establish a clear course of action and deal with the problems that confront us. Your situation may be dire, you may even die, but while you're breathing, you are going to TRY and get to safety. Let's examine each situation you could find yourself in.

- Is the disaster over, or stable?
- Are you alone?
- Are you injured to the point where you cannot move?
- Is there an immediate threat to your life?
- Do something, even if it's only thinking about how long you can last.

Every disaster, earthquake, tsunami, fire, or flood will eventually revert to a stable condition. How long this takes will depend on the type of disaster; earthquakes can last a few minutes, with some aftershocks; tsunamis roll inland and then the water recedes; fires consume all within its path, but eventually will burn itself out; floodwaters can rise and stay at a dangerous level for weeks. In all these cases you must decide when the situation is stable enough for you to move to safety.

Are you alone? The answer to this is simple: look around, shout or call out if you cannot see anyone. If there are others, you will have an immediate boost to overcoming your fear. If others are present, find out what their condition is and if they need help or if they can help you. In any survival situation, it is always best to join forces and assist each other; a group of people have a much better chance of survival than an individual. If you are alone, continue to listen for others.

Are you injured? Can you stand up and walk, or crawl? Can you see an immediate place which will offer better safety? If so, can you reach it? If you are injured and immobile, is there anyone that can help you? Make sure you think, "Can you improve your situation in any way?"

Is there an immediate threat to your life and can you do anything to avoid it? After an earthquake, you might find yourself trapped in a building below rubble. Take notice that, if you are alive, then somehow the collapsed building has fallen on you in such a way as to make it a "temporary" shelter. Likewise, in a flood, have you managed to reach high ground, or get above the water level? After any disaster, there is always the threat of further risk to life. Think, "Is there a way to avoid further harm?"

All these questions will be addressed fully in this book, and the answers depend on the individual type of disaster. Nonetheless, there are several common attributes following a natural or man-made disaster that help us form a rough benchmark. Of all the disaster victims interviewed, there emerged a pattern. These included immediate protection by finding a place of safety; clean water was also high on the list, as was a safe place to sleep; these were followed by seeking medical aid and locating loved ones.

MAKE A DECISION

Perhaps the earliest and most vital decision will be the choice between staying where you are and awaiting rescue, or attempting to make your way to safety. There is no single, simple answer to this question. The circumstances of your survival situation will, to a greater or lesser extent, influence the choice you make.

If it is safe to do so, check the surrounding area without wandering too far away. You will be able to make a better assessment of the ease or difficulty of moving around in the locality. You will also gain information regarding the availability of food, water, and shelter.

Having taken time and trouble to collect the best information, be sure to make good use of it. Remember, you are looking for the SAFEST option—the choice that will give you the best chance of survival.

Stay Put

- If you suspect that a rescue is imminent, where will they come from?
- Where are they likely to start searching?
- How are they going to come?
- What signs will they be looking for?
- How can you make these signs more obvious?
- If injured, you may not be able to meet them physically.
- Do you have a means of communication?

Moving

- Do you know where you are going?
- Can you access information about the disaster?
- Do you have a mobile phone or iPad with satnav with you?
- Is the way clear for you?
- In a war zone disaster, do you know a safe route through the streets?
- When is the safest time to move, by day or under the cover of darkness?

If you have decided to move, consider carefully what you can take with you. Your choice may have to be a compromise between what is available and how much can be conveniently carried. If you are in a group, make sure that all available protective clothing has been shared equally, and that everyone is as fully protected as possible. Select what you are taking with great care. You will, of course, regard any survival supplies—first aid, food, water, survival kits, flares, etc., as priority, adding to them anything which may be useful but is not bulky or heavy. Look to your traveling with imagination and a wide eye for adaptability when selecting items. You have to be able to obtain or

A place of safety is not always safe, as many discovered during Hurricane Katrina. (Staff Sgt. Jacob N. Bailey)

provide shelter, warmth, food, and water, especially during overnight stops.

PLACE OF SAFETY

If you are alive, injured or not, providing you can move, or others can move you, your first priority should be to move to to a place of safety. This may be moving to higher ground, or a place where floodwater or a firestorm cannot reach you. In a war zone, try to find a strong building; reinforced concrete is better than brick, for example. Likewise, cellars offer more protection than high-rise buildings. Once again, reaching a place of safety, even on a temporary basis, will lift your spirits and help reduce the fear factor.

A place of safety is where you can assess your body for damage and possibly try to repair it. This should be a place where others can join you, or from where you can be seen by others. A place of safety should offer the following:

- Immediate protection from the hazards of the disaster.
- Shelter from the elements.
- Clean water supply close by.
- Room for others to shelter with you.

It is impossible for anyone to predict where they will be immediately after a disaster, or what condition they will be in. The only real advice I can offer is to THINK. For some people this will come naturally; while for others, especially those trapped or seriously injured and immobile, it will be difficult to focus on anything other than your immediate situation.

For others, a place of safety might simply mean getting out of the water and onto dry land, or fighting your way out of a forest fire. No matter the situation, if you are alive, there is always something you can do; even the simple act of thinking can help.

In some cases you may find yourself in charge of a small group of survivors. While this will help you personally relinquish your fear, be aware of mental and physical exhaustion. Help others, but don't try to do too much at once. Make sure that you pace yourself and have priorities. Give others in your shelter simple tasks, even the older children, and make sure that everyone gets enough rest.

If you must forage for food and water, send people out in pairs. Talk to them before they leave, give them some idea as to what to look for and what places to avoid. Here are a few tips:

- Stay off the streets where there are crowds of people or a mob.
- After an earthquake, watch out for fallen objects: downed electrical wires and weakened buildings or bridges.
- Stop and retrace your footsteps if you see looters.
- Think of where the nearest food supply or water may be found before setting out.
- If you encounter small parties of other survivors, welcome and guide them to your shelter.
- Give each forage party a distinct area to search.

When choosing a safe place to shelter and rest, use your basic instincts. If a place feels right, then it generally is safe. If you feel trapped or nervous, always look for a better location. After the trauma of a major disaster when your world is upside down, you will need somewhere to relax and contemplate your next move.

IMMEDIATE PROTECTION

The aftermath of many disasters leads to people being homeless and living on the streets. This happened in Haiti, where thousands of homes and families were destroyed instantaneously. Those that survived were left in a state of shock and found themselves alone with no home and no food. While we all sympathize with their plight, a similar situation is normal for millions of people around the world, and none more so than in India.

In a detailed report on the homeless carried out by the Indian government, many aspects of homelessness were identified. However, the two main problems facing home-less people were food and shelter. From their experience, we can gather vital lessons which will serve us well when surviving a disaster.

For the homeless, the worst experience is not having a permanent place to rest your head and store your belong-ings, meager as they may be. Living on the street is itself living in a state where one does not know what is going to

Band together for safety; share your accommodation and food. (Barry Davies)

happen from day to day. In addition to having no fixed abode, anxiety about the future also takes its toll. In our world today, we have two types of people; those that live in cities and those that live in the countryside. After a disaster, where you are makes a vast difference.

It has been found that the homeless have a tendency to stay within the city boundaries, and would eventually form into groups which would work and sleep together for protection and self-help. These groups would form units of up to thirty to forty people. By comparison, the homeless living in the countryside would gather in numbers no greater that three to five people. The conclusion is that people feel less threatened in the countryside, where the people are more generous.

You must also consider what other survivors are doing. A place of safety does not have to mean being alone in a protected place; being in a strong group with shared principles also qualifies as a place of safety. The desire to join with others is a natural emotion, however, this is best done by joining others you know and understand; family, relatives, close friends and neighbors. Often, people sharing the same experience within a confined area will band together in the immediate aftermath of a disaster.

On the other hand, people will band together in gangs, most of which are intending on looting, stealing, raping, and even murder. With law and order weakened by the disaster, some will see this as an opportunity to commit crime. This is the story of one inhabitant of New Orleans following Hurricane Katrina.

"When I got there, I looked through the pedestrian gate that surrounds the building and I saw a group of five men circling my Blazer, looking through its windows. One of them was clearly trying to read the fuel gauge. Knowing what they were about to do, I dashed through the gate and yelled at them to get away from the vehicle. As I charged through the gate, I unslung the AKM. At first, the malice in their eyes and their threatening moves could not have been more clear. It wasn't just about the Blazer anymore. Then, they each saw the rifle and, without hesitating, turned and ran. If I had been unarmed, I would have never done this, and they would have taken the only means of escape that was available to us. I watched the impulse that shot through each of them the second they saw my AKM. It was the unmistakable and immediate impulse of complete terror. They responded dramatically to the sight of that AKM. It was better than having a team of Rottweilers."

While it is true that having a gun will certainly deter people from stealing your property, very few people outside of America can legally carry a firearm, never mind a fully automatic AKM. The argument is, should you carry a gun and use it to defend yourself? The answer to this is simple: it depends on where you are. Had I found myself in downtown New Orleans, or in Port-au-Prince, Haiti, and all alone, then a gun would have come in very handy. Would I have used it? Again, the answer is an easy YES. As a soldier, I have been carrying a weapon most of my early life. I respect weapons and know what they can do to a person, so if I had to fire one, then you can bet your life it would be for the best of reasons. Once again, we return to the behavior after a disaster and the moral fiber and character of the individual.

TRAVELING ALONE

Today, many young men and women travel the planet to enlighten themselves of the wonderful world we live in. I use the word 'wonderful,' because I have traveled to every continent and just about every country. Everywhere I have traveled, I have found one thing in common: the people. People are basically good; they will help a stranger, or foreigner, and there is also a very small fraction that will harm you.

Before you leave home, do a little research into the countries you intend to travel to. Asia, in particular, is very prone to earthquakes, tsunamis, and extreme weather conditions.

A simple check will tell you if the country has enforced building regulations and laws regarding resistance to earth tremors, etc.

Talk to your family and friends; provide them with a rough plan of your travels. Make arrangements to stay in touch with a least one person back home; Facebook or Twitter is extremely handy. Always carry a smart phone such as an iPhone or BlackBerry. This will serve you well if you look after it and make sure you always have a full battery and network signal.

If you don't have a smart phone, check in at regular intervals; most locations, even remote villages, have internet cafes these days. Just send a quick email so the IP address can be traced. If you are lucky enough to have an iPad, use its tracking capability so family and friends can keep track of your location. Leave a copy of your documents, i.e., passport, flight tickets, credit card details, etc., with a family member. If yours are stolen you will not remember all the details.

While most people are honest, in towns and cities you will always find some criminals, or they will find you. It's a sad fact of life but there are some lowlife scum out there that have absolutely no respect for themselves or you; they simply want to take from you.

- If distracted by a stranger, stay alert, as most crooks work in pairs.
- Be wary of pickpockets when you arrive at a railway, bus station, or airport.
- Hold onto your valuables when in a crowded market place.
- Keep your mobile phone in your pocket when it's not in your hand.
- Keep your travel documents on your person, preferably in a waterproof container.
- Never carry all your credit cards and money in one wallet or purse. If you get robbed, you do not want to be completely penniless or be denied access to additional funds.

- Arrange with your bank to have a number whereby you can draw out emergency cash at any ATM.
- Only drink bottled water, don't eat the local ice cream (crushed ice with flavored juice), wash fruit, stay clean and hygienic—this way you will avoid getting sick. Make sure you have adequate health insurance.
- If you stay in a hostel or hotel, use the safe deposit box, if one is available.
- For women, try to avoid the advances of men by silence; make no eye contact, or if in doubt, move away from the cause of annoyance. In many societies the male is dominant, and any affront to their ego is seen as a humiliation, so don't get involved. In some countries, the male population's impression of the West, is that our women are loose and easy (they have seen *Baywatch*), and for a woman to be traveling alone is just not culturally acceptable. In such countries, see if you can find a fellow traveler as they will be equally as keen on teaming up. Wear sunglasses to avoid eye contact. Dress and respect the customs and culture you are in.

A lot of people are forced to sleep rough every day. (Barry Davies)

- Avoid romantic encounters, especially if you are female. You could soon find yourself part of the human trafficking trade.
- When traveling alone, ALWAYS have an emergency call button pre-set on your cell phone. (There's information about a free application at the back of this book.) Special agents have such devices, so why not you? Problems can quickly arise, so in the event, press the button and let people know your last known location and that you are in trouble (see Annex B).

Author's Note: I have been robbed twice in my life: once at an airport and once while on vacation. The second instance involved two people working together, and the guy kept me occupied for no more than 5 seconds, while his accomplice, a female, opened my pocket and removed my wallet—I never felt a thing. This event proved very useful, because from that day on, I only ever kept one credit card in my wallet and only enough money for the day's journey. I also only carry what is required for the journey.

- Make sure you always have somewhere to sleep. Never sleep in a remote or deserted building in poor countries—alone, you are vulnerable and may get set upon. If you are on a budget, always check out the accommodation. Make sure the door has a good lock. Check out the escape routes in the event of a fire.
- If you need to seek directions, always ask in the hotel before you leave or if in the street, a family or a woman with a child, and never a single male.

SLEEPING

While sleeping might seem like a strange subject for survival, it happens to be an important one, as it will fill a third of your time. Even if you are injured during a major disaster, the chances are that you will not have a medical pack with you, or that one will be present within the surrounding area. Emergency teams can take days to find you, so the best that you can hope for is rest, care, and self-attention.

Moreover, sleep is advantageous to your health and helps your body recover. It is vital to make this time as comfortable as possible, as it will help both your mental and physical being. Sleep will help mask any pain you may be suffering. In any situation, getting the best night's sleep possible is always beneficial. Furthermore, when you awaken you will be filled with new hope.

A good night sleep can be achieved when you are comfortable, preferably in a darkened room. Not too hot, not too cold, with a good circulation of fresh air. If you are with others, share your body heat and cuddle together.

Author's Note:

Did you also know that heart attacks and strokes are more common during the early hours of the morning, and that lack of sleep has been associated with worsening of blood pressure and cholesterol? Your heart will be healthier if you get a good eight hours of sleep each night. Sleep deficiency will also make your body stressful.

On the bright side, sleep can help reduce inflammation, improve your thought pattern and make you more alert. Just taking a nap during the day has been proven to be beneficial, making you brighter and more efficient when you wake. Sleep also reduces depression.

Place those most at risk, such as older people and children, in the middle of the group. Here are a few more tips.

- Eat your main meal just before you go to bed.
- Exercise to warm your muscles, but do not perspire.
- Strip and rub your body with a dry towel.
- Put on extra clothes and socks.
- Wear a hat to bed.
- Go to the toilet just before going to sleep.
- Four hours sleep before midnight is better than four hours of sleep after.
- Make sure your shelter is windproof.
- Sleep on a good bed of insulated material.
- If it's cold enough for a fire, have a plentiful supply of fuel handy.
- If you cannot sleep, plan what you will do the next day.

Avoid rough areas, or an area close to any danger. Never try to sleep directly on the ground, because the cold and damp floor will get through to your body. Instead, make a bed of cardboard boxes. These can always be found at the rear of most supermarkets; at the same time, look for any food disposal. Collect dry newspapers and use them to line your clothes, this way you will have a warm sleep.

If you are lucky enough to have a sleeping bag make sure that you turn it inside out each morning and give it a good shake before storing it away. Likewise in the evening, fluff out your sleeping bag to give maximum insulation. Never get into your sleeping bag if your clothes are wet.

Improvised sleeping bag. (BCB Int Ltd)

If you don't have a manufactured sleeping bag, learn the benefits of finding a large plastic bag. You can find plastic bags everywhere; almost all homes put their trash out in one, and in the countryside, farmers use them for animal food. A good, strong, black plastic bag can be turned into a mattress when stuffed with grass or straw; two bags, one inside the other, and with the space in between, stuffed with any insulation material will make

a temporary sleeping bag; plastic bags can also serve as a rain coat, or makeshift shelter. After a major disaster, the humble plastic bag really becomes valuable. In 1989, three men were caught out in a blizzard in Northern Sweden. One of the men used two plastic bags to construct a makeshift sleeping system, using frozen moss to fill the cavity. He was extremely cold and had a rough night—but, he was alive in the morning, while his two friends had died.

A simple polyethylene sack will help protect you from both wind and rain. Better still, a hessian sack inside a plastic sack will make a very comfortable sleeping bag. Insulation can be improved by filling the gap between the inner and outer sack with insulating material: straw, grass moss, etc. Once again, the same rules apply, so shake out your improvised sleeping sack and keep it dry. Change the insulation material on a regular basis.

Many public places such as bus/train stations, local sports centers, libraries, and even airports have seating. Restrooms offer shelter, if these are still standing after a disaster. However, you will not be the only survivor, so make sure you check any place out before you enter (look for good order, and some security in the building). Avoid places where gangs and mobs tend to gather, such as supermarkets and liquor stores. Think about where you are. Do you know the area? Can you walk to an area you do know well? Wealthy areas may offer better pickings, but they are also well policed.

If you are alone, it is always best to sleep in an area where no one can see you. Believe it or not, a graveyard can offer a quiet night's sleep. However, during the day, it's often better to sleep in open areas, such as parks. The amount of people around will help stop you from being pestered if you are female.

If the area you are in has lots of people milling around and you want to be alone, try making camp for the night on a large traffic island or side of the highway. Select a spot that has lots of trees and bushes on it, which will provide cover from view. When it is safe to do so, and when no one can observe you, make your way to the center and find a good place to sleep. True, the traffic noise or voices can be a little bothersome, but by and large you will be very safe and remain undiscovered.

Author's Note: If you should ever find yourself looking for a free place to sleep and are close to an airport, simply go to Departures and you will find not only a warm place to sleep, but also good bathroom facilities. Plus, there is always something to eat and drink. If you do use an airport, make sure you look fairly tidy. It's a good idea to have a look at the departures board to see which flights have been delayed (just in case security asks you), or simply tell security you missed your flight. However, be warned: many airports (especially in Delhi, India) will not let you enter unless you have a valid ticket for that day. Likewise, after a few hours, security will start taking an interest in you.

WATER

Water is undoubtedly the most important nutrient and the most abundant substance in the human body. It comprises three quarters of our body mass and affects every one of our cells. When we eat food, water is needed to help convert that food to energy. Water helps the body remove toxins through the bowels, urination, and perspiration. Water keeps your body in balance (if you become 3% dehydrated, you will see a drop in physical and mental functionality; a drop of 15% is likely to lead to your death). Dehydration can kill you in just a few days.

After any disaster, but especially a tsunami or severe flooding, the streets will become a soup of dead bodies, animals, sewage, oil, chemicals, and waste. Even as the waters recede, the bulk of the solids will remain. Almost all surface water, rivers, and streams will become contaminated.

Check your water intake as to how much water you have consumed in a twenty-four hour period. If you are not sure if you are drinking enough for the current conditions, then check your urine visually. It should be light yellow in color, the brighter or darker the yellow, the more water you should consume. Remember if you are sweating, you will also need to replace the lost sodium in your body.

When you are dehydrated, the body will try to conserve water and minimize the amount it allows you to pass by forcing the

Drink water as regularly as you can. (Barry Davies)

Personal hygiene is important and healthy. (Barry Davies)

liver to take on a more productive role. However, your body can only handle this for a few days.

Thirst is probably the best-known enemy of survival, especially in its extreme form. Well before this stage, however, thirst can begin to pre-occupy the mind. Nevertheless, like pain and fear, thirst can be kept in its proper place. If you have water with you, it is important to drink it in a rational way. If you are injured, do not use your emergency water for washing the wound—keep it for drinking. Even then it must be used sparingly, but not so sparingly that you run the risk of significant dehydration. It is pointless, not to say harmful, to reduce your effectiveness in a survival situation while you still have resources at hand.

If water CAN be obtained, save it and use it wisely. Taken that the disaster has cut off all normal water supply, you will need to look for sources of water. In a city, there are numerous places and water catchments, and while the water might not be pure, it can be cleaned and purified for drinking.

The amount of water (and its purity) you drink is vital to maintaining a healthy body. After any disaster situation, either natural or man-made, water is likely to be scarce and impure. It is, therefore, a priority in your survival plan (see Chapter 11).

PERSONAL HYGIENE

If you are traveling or live in a disease-prone area, it is advisable to make sure that you are immunized against as many diseases as possible, and that your immunization record is kept up-to-date. Typhoid, Paratyphoid, Yellow Fever, Typhus, Tetanus, Smallpox, and Cholera are among the preventable diseases. Seek medical advice regarding any special precautions needed prior to any disaster prone area.

Personal hygiene, while not a priority, should be carried out on a regular basis when clean water is available. Bodily cleanliness is a major protection against disease, germs, and infestations. A daily wash with warm water and soap is ideal. If this is not possible, concentrate on keeping your hands clean, and wash and sponge your face, armpits, crotch, and feet at least once per day. In desert conditions, scrubbing your hands and feet with sand will improvise, as will snow in cold conditions. In the absence of another method, take an air bath, rubbing your body briskly with a clean piece of cloth. Clothing, especially underclothing, must be kept as clean and dry as possible. At the very least, shake out clothing and expose it to the sun and air each day. Check for and remove any ticks, lice, and fleas regularly. You can protect your teeth by improvising a toothbrush from the crushed end of a small twig. It is possible to use dry charcoal ash as a toothpaste substitute.

Make and use an improvised tooth brush. (Barry Davies)

Water is precious, so make you that you use it wisely. Long hair can be washed in a one-and-a half liter, and the whole body in two or three. Use little pots and pans, with water, lukewarm or cold. Remember that hygiene does not stop with your body. Eating utensils can contaminate your body as quickly as your fingers if not cleaned properly. Collect clean water or paper after you visit the toilet.

CLOTHING

Man is a tropical animal, and in most parts of the world needs clothes to protect himself against the elements. The body temperature functions best between 96ºF and 102ºF, and preventing heat loss or heat gain is of primary concern to the survivor. Factors which cause changes in the body temperature are weather, climatic temperature, wind, moisture loss, and illness. Heat gain or loss is transferred by:

- Conduction.
- Convection.
- Radiation.

Heat gain or loss is exacerbated by:

- Evaporation.
- Respiration.
- Wind chill.

Of the above, the wind chill factor is the greatest threat to any survivor. It can rob the body of heat in cold, wet conditions, and moisture in hot conditions. Do all in your power to prevent it.

The principle of using a layer system in order to trap warm air has proven itself to offer the most benefit in cold conditions. Thin cotton underclothes, covered with one or more layers of warm wear made from wool, fiber pile, or fleece is ideal. The outer garment should be windproof, and preferably waterproof. It could be made from tightly woven cotton, polycotton, fiber-pile material, or nylon. If the clothes you have are insufficient, just improvise: use a plastic bag as a poncho and newspaper for insulation. The most important factors to remember about clothing are:

Use a layer system of clothing and stuff newspaper inside for insulation. (Barry Davies)

- Keep clothes clean.
- Avoid overheating and sweating.
- Keep clothing dry.
- Repair defects immediately.
- Improvise.

Overheating results in perspiration, which wets the clothing, reducing the insulation qualities. Ventilation is essential when physical exertion is necessary. Wet clothing from rain or sweat will lose heat up to twenty-five times quicker than dry clothing. A combination of wet clothing and strong winds can mean a swift death. By keeping your clothes clean and dry, you help prevent the build-up of grit that destroys the fibers. Additionally, dirt will reduce the effectiveness of the garment. If washing is not practical, then a good daily shake or beating will suffice. In tropical conditions, cloths need washing more frequently or they will rot. Likewise, cloths that fit next to the skin (socks and underclothing) also require daily attention.

AFRAID OF THE DARK

For a mixture of reasons, so many people are afraid of the dark. They imagine enemies that are not there, and their own head gets the best of them. Let me assure you that in a survival situation, darkness is your friend; darkness hides your presence; darkness keeps you safe.

There are many reasons why we are afraid of the dark, and most of these originate from our childhood. Let me assure you that there are no bogey men; plus, any other human walking around in the dark is just as afraid as you are— or they are rescue workers, in which case you will be safe. There are two things to do if you are trapped in darkness.

1. 'Listen'
   Identify any sound and its direction. The best thing to do is to open your mouth and turn your head slowly; this will help increase the sound and identify its location.
2. Do not be afraid of small insects or rodents.
   They are not going to eat you alive. Trust me, they will try to get as far as possible from a human presence. Remember that they are frightened of YOU. Try to catch them if possible. You may not feel like eating it right now, but in several days' time, it could turn into a small feast!

If you are in total darkness and you clearly hear a sound, try to identify it. After an earthquake, it will simply be the rubble moving or falling. In the event that another person is trapped near you, you will soon learn the difference in sounds; in which case you will have company, and with company, comes HOPE.

LIGHTS

Light is very important to us, especially from fire, which brings with it a source of comfort, plus the ability to see into the darkness. After a disaster, light can become so much more: it can signal your location (not always a good thing),

Using a mobile phone as a torch. (Barry Davies)

guide your path, should you have to move at night, or survey your surroundings, should you decide to stop and rest. If you think there are other humans within sight and sound and you do not wish to make your presence known, do not make a sound and do not use any form of light. If on the other hand you are confident that there is no close threat, use any light source to survey your surroundings. The moment you produce light in a dark area, you will provoke some reaction, especially in a forest. These sounds are simply the creatures of the night making you aware of their presence.

If you do not have a source of light, such as a flashlight or mobile phone, then use the ambient light supplied by nature. Rest, and let your eyes adjust to the light. Even in a forest there will be some ambient light to guide you.

Remember that if you use a flashlight, your night vision will be rendered useless. That is to say, when you switch your flashlight off, you will not be able to see much. The same thing is true if you have achieved good night vision and someone approaches you with a torch or you look directly into a vehicle's headlights. To maintain your night vision, always cover one eye.

It is a good idea to close your eyes for a few minutes before moving in the dark. When you open them, try to look at shapes using your peripheral vision. By using your peripheral vision, you are using more rod cells in the retina, which work much better in low light. You will need to be patient, as good night vision can take up to twenty minutes to achieve.

If you're walking in the dark, and you're unsure of the surface beneath your feet, slide your feet rather than taking steps. In areas of high-rise buildings or forest areas, keep your head slightly up so you can see sky (this normally produces more ambient light and offers good guidance). There are many sources of light available to us today, and if you live in a disaster prone area, you should keep several on hand. Remember: disaster strikes at any time of the day or night, so keep a flashlight in your bedside locker.

HOW WILL YOU DEFEND YOURSELF?

Surviving a disaster is one thing, but remember that even though you've survived, it doesn't mean that you're still not in a dangerous place. People react differently after any major disaster that has taken lives and still threatens to take more; the animal instincts rise quickly to the surface in some people. If you're alone, you could be a target for theft, assault, and rape. You need to take some precautions, such as letting people know where you are (such as texting people). Once safe, try and stay in a location where there is a reliable signal. In addition, always know where you are so when you call for help you will be able to give them a specific location. For this reason, it is often best to find shelter with others. Remember . . . there is safety in numbers.

Defending yourself does not necessarily mean fighting. Long before you have to consider violence, you should try avoidance. Avoidance is something we all practice on a daily basis: a bill drops through your letterbox, you know it's a bill so you tend to avoid it. You see something in the supermarket you can't afford, you avoid it. All you have to do is simply adopt the same principles when defending yourself.

Problem: You are sitting on an underground train and at the next stop the train fills up with drunken football fans, or a gang of youths looking for trouble.

Solution: Get off the train and wait for the next one. The same principles apply to any natural or man-made disasters.

If avoidance is not possible, you have a number of options when it comes to defending yourself. During any disaster, people will be in panic mode, which is natural. Everyone will want to evacuate, escape, and move themselves and their family to a safe location. How you do this will depend on your individual situation, as different types of disaster present different scenarios. The first and best way to defend yourself is to band together with family, friends, and neighbors as soon as reasonably possible. There is strength in numbers; violent gangs will not readily attack you. Seek the nearest government safe zone, one that has armed police or military for protection.

Self-defense means using anything at hand; a handful of coins will weight your punch. (Barry Davies)

Defending yourself when you are alone can prove difficult, especially when armed gangs roam the streets. Make yourself invisible; move only when you can see that the way forward is indeed clear. Move out of any built-up area, as the countryside is always a much safer place to be in than any large city.

In cases where there is visible violence and no sign of law and order, ARM yourself. In countries with a poor security record, such as Haiti, where law and order has steadily deteriorated, arming yourself is your only chance of survival. Kidnapping, death threats, murders, drug-related shootouts, armed robberies, home break-ins, and carjacking are common in Haiti and many other countries—defend yourself with any means, including firearms if you can get them.

Do you ever wonder why the police, or soldiers on military duty always feel confident? Because they have a weapon. Take that weapon away when they are facing an angry mob, and they will be just as vulnerable as everyone else. It is true that both the police and military have a lot of training, but when unarmed and massively outnumbered, their confidence will not be so high.

In many Third World countries, it is easy to buy an automatic weapon such as an AK47 for just a few dollars. If you do go down this path, make sure you also purchase lots and lots of ammunition and spare magazines. Make sure the weapon you have purchased works, and works well all the time. Practice firing it if at all possible, get used to changing magazines rapidly, and get to know your weapon. If you have the opportunity, teach other sensible family members. Remove a weapon from anyone acting erratically, or in a precarious manner.

In conclusion, by all means, defend yourself and your family, but do not use your weapon to demand from others. Always treat a weapon and its usage with responsibility and respect.

Author's Note: I do not proclaim that everyone should rush out and buy a gun; in many countries, this would be extremely difficult and totally unnecessary. But one thing I have learned is that the types of people you find in armed street gangs have no respect for human life, especially in Africa. The only sensible reaction is to fight back, and fight back aggressively.

UNARMED COMBAT

If you do not fancy carrying around a gun, there are several other alternatives when it comes to weapons for self-defense. Just look around and you will quickly find an object that can be useful. One of the best is a baseball bat or a pick handle. Believe me, if used correctly, they are better than a gun. During the London riots in August 2011, when gangs of youths roamed the streets looting, the fastest selling item on the internet was a baseball bat. In a twenty-four hour period, Amazon UK reported that sales of the Rucanor Aluminium Baseball Bat climbed in ranking from 6,974 to 105. The main reason for this was people wanting to protect their property from the looters. In addition to a baseball bat, the list below details some other items to get you thinking.

A tightly rolled newspaper or magazine makes a great improvised weapon. (Barry Davies)

Coins: Filling your hand with loose pocket change and forming a fist will greatly increase the force of any blow. Additionally, several coins tied into the corner of a handkerchief will form a very effective cosh or blackjack. Use it by swinging at the assailant's temple or general skull area.

Magazine or Newspaper: Roll any magazine into a baton and carry it with you quite naturally. Hold it by the center to stab with, using either backward or forward thrusts. Hold the end of the baton if you intend beat your assailant around the head. A rolled up newspaper is a great defensive weapon for fending off any knife attack.

Walking Stick: This item offers excellent protection for the elderly, although it is not uncommon for hikers of all ages to carry a walking stick. The best type is the one with a heavy ornate top, and a metal tipped, strong wooden shaft. Use the walking stick as you would a fencing sword; slash, and rain blows at the assailant's head and solar plexus. This is very useful against any knife of bottle attack, by slashing down hard at their wrists. You may be able to stop the assailant pursuing you if you can strike his kneecaps hard enough. It's also a good idea to have a small strap securing the walking stick to your wrist.

Bottle: The bottle is the weapon of many a street fight. Beer, champagne, or wine bottles all have a good grip at the neck and heavy base. Do not bother to smash the end of the bottle off, as this normally results in the bottle disintegrating altogether. Use the bottle as you would a club, and strike for the head and temple. The joints in the body are particularly sensitive, so the elbow and kneecap are particularly good to hit with any bottle.

Flashlight: It is common sense to carry a flashlight with you while walking out on a dark night. Additionally, several flashlights should be positioned around the home for emergencies (see Home Protection). Although expensive, the more modern Mag-light type flashlights are extremely good, and make an excellent weapon (the Special Forces have used them for years). In any attack, use the flashlight as you would a hammer.

Rocks and Soil: If you are attacked outdoors, throwing rocks at your assailant will help keep him at bay. Closer up, a handful of sand or dirt thrown in the assailant's face will temporally blind him.

Socks: Silly as it may seem, a sock will readily make a very effective cosh or blackjack. Fill it with sand, chippings, or soil. In the home or street, use loose pocket change. Swing it hard at the assailant's head in the same fashion as you would use any cosh or blackjack.

Balled fist, or a torch—a hit quick and hard, and then run. (Barry Davies)

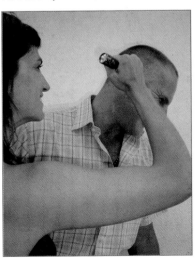

In a situation where no other weapons are available, you must defend yourself with the weapons you were given. Select which is appropriate to the situation and when you decide to strike, move with all the speed and aggression you can muster.

Balled fist: It is normal for us to fight with a balled fist. Use your first punch to hit a vital target area of your assailant. Aim for the nose, chin, temple, or stomach. If time permits, fill your hand with loose pocket change, as this will increase the weight of any blow. Rain several blows in rapid succession and then try running off.

Heel of the hand: The chin jab is delivered with the heel of the hand, putting the full force of your body weight behind the punch. When attacking from the front, spread the fingers and go for the eyes. If attacking from the rear, stick the back of their neck just below the hair line for a very effective punch. As the head snaps forward, use your fingers to grab the hair and snap it back quickly. You are less likely to injure your hand with the heel of the hand techniques.

Elbow: The elbow is a great weapon when you are side on, or have your back to the assailant. Jabbing the elbow into your assailant's stomach will almost certainly drop them to the floor. If you have been knocked to the ground, try elbowing up into the privates. Any well connected blow from your elbow will give you time to break contact and run.

Knee: Although it is one of the body's more powerful weapons, it is limited by its movement, restricting it to the lower part of the body. However, its battering ram effect can cause severe damage when driven into the private area or aimed at the outer thigh causing a dead-leg.

Foot: A hard kick is as good as any fist punch, and can be used just as readily. Keep your kicks below waist height, unless you have had some special training. Remember, the moment you lift your foot from the floor, you become unbalanced.

Heel: The heel is excellent when grabbed from behind. Drive it down the instep of your assailant or stamp continually on his foot. Another effective way is to kick at the ankle bones.

Teeth: Biting into any part of your assailant's body will cause severe pain and discomfort. The ears and nose are the favorite places to go for, but any exposed skin will do.

Chapter 2

SURVIVING IN A THEATRE OF WAR / CIVIL UNREST / TERRORISM

A war zone is not a good place to find yourself.

No matter where we live on this planet, we all face a wide variety of risk: floods, earthquakes, hurricanes, tornadoes, and wildfires take many lives. But it is not just natural disasters that kill the innocent; civil unrest, war, and terrorism all produce high numbers of deaths and injury. The question then lies, which one is worse?

In 1918, the Spanish Flu Pandemic, which was a highly contagious disease, took the lives of some fifty million people around the world, including a lot of young and healthy people (that's about thirty-four million more than were killed in the First World War). It was dubbed the 'Spanish Flu,' as Spain showed the first amount of serious deaths. There were rumors that the pandemic started as a result of trench warfare in Western Europe, which had degenerated to soldiers living in the most appalling rat-infested, damp, and diseased conditions.

While it would take a volume of books and data to argue which was worse, one thing is for certain: there is a difference. Wars and civil unrest can be prevented or stopped, and terrorism can be abated. Natural disasters, on the other hand, can happen at any time, to any country, and with any degree of intensity. Let's face it, life is unpredictable!

Wars are no longer fought on battlefields where both sides line up and face each other, with none of the combatants sent to the rear for safety. They are fought in the streets and rubble of towns and cities, where the only criterion is to gain control. Pilots of sophisticated aircrafts release bombs and missiles from thousands of meters away with little knowledge of the damage they cause on the ground. In many cases, the pilots are elated at the accuracy of their guidance systems, and rarely give a thought to the collateral damage caused. Armed un-manned drones (UCAV's) fly overhead, carrying massive destructive capability (guided by pilots sitting in a bunker, drinking coffee).

People, mainly adolescents, seniors, and women, cower in their homes as the explosions take place, doing their best to protect their families. When the bombs and missiles stop falling, the lucky ones emerge to see the damage caused, while those not so fortunate wail over the dead. Living in a war zone is equally as dangerous as any natural disaster, and in many cases, more so. You will experience terrible sights: the death of loved ones, parents, children, and friends. You will suffer hunger and thirst and have to endure freezing cold or extreme heat. To venture outside is to risk being shot by a sniper, or worse, being captured and tortured.

It is difficult for me to tell you how to survive in a war zone, because most of my life, I have been on the other side of the street. I was a soldier within the war zone, and as such, belonged to a military unit. I always had food and water, and even after several weeks of fighting, I would be passed back to base for a little 'R & R' (Rest and Recuperation). I would be given a shower, a hot meal, and was able to swap war stories with my friends over a cold beer. Rarely did I ever think about the civilians who had been caught up in the war: their homes destroyed, their main water supply disrupted, no electricity, and food in very short supply. To make matters worse, many civilians would be wounded, and the hospital facilities, for those that could reach them, would be stretched to capacity.

Civilians caught up in a war can suffer in many different ways, partially due to the type of war and its geographical location. In Afghanistan, the war is fought over the towns, over the land, and in the mountains. In such a war, the civilian population tends to stay in their homes and villages, although many have moved to the larger cities where they feel safer. Back in 1975, the once beautiful city of Beirut in Lebanon fell to civil war. In the West, the Muslims seized control, while the Christians took over the Eastern part of the city. Many factions entered the war, which devastated the city, and by 1982, most of West Beirut was under siege by Israeli troops and both American and French forces suffered heavy losses at the hands of Hezbollah. Amid this destruction, many civilians fled.

In the jungles of Vietnam and Borneo, the village people could leave their homes and hide temporarily in the jungle. In Southern Thailand, where there is a large Muslim population, the people are split between their religion and loyalty to their country and crown. But as with a natural disaster, people living in a war zone do survive. They are still breathing, which proves that there is hope in surviving war conditions.

A war zone can develop very quickly in today's world, but there is always a few days' warning. Heed this warning and discuss the problems and possibilities with your family. It will always depend on your individual circumstances, but below I have laid out a list of useful questions you should answer and some ideas of how to survive in a war zone.

- Do you have any place to send your children away from the war?
- If yes, do so without delay.
- Can a member of the family accompany your children?
- If yes, do so. You should try to make sure that it is an elderly member.
- Is it safe to travel?
- If yes, do so.
- Is this war based on religion, ethnic, or tribal differences? How do you and your family relate to this?
- Who is the dominant force? Are you on the winning side?
- What non-perishable supplies do you have available?
- If you are not sure, remember the basic rule:
  If in doubt, move out!

CIVILIANS IN A WAR ZONE

Unless you have lived through a war zone, you will never understand the full range of feelings and emotion that are provoked. So far, we have talked in this book about overcoming and controlling the two worst enemies of survival, fear and pain. For locals in a war zone, there is a lot of fear and pain, but unlike a natural disaster, where it is short-lived, in a war zone it continues for months or even years.

I am truly amazed at how the locals seem to go on with the business of living, right in midst of the terrifying war zone that their country has become. Bombs rain down, building and debris are scattered at the speed of 24,000 feet per second, and bodies and body parts fall as the dust settles. Then in the distance, you hear

Rebels, young people with guns, can be a real threat. (Barry Davies)

the sound of machine gun fire, and it comes ever closer. The nightmare becomes terrifying.

At this stage, the petrified local people are holed up in the basement of their homes. They are too terrified to move, paralyzed by the fear of what might happen next. A woman, eight months pregnant, wonders if her child will ever be born. People peek out of their holes, and run through the bomb damaged streets looking for food or water to feed their children. This is just the start.

Gone are the dreams of going to school and becoming a doctor. There is no play time, no laughter, no sports, and no time to relax. Out of the silence comes another deafening explosion as yet another bomb hits nearby. This you can deal with, but when the soldiers come in the night, you fear for your sanity as the violence they inflict is beyond description.

While the above might seem a little dramatic, it is all true. If the truth were known, living in a war zone can get far worse; trying to put fear and pain in its place is almost impossible and the best you can hope for is to survive.

Staying Alive in a War Zone

It is not easy to tell everyone how to survive in a war zone. The country, the conflict, and the climate all play a major part in your survival. In a remote African village, there may very well be ample food and water, but the conflict could be ethnic or tribal. The soldiers on both sides

Author's Note: I have seen many cities, towns, and villages where war has turned civilization into savagery. Many people think that this only happens in places like Africa, but they would be wrong. Some of the worst atrocities were committed in Europe during the siege of Sarajevo in the war in the former Yugoslavia (1992-1996). Mass murder, torture, rape, genocide, and worst of all, ethnic cleansing all took part in this once beautiful city. Every day, hundreds of innocent people were shot by snipers as they ventured out of their hovels looking for food and water. A mortar round would land and kill children playing in the street, while hospital patients died as a rocket smashed into one of the wards. The list of atrocities cost the lives of over 10,000 people with another 58,000 wounded. In 2011, the commander of the Serbian army controlling the siege, Ratko Mladic, was arrested and flown to The Hague to stand trial for War Crimes.

will steal food and murder the villagers in a frenzy of violence. In Mogadishu, there is no food, other than that stolen by war lords from the relief agencies. Water is scarce and medical assistance almost nonexistent. But if you are alive, there is always hope. Climate is important because you will have to deal with the rigors of heat and extreme cold, both of which can kill as efficiently as any bullet.

Here are a list of things you can do to try and improve your situation and living standard; some may be applicable, some may not. Always remember, humans walked this planet thousands of years before supermarkets, shops, farms and industry, and we are still here!

Providing you are alive and not injured, your first priority in a war zone is to find a safe shelter. This maybe an underground cellar in the city or a safe place away from your village in the jungle, but the location and situation of the war will determine which is best. Whatever you choose, make sure it is protected from any further bombing or mortar fire. Try to get to a place where there is only one main entrance, but has a small bolt hole in case of emergency. Here are some points to keep in mind when selecting your secure shelter.

- Stay away from windows. Replace glass (if not already broken) with clear plastic sheets.
- Keep everyone together in one corner.
- Keep your belongings with you and within reach.
- Share your shelter, as there is safety in numbers.
- Devise games for the children to distract their fear.
- Use water as if you were a Bedouin Arab crossing the desert. Make sure all drinking water is clean (see Chapter 11).
- If there is no electricity, then use candles. Remember, light gives away your location, so use it sparingly at night.
- Sleep when you can, day or night, when it is safe to take an hour or so.
- Research has proven that a 15-30 minute power nap is as good as a full night sleep for some types of memory tasks.
- Collect food, save any tinned food for an emergency, and preserve perishables for as long as possible.

- Scrounge from the soldiers. One American or British ration pack will feed five people.
- If you can, make a running bag. In this, put as much food and water as you can spare. Include your passport if you have one, as you may need to cross into a safe country. Keep your running bag in a safe place, but a place where you can grab it quickly.

Make a War Zone Grab Bag

When hell is unleashed and the bombs start to fall, you may need to move from your home and move quickly. In such as case, just like a natural disaster, have a grab bag ready. A War Zone Grab Bag differs slightly from that of a normal Disaster Grab Bag because the danger you face is not caused by nature. Your grab bag should not be too heavy and only filled with the real essentials to sustain life. If you live in an isolated village or a jungle area, it may also be prudent to prepare a hidden cache which you can visit. Use a simple thirty liter rucksack to hold the contents of your grab bag and fill it with these items:

Refugees carrying their basic possessions move away from the war.

- Cell phone, if coverage is still available.
- Passport, as you may need to cross borders.
- Some currency or gold items to barter (the SAS were issued gold coins in the Gulf War).
- Non-perishable dry foodstuffs, such as rice, grain, flour, or biscuits.
- Water, but remember that this can be heavy.
- Salt.
- Matches (suitably protected against dampness—wax coated matches).
- Candles.
- Water purification system or iodine tablets.
- First aid kit containing mainly bandages and wound cleaning supplies, such as iodine.
- Small radio (wind-up type that will never run out of batteries).
- A weapon if you have one.

Author's Note: Outside of America, many people will challenge the thought of carrying a weapon in a war zone. Trust me, many men, members of some paramilitary factions including regular soldiers, see a war zone as a killing field where they are free to murder, rape, and pillage at will. Your life and the lives of your children are at serious risk. The only answer in a war zone when threatened with a gun is another gun. Do-gooders and unarmed non-combatants die very quickly, and often for no reason at all. In Africa, children as young as six are drugged and taught to fire a weapon. They have no qualms about killing you. They simply don't know any better!

Before you leave your home, make sure you have a pre-arranged place to meet up, as things get disorientated in a war zone. Keep one adult with each child if possible, just in case you get split up. Dress with as many layers of clothes as possible. You can always discard some later, but if you need to sleep on rough terrain, you will need some warmth.

While you remain in your safe shelter or home, your first priority is to locate a water source. Most advancing armies will knock out the essential services such as the power grid, which in turn may disrupt the water supply or filtration. Always have available the means to purify your water (see Chapter 11). If you have to fetch water from a point in the street, remember that you will not be the only one doing so. Soldiers have a nasty habit of waiting for civilians to fetch water, and they may have booby-trapped the water source or have a sniper watching.

Children war fighters.

Military snipers are trained to shoot from over 1,000 meters. They often wait and watch places where they know people must go: water supplies, hospitals, and schools. If you must go out, look out for bodies, especially with head wounds, and avoid the area.

In your home, you are safer on the ground level or in a cellar. Stupid as it may sound, you might consider constructing the shelter in your garden if you have the materials and time. During WWII, many Londoners were saved due to the construction of Anderson air raid shelters. If you don't have a garden and live in a city or town, is there an underground car park or underground concrete structure that will withstand the bombing? Never seek shelter close to any military target, such as army barracks, government buildings, or main power generators. In Beirut, many people found safe shelter and hid in the ruins, from where they would only venture out at night. If you have to move, do it quickly and quietly. Look after your feet, as they are your only means of transport. Additionally, you will need to run like a rabbit, dodge and roll like a football player, and dive like a goalkeeper.

The buildings and streets of Sarajevo were not safe; for years people cowered in cellars and debris.

Some Advice from a Survivor of the War in Sarajevo

- Stockpile as much durable food as possible; potatoes are always a good choice.
  - Tinned meat and rice are also worth considering. Tinned food that does not need heating was best.
- To have a gold bracelet is OK, but to have real toilet paper is wonderful.
- Don't worry about losing electricity, you soon get used to it.
- Boredom is terrible, so always have a few books with you, or you will go insane very quickly.
- The feeling to be human can fade very quickly and I would happily have exchanged a full hot meal for a bit of soap, or toothpaste.
  - You have no idea how happy I was to actually brush my teeth with toothpaste and wash my face—after two months, it was a real morale boost.
- There are also the basic things, such as candles and lots and lots of matches (or a very good lighter).

I would advise you not to keep everything that you have in one location. I was forced to leave my house and take off with just my backpack and weapon. If you can, keep a cache a few miles away from your home so that you could go to it, if you are forced to abandon your residence. Be prepared to not return to your home for years and try to have another

Man using a dead body as cover from return fire. (Barry Davies)

place to live in another part of the country or even some other country. (I was not able to go back to my home until years later.) Stash as much ammo in different locations as you can. I did not have enough ammo in the first place and whatever I had was used or traded within the first month of me leaving my home. Ammo was a good trading currency and could get you a meal at any time. Local paper currency was basically worthless, but if you had foreign currency, then you were in better shape. Gold and silver were good to have, but it was harder to find someone that would accept gold and silver as a form of payment.

People that lived in big towns also had their share of problems. If they lived in apartment buildings, they were dependent on central heat; when things started to go bad, there was no more fuel to heat these apartments. The people that had stoves or were able to obtain them or make them then had another problem: getting the firewood. If you live inside of a city that is surrounded by soldiers and you can't go outside of the city, obtaining firewood can become your daily battle for survival. Burning your furniture, books, park benches, trees from the parks, and every other tree that you can find will be normal. Most of the people were forced to make daily runs to water points and bring the water back to their families. Water points were favorite targets for snipers. Having extra water jugs will help you minimize your visits to water points.

BULLETS, EXPLOSIONS AND EXPLOSIVE DEVICES

In war, civil strife, or terrorism, the two main elements that will harm you are bullets and explosions. Bullets can be avoided (if not, having read this book will be of little use to you). Explosions can go off all the time, and for any number of reasons, but bullets are only normally fired when two enemies come face to face. Having been in many battles both large and small, the bullets fly around like angry little bees. When you hear them going 'zip zip' they are too close, so get your head down. Those people who do get shot and killed are very unlucky, as most bullet wounds are in the limbs and they have to hit you in the head or in the center of your chest to do any real harm. Why am I telling you this? Well . . . it's to put your mind at rest. True, bullets can kill, but they are not what the television programs would have you believe. Soldiers will tell you that being shot is preferable to being blown up. If you are shot and still alive, and provided the medics get to you quickly enough, your chances of recovery are very high. Triggering an IED is a totally different story. At best, you're going to lose at least one limb. The story below is true and highlights the extraordinary feats the human body can do when shot, to overcome pain and fear.

Author's Note: On February 26th, 1966, Sergeant Geordie Lillicoe, a member of the British SAS, led his patrol into the area of an old Indonesian camp which was situated close to the border of Borneo. Cross border raids known as 'Claret Operations' were top secret and designed to hunt down and harass the Indonesian army on their own ground. The patrol, which numbered some eight men, had withdrawn for the night on the slopes of Gunong Rawan, where they 'bashered' (SAS term for sleeping place) up for the night.

The next morning, Lillicoe decided the camp was worth a second look, but decided to split his forces. His reasons for doing so were based on clear military thinking. The patrol was large enough; secondly he would leave the four new recruits in the relative safety of the overnight camp. Lillicoe and the only other experienced SAS soldier, Trooper 'Jock' Thomson, moved off. They made good time quickly covering some 1,500 yards when Thomson reached the outskirts of the Indonesian camp area. He stopped, and motioned discreetly for Lillicoe to do likewise. They waited, listening to the jungle, and all seemed quiet. Nothing was suspicious, and Thomson turned his head slowly to query Lillicoe. A perceptible nod told Thomson to continue. Ducking under some bamboo which lay across the track, he emerged on the other side. There was a soldier with a light automatic no more than twelve yards away to his right. They had walked directly into a well-prepared Indonesian ambush.

Almost immediately, the soldier fired. At this signal, several more guns opened up on the two SAS men. Jock Thomson was hit in the first burst, taking a bullet in the left thigh, shattering the bone. However, the hit knocked him off the track where he landed in thick bamboo. Here, Jock found himself confronting yet another Indonesian soldier. The soldier was very young and extremely scared; he seemed to be having trouble with his rifle. Jock raised his Armalite rifle and shot the soldier. He then crawled out of the immediate danger zone. The sight of bright blood pumping from his wound made him want to stop, but he knew that if he did not clear the Indonesian ambush area, a second and third bullet would find him. So, with the life blood flowing from him, he crawled into the thick bush. Although not out of immediate danger, Jock Thomson felt it was safe enough to dress his wound and stop the bleeding. The pieces of the shattered femur led to excruciating pain, so Jock injected himself with morphine. (Every member of the SAS carries two syringes operated by squeezing the flexible container.) While he did this, the gun fire died down to a few sporadic shots. Even so, he felt it necessary to keep his senses about him and make his way to safety.

Lillicoe was a short way off, and was lying quite still, with blood all over him. As patrol commander, he was immediately behind Thomson and also hit by the initial bursts of Indonesian gunfire. As Thomson was thrown to the left of the bamboo clump, Lillicoe leapt to the right, firing to his front as he did so. Almost immediately, he was knocked off his feet. Hit in the legs, he was unable to move and forced to return fire while sitting in the center of the track. Despite their injuries, both men continued to lay down suppressive fire. Then as quickly as it had began, the firing stopped. Both men immediately crawled out of the ambush-killing zone. Then, Thomson saw a figure stand-up and move out into the open. It was an Indonesian soldier coming out to check the killing area. It was a serious error of judgment, as both Thomson and Lillicoe fired together. Once more the area fell quiet. This time, Lillicoe and Thomson exchanged words telling each other of their injuries. At this time, Jock came forward to give Lillicoe covering fire.

As Thomson was on his feet, Lillicoe thought he could walk and ordered him to get the rest of the patrol. Thompson shouted that he was also hit and would try and make it back up the ridge where he could reconvene with the rest of the patrol. The balance of the SAS patrol had decided that the best course of action was to move to the nearest infantry post, which was close by, and lead back a stronger party to search the area. This they did, starting back towards the scene of the contact later the same day.

Thomson and Lillicoe became separated. Thomson reapplied a fresh field dressing to his wound and injected himself with more morphine. Then very slowly, he continued crawling his way towards the ridgeline above him. Darkness fell and gave him some protection; to provide camouflage, he settled down in the mud of a pig-hole to wait out the night. By morning of the second day, Thomson managed to cover half the distance back to the infantry camp and finally managed to make it back to the RV where he was discovered by a Gurkha patrol who had been sent to look for the wounded men. He was extremely weak from loss of blood and required immediate medical attention.

Geordie Lillicoe managed to extract himself into the nearby bamboo and like Thompson, dressed his wound and gave himself morphine. His left leg felt numb and detached, and there was no sensation in it. His right leg felt better, although it would not support him, as he was losing a lot of blood. The bullet had entered his left leg a little below the thigh and exited by blowing an enormous hole through his backside. Luckily, the nerve had been severed, so fortunately there was little pain, added to which the main artery was undamaged. Bandaging the entry point was easy, but trying to stem the bleeding from his buttocks proved to be an ordeal. These wounds to his legs made it almost impossible to move and the blood loss seriously worried him.

By hiding under the trunk of a fallen tree, he, like Thomson, waited out the night. By this time he had lost a tremendous amount of blood and after a while fell unconscious. It was daylight when he recovered and heard the Indonesian soldiers all around him. One of the enemy had climbed a tree about forty yards away and remained there for about half-an-hour in full view as he looked around. By this time, Lillicoe could hear a helicopter searching for him; however, the close proximity of the enemy deterred him from deploying his Sarbe rescue beacon. It was only when he was absolutely certain he would not be detected that he risked using the survival radio, calling in a helicopter which managed to winch him out. Both men survived and were fit enough to continue service in the SAS. The story is true and a good example of how to live with fear and pain.

Explosives

Explosions, on the other hand, come in all shapes and sizes, from small hand grenades to very large bombs and missiles. As I stated earlier, **'Knowledge Dispels Fear,'** so understand what explosives are and what they can do so you will dispel some of the fear.

Explosions are caused by a rapid chemical conversion of a solid or liquid into a gas with resultant energy release. Explosives are either high or low order. High produces shock waves of up to 9,000 m/s, while low explosives, mainly gun powered, tops out at around 400 m/s. Low explosives are mainly used for propellant, i.e., to fire something out of a barrel, while high explosives are usually found on the receiving end, i.e., the warhead.

For the purpose of this book, we will stick with high explosives and the effects on the human body. When explosives are detonated, they produce a supersonic over-pressurized shock wave that moves out in every direction. The pressure in the shock wave can equate to 700 tons, this coupled with the speed causes a shattering effect, so you can start to see what this is going to do to simple flesh, bone and blood.

Not surprisingly, most of the high-end explosives are used by the military: TNT, C-4, PE4, Semtex, Nitro-glycerine, Dynamite, and Ammonium Nitrate Fuel Oil (ANFO) are a few common ones we all know about. The newer variants are such things as HMX, which is an insensitive Nitro-Amine high explosive. HMX has a high molecular weight and is currently the world's most powerful chemical explosive. In

This mine is sensitive to human approach. (Barry Davies)

the main, HMX is the explosive of choice for detonating a nuclear bomb, and is also sometimes used for rocket propellants. Then, there is Octanitrocubane; a truly powerful explosive, which has a twenty to twenty-five percent greater explosive power that HMX. One interesting fact is that Octanitrocubane doesn't require an external oxygen source to decompose, which means it could be used in the vacuum of outer space. The good thing is that there is not much of it about as they have only managed to produce a small amount, but look out for it in the future, as it has an explosive velocity of 10,100 m/s!

The problems we face is that it's not necessary to have sophisticated material in order to make high explosives; you would be surprised at the chemicals normally found in your own home, the local supermarket or hardware store. The recent bombing and mass killings in Norway by Anders Behring Breivik is a perfect example of how easy it is. Breivik bought around six tons of fertilizer and made up various types of Ammonium Nitrate (when mixed with diesel, this produces an explosive known as ANFO). Variants of ANFO have been used by the IRA in Northern Ireland and ETA in Spain. ANFO was used in both the World Trade Center bombing in 1993 and the Oklahoma City bombing in 1995.

Improvised Explosive Device (IED)

The IED has supplanted the Kalashnikov to become the insurgent weapon of choice for the 21st century. In 2010, insurgents planted 14,661 IEDs, a sixty-two percent increase over the previous year. During this period (2008-2010), IEDs are known to have caused approximately sixty percent of all fatalities in Afghanistan. IEDs can be assembled by villagers in their backyard and provides such groups as the Taliban with a very effective way of demoralizing our troops. Ironically, it is what the Stinger surface-to-air missile (supplied by the American Military) enabled the Mujahedin to do to the occupying Soviet forces: knock out their air power and demoralize their army. I think someone at the CIA in Langley forgot the old adage; today's friend is tomorrow's enemy.

However, the IED is so much more. It can be a simple device, nothing more than an old artillery shell with a pressure plate or trip wire to activate it, or it can be complicated or undetectable, especially when it's made of wood or non-reactive material.

Patrolling in Afghanistan is extremely dangerous, and troops are constantly aware of the IED threat. (Staff Sgt. Adam Mancini)

Author's Note: I have worked with explosives for many years and have constructed many IEDs, as well as taught their usage and capabilities. The use of IEDs in Afghanistan, which are being planted today, has become an art form. While not as sophisticated as those in Iraq, they tend to be much larger and more effective. Above all, in order to stay in one piece, you need to know what signs to look for and where to look. Remember this one thing I always told my students, if it don't feel right, don't do it, and 'NEVER' touch or pick-up an object in a war zone unless you are absolutely sure its one-hundred percent safe to do so. Finally, never pull a tight pin from any explosive device; blow it in-situ.

With any luck, those who are most at risk from IEDs will have received the full package of what to do and what not to do prior to deployment. The only thing I can add to this is to listen to the voices of experience, the men and women of our armed forces who have just finished their tour. The enemy keeps pace with what we do, i.e., if we find a way of disarming an IED, they find another way of killing you. The most common types of IEDs are:

- Victim-initiated.
  - This simply means the first person to step on or near the IED will be killed or severely injured; makes no difference if it is a soldier, Afghan civilian, or child. The IED requires no command wire or wireless detonation, just a simple pressure plate. Manufactured mines, both anti-tank and personnel, left over from the Afghan war with the Soviet Union fall into this category.
- Command-detonated requires a trigger man to sit and wait for his victims. The IED is detonated either by a hand wire cable connected to a battery or remote-controlled via a wireless signal such as a cell phone. This means the IED is selective in who it kills.
- Suicide IEDs are set off by an attacker wearing an explosive vest or driving a vehicle laden with explosives (vehicle-borne IED). This is by far the most effective type of device, as the suicidal operator can detect and select the best target. In the event that he has more than one target, he can switch to what will cause the most damage.

Major supply routes (MSR) are frequently cleared of IEDs, and in some cases a watch is kept on the route. Nonetheless, there are times when you will be driving or walking along a route that possibly has an IED planted, maybe even more than one. Look for unusual activity patterns or changes in normal community movement (fewer people or vehicles in a normally busy area, open windows, or the absence of women or children). Vigilance is the key and there are many things you should look out for:

Once an IED has been detected it must be revealed and destroyed.

- When out on patrol, study the amount of locals around you or traveling on the same road or pathway. The Taliban are not keen on blowing their own people up (unless they don't cooperate). If an IED has been planted, the chances are they will tell the local villagers or townspeople to stay clear.
- The local population may know of a newly planted IED and will use markers to identify it, such as tires, rock piles, ribbon, new graffiti symbols, or writing on walls and buildings. The same markers could be used by the trigger man who is using it as an aiming reference.
- The enemy will rarely plant victim-initiated IEDs close to locally populated areas. But this is not to say they will not use a command-detonated IED, which is detonated directly under your vehicle or patrol. Selective targets have been blown to bits while traveling among the busy highway where jingle trucks, taxis, and coalition forces are all in high numbers.
- If the enemy knows you're going to be traveling to a certain point via a specific route, then there's a good chance they will plant an IED. Maintain good security discipline. NEVER say to a friendly local 'we will be back tomorrow,' because you won't be!
- On dirt roads, the enemy can plant an IED in a matter of minutes, while on a metal-bordered road this will be much harder. Quick, opportune target IEDs are normally easier to spot than one which has been planted with care.

Dealing with IEDs is one of the most dangerous tasks the military must face. (Sgt. Michael J. MacLeod)

- Watch for vehicles following a convoy at a distance and then suddenly pulling to the roadside, people standing on an overpass, or vehicles flashing headlights.
- The enemy has been known to record their actions, so be aware of anyone using a video camera nearby.

IED Prevention

Defeating the IED infrastructure requires a whole army of different approaches. It necessitates the need for good intelligence, so we can locate the IED factories and raid them. It needs a strong technical element of counter-IED detection and deactivation. It also requires excellent training and dissemination of all that is known about IEDs to the war fighter on the ground. The growth of the robotics industry has done much to elevate the need for humans to venture close to an IED. The use of robotics on the battle field has grown mainly in support to counter the IED threat. An estimated $24.6 billion is being spent on new electronic techniques to defeat IEDs. Their preventative methods include:

- Protecting the war fighter with better clothing and equipment.
- Improvement in vehicle armor.
- Imaging techniques that can identify or indicate the location of an IED.
- Surveillance of key areas.
- Radio jamming on commonly known triggering devices, such as cell phones, walkie-talkies, and car door fobs.
- Chemical detection of explosives on the hands of local suspects.
- Ground penetrating radar.
- Deployment of rapid UAV strikes.
- Specially trained search dogs.

Search Dogs

It is worth a small paragraph to mention the work done by specially trained search dogs and their handlers. These

teams go a long way towards minimizing the risk posed by IEDs and
other explosive devices to the war
fighter. While there are numerous
robotic machines on the battle field,
dogs can go where machines cannot.
Most will work off leash and out in
front of the handler. They are not
aggressive to the local population
and their mild manner is normally
well received. Breeds such as Labs
and Spaniels are ideally suited to the
task, and after training, they are not
influenced by gun fire, but go boldly
sniffing around. The good thing about

a dog is that it is not affected by human emotions or peripheral factors. They serve in the capacity of detecting IEDs,
explosive hides, and other bomb making equipment (and
are excellent at this).

Search dogs play
a significant role
in the detection of
IEDs. (Pfc. Jesus
J. Aranda)

While there remains no real answer to the detection of
IEDs, other solutions, especially the prevention of injury,
has progressed. Both the American and British army has
supplied 'ballistic boxers' to soldiers working in Afghanistan. Officially known as protective underwear, they are
made from heavy duty silk. Silk has been used for centuries
as a form of protection, when knights would wear silk
garments under their chain-mail. Many soldiers in the army
of Genghis Khan would wear several layers of silk, which
was enough to stop an arrow or deflect a sword.

In addition to silk, some soldiers also have extra protection for the genitals; this comes in the form of a codpiece or
cup which fits in the genital area (but is very uncomforta-
ble). Extra Kevlar plates can also be inserted to help protect

Author's Note: It is worth relating the story of Lance Corporal Kenneth
Michael Rowe of the Royal Army Veterinary Corps, attached to 2nd Battalion
of the Parachute Regiment. This dog handler, at age twenty-four, died on
Thursday, July 24 2008, on a routine patrol operating from Inkerman in the
Sangin area of Helmand Province. The patrol came under heavy enemy fire
resulting in Rowe's death and five other soldiers being injured. His explosives sniffer dog, Sasha, was also killed in the incident.

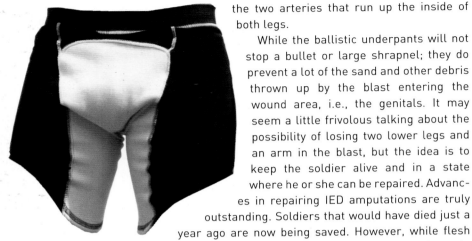

Blast Boxers protect the soldier's groin area from serious damage when an IED explodes, giving them a fighting chance of survival. (BCB Int. Ltd.)

the two arteries that run up the inside of both legs.

While the ballistic underpants will not stop a bullet or large shrapnel; they do prevent a lot of the sand and other debris thrown up by the blast entering the wound area, i.e., the genitals. It may seem a little frivolous talking about the possibility of losing two lower legs and an arm in the blast, but the idea is to keep the soldier alive and in a state where he or she can be repaired. Advances in repairing IED amputations are truly outstanding. Soldiers that would have died just a year ago are now being saved. However, while flesh and bone can be replaced by metal and plastic, the groin area is a different subject altogether. Serious damage up and inside the genital cavity is difficult to repair and death is almost certain.

One company is selling a set of underwear called 'Blast Boxers,' which are designed to protect against IEDs. Blast Boxers are manufactured both in Europe and America. They are constructed from Kevlar fabric that purportedly protects soldiers in areas where standard body armor is absent. Weighing in at just under seven ounces, the Blast Boxers are lightweight and comfortable, as all the stitching is done on the outside. Their main job is to shield the femoral artery, which is located in the thigh and when severed, produces rapid blood loss. They also help protect against a ruptured colon or loss of genitalia (which is a major plus in any man's book).

On Discovery of an IED or Possible IED

When it comes to IEDs and bombs, no matter if you are a soldier or a civilian, if you spot something unusual, no matter how trivial it may seem—**CALL IT IN.**

For those soldiers that enter a war zone where IEDs are prevalent, it is almost certain that they will receive good training in the practice of dealing with the situation. However, many others that enter a war zone will not be so prepared (personnel working for NGOs and AID agencies may only have an inkling of what to do). Advice on dealing with IEDs is constantly changing, as more intelligence comes to the forefront. However, I have outlined a simple procedure below, which at worst should keep you alive.

- Clear the immediate area.
- Watch which way you move and the cover you take; secondary IEDs may be present.
- Establish a cordon: 300 meters for a small device, 1,000 meters for a vehicle-borne device.
- Request explosive ordnance disposal (EOD).
- Maintain observation of the device until EOD is on the scene.
- Inform your command of the following:
  - Your Unit call sign—organization.
  - Time the IED was found.
  - IED type, if known.
  - Eight figure grid reference, or close GPS location.
  - Contact location and route in to meeting point.
  - Any immediate threat, to personnel, property or mission.

IED wounds are simply horrendous; despite this, through the brilliance of our surgeons, many survive.

Immediate Treatment for IED casualty

When an IED is initiated, anyone within the immediate vicinity will be caught up in the blast. If the detonation was caused by victim-initiation that person will almost certainly lose at least one limb, more likely two, sometimes even three or four. The limb that steps on the mine will take the blast, with the other limb coming in at a close second. The outstretched arm holding the rifle is also at risk, as is the groin area. Most current IEDs are powerful enough to remove one limb, if not several.

Damage caused by an IED includes immediate amputation of extremities, contusions, ruptures, lacerations/punctures/avulsion, fractures, subdural hematoma, concussion (traumatic brain injury), burns, loss of hearing, flash blindness, etc.

The speed at which the injured soldier can be moved from the point of IED impact to the hospital is vital to his or her life. Where there is more than one victim, effective triage is crucial. Those victims with a good potential for survival should receive immediate medical attention, while those with a poor diagnosis for survival should receive minimal care but with maximum pain control. Soldiers with lesser injuries should be checked and placed in order of injury degree.

All trauma care should start with the ABC (Airway, Breathing, and Circulation). Once the victim is stabilized, as much history as possible should be obtained. A systematic physical examination should be performed with the patient completely naked and exposed. The finding of the examination will address the priority of recovery procedure (see Chapter 12).

TERRORISM

While we talk of wars and civilian unrest, we must also include acts of terrorism. Without a doubt, modern terrorism poses a much greater threat than it has in the past, as modern weapons bring the threat of nuclear, chemical, and biological attack within the grasp of radical terrorist organizations. Terrorism is not only on the rise; it has increased in brutality, producing ever more casualties. For example, the hijackings of the late 1960's produced few casualties, compared with those incidents that have taken place at the start of the 21st century. The attacks on America, the Bali bombing, the Chechen siege in Moscow, and the bombings in London are all evidence of this. Such incidents provide governments with an insight into the future of terrorism by indicating what is feasible.

We must recognize that a new breed of terrorist has emerged; one that has developed outside the normal target confines. Remember, a terrorist is a person, not some ghostly aberration. They think, learn, adapt, and improve.

The Possibilities

Nuclear bombs, nerve gas, suicide bombers, assassinations, and even conventional warfare are all possibilities open to a terrorist group. In reality, most of these possibilities are restricted by governing factors. While it is possible in theory to construct a nuclear bomb, it is almost impossible in practice. Therefore, it will be a long time before we see a terrorist group with its own nuclear bomb. Unfortunately, the same cannot be said for biological or chemical agents, some of which, although highly dangerous, are simple to produce. The Sarin gas attacks on the Tokyo subway in March 1995 is one example.

For the moment, the growth of terrorism remains within the realms of the suicide bomber, IEDs, and shootings. Used intelligently, the suicide bomber offers any terrorist organization a weapon with a perfect guidance system and full stealth facilities. The suicide bomber is able to identify its target with one hundred percent accuracy. If threatened or prevented from acquiring its primary target, they can abort, and go immediately to a secondary target without being re-programmed. The lethality of a suicide bomber is indefinable.

Why Does Terrorism Exist?

I have spent most of my life fighting terrorism, but I have always found it difficult to define, let alone understand it. Like the rest of us, I have made comments and judgments, while ignorant of some very basic facts. The problem for most people is being able to understand the layered history of each terrorist group as it is defined by its individual struggle. For example, in the conflict between the Israelis and the Palestinians, awareness of their past history prior to 1948 influences comprehension of the situation created by the establishment of modern Israel. I make no apologies for my simplistic version of events, nor do I swear to the dates, but it does clarify and set the scene of how a terrorist conflict can be created.

We all usually feel that our governments are doing their best, acting on our behalf to provide us with a stable society, controlled by laws, and enforced by penalties. Yet, not everyone agrees with the government, and therefore seeks to make changes. When these changes cannot be made via the ballot box, some try to make changes by force of arms.

Terrorists normally target crowded places or high value targets. This picture shows the damage caused by an IRA bomb on a hotel where the British Prime Minister was staying. (Barry Davies)

Sometimes, governments interfere in the domestic affairs of other countries, this too can spout terrorist activity.

I have long pondered why people turn to terrorist acts as a means of expression or defiance, where in all cases, it is the innocent that suffer. There are many definitions and reasons why terrorism exists, but the question is who is the terrorist, and who is the victim? What happens when the 'good guys' deliberately commit acts of terrorism? Since September 11, 2001, America has seen itself as the victim of terrorism; yet this same nation is equally guilty of terrorism and vicious, heartless violence. Which brings me back to the original question: how can we define a word for terrorism when the execution of military actions taken by governments is, in the expression of violence, equal or greater to that of any terrorist act?

In 1950, Jacobo Arbenz Guzman became the second legally elected president of Guatemala. His first task was to change the rules under which a minority select elite had previously governed. These changes included the recognition of the Guatemalan Communist and some serious land reforms which threatened U.S. companies, like the powerful United Fruit Co. America did not see the democratically elected President as an ally, and therefore set about organizing his downfall. This task was given to the CIA (Operation PBFORTUNE) and a plan of action was developed that included assassination plots and sabotage. The CIA planned to attack Jacobo Arbenz Guzman from all angles, but mainly the campaign was aimed at undermining the backing of the Guatemalan military which Arbenz needed in order to control the country. The CIA succeeded and in 1954, as Arbenz relinquished power to the military, which was later seen by America as the only power capable of maintaining order. After the coup, the CIA (Operation PBHistory) collected over 150,000 documents to establish the direct link between Guzman and the Soviet Union. (There was none!)

In the aftermath, the military junta was nothing more than another dictatorship: do as we say or you will be killed. When a small insurgency developed, Guatemala's U.S. equipped and trained military let loose a savage wave of repression that left thousands of peasants dead. This oppression has lasted forty years, totally destroying the fabric of Guatemalan society and causing the death or disappearance of almost a quarter of a million people. This type of story is not new. Ask any Special Forces soldier and he will tell you that they have all participated in something similar.

> "As a CIA operative, I trained Guatemalan exiles in Honduras to invade their own country and unseat the elected president . . . . The coup I helped engineer in 1954 inaugurated an unprecedented era of intransigent military rule in Central America. Generals and colonels acted with impunity to wipe out dissent and garner wealth for themselves and their cronies . . . . Later I realized we weren't fighting communism at all, we were fighting the people."
>
> —Philip Roettinger, a retired U.S. Marine Corps Colonel and CIA operative

On January 27, 1971, Arbenz, now living in Mexico, died in his bedroom. The Guatemalan government signed an agreement with his surviving family in 2011 to restore his legacy and publicly apologize for the government's role in ousting him.

Oppression, tyranny, dictatorship, political motivation, and religious zeal all play their part in promoting terror; yet in all my years of fighting terrorism, the best and closest quote that answers 'why does terrorism exist' is one given by a terrorist leader himself.

> " . . . In today's world, no one is innocent, no one is neutral. A man is either with the oppressed or he is with the oppressor. He who takes no interest in politics gives his blessing to the prevailing order that of the ruling classes and exploiting forces . . . "
>
> —George Habash, Leader of the Popular Front for the Liberation of Palestine

You can put George Habash's words into a simple scenario that is factual. Let us reduce the problem to one of them or us.

There are only one hundred people on the planet of which ten are terrorists; they want everyone to join their religious sect. They bombed and killed five of our number last month, this month their success has been more fruitful as they have managed to blow up another eighteen, including five children. Everyone was very angry. We have tried all the normal things like negotiations, peace talks, giving into their demands and threats of retaliation without actually carrying them out. We even took two of them into custody but these had to be released when they threatened to blow up a school bus. At the present rate of attrition, the good guys will be powerless within a period of six months.

Then one of the good guys asks, 'Why don't we fight back. We know that of the ten terrorists only two are the real instigators. Let's kill them and the problem goes away.'

'Kill them. Are you mad? We will not sink to their level!' So the larger group gave their blessing to the prevailing order but still remain the weaker group.

Terrorism in Perspective

On October 12, 2002, at 11:05 p.m., huge explosions tore apart the peace of the idyllic island of Bali. This tropical island, with its beautiful beaches and friendly people had long been a holiday magnet for young people from around the world (especially Australians). Many Australians were in the Kuta, enjoying the nightlife and music of the bars and nightclubs. Some were having a drink in Paddy's Bar, the prospect of terrorism the furthest thought from their minds. In just a few seconds that changed forever as a bomb, placed on a stool or table near the DJ's booth, exploded in a blast that was strong enough to wrench a row of concrete seats from a wall.

Fifteen seconds later, a second massive blast destroyed the nearby Sari Club at Kuta Beach, a popular nightspot packed with clubbers. This bomb had been placed in a white Mitsubishi van parked in front of the building. The blast destroyed the building and caused massive damage to those in the surrounding area. The two blasts killed more than 180 people and injured 300 more, some very seriously.

Aerial shot of the Bali bombing which killed some 202 people, many of which were tourists.

As the bombs had been aimed at soft targets frequented by westerners, terrorism was immediately suspected, with the possibility of Al Qaida being behind it. Subsequent forensic examinations of the scenes revealed that chlorate-based explosives had been used.

Like so many other aspects of everyday life, terrorism is just a part of the fabric which interlaces the individual, social, religious, and national characteristics of human behavior. As with other elements of life, it appears on every continent and in almost every country, even those peaceful countries like Norway. On July 22, 2011, Anders Behring Breivik left a car bomb near the government offices in central Oslo. The blast killed eight people and wounded many others. Two hours later, dressed as a policeman, Breivik arrived on the tiny island of Utoya where hundreds of young people were having a summer camp. He shot and killed sixty nine people, many of them teenagers.

Despite these terrible disasters, we still need to put terrorism into perspective, especially when countering the threat and putting the contributors to death. For example, in 1999, some 500,000 people died in road accidents around the world. In 2006, the CDC reported some 30,000 gun-related deaths in America alone; however, in the previous year some 652,000 died of heart attacks. We should not be afraid of terrorists or terrorism.

How a Terrorist will Strike

A suicide bomber is normally a young person between the age of 20-30; with that said, children as young as six, as well as cripples, have been used by terrorist organizations to deliver suicide bombs. The bomb itself is mainly strapped to their chest, but it can also be transported in a suitcase, child's push chair, or more recently in a backpack. The bombs are normally high explosives surrounded by nails, nuts and bolts, ball bearings, or anything that will kill or maim. The bomb is normally detonated by the bomber themselves, although they have been known to be set off by remote control (this stops them from having second thoughts). The suicide bomber will do their best to blend in with the local people. They will dress in a similar manner, but sometimes you can spot the difference.

Author's Note: It is not easy to prevent a suicide bomber from detonating their bomb and killing many others. Conversely, in the last decade, the majority of suicide bombers are from the Islamic nations. Some consider that their struggle, whether political, religious, or whatever, to be more important than their own lives. Additionally, suicide bombers do not happen overnight, as there is a huge build-up: cautious target planning, the assembly of the bomb, the approach, and finally the personal determination to trigger the bomb.

- The behavior of a suicide terrorist differs from that of people surrounding him (it has to). They may be drugged, sweating, or have pasty skin. The more religious bomber may be whispering a prayer.
- Male-Muslim bombers are normally clean-shaven (preparation for burial ceremony) and will have clean footwear.
- Both male and female bombers will be wearing bulky clothing to conceal the bomb. This this may not fit into the current weather pattern, i.e., it's a very hot day, but they are wearing a lot of clothing. Some female bombers may also simulate pregnancy to conceal the bomb.
- Clenched fists or any external wiring showing from the hand or clothing.
- People who look out for police, avoid eye contact, or keep touching their chest.
- People perspiring profusely, acting in a nervous manner, or jittery and frequently glancing over their shoulder for fear of pursuit.

The suicide bomber will simply drive or walk to their target—Oslo 2011. (Source unknown—multiple usage)

- People who return to the same spot each time, especially in a crowded place.

Most people go about their business observing nothing, but some people automatically take note of odd movement. Marketplace stall holders watch the crowd, as do other street vendors; children are also good at observation, but rarely tell their parents what they see.

If you think you have spotted a suspicious person, do not attempt to attack them yourself. If a suicide bomber suspects any danger of discovery they will almost certainly detonate the bomb. You should leave the danger zone and notify the nearest policeman or security agent. If at all possible, continue to keep an eye on the suspect; at the very least, be able to give a good description.

What to Do During a Bomb Attack

While soldiers suffer the threat of IEDs, many civilians become caught up in terrorist bombing campaigns. Most terrorist explosions take place in crowded areas with little or no warning, and the effects are always horrific. If you find yourself in the immediate vicinity of a bomb blast, your main priority is to get out of the area. This increases your chances of survival in case a second device is set to go off once the rescue services arrive. It also reduces your exposure to smoke, dust or any hazardous gasses that may be released as a result of the blast. Many survivors of 9/11 in the U.S. have subsequently died of mystery cancers thought to be related to the inhalation of particulates from the collapsed buildings. By removing yourself to a safe area, you are also making the way clear for the rescue services that will then be better able to assist those who are critically injured and cannot move.

If you are given a bomb warning, it is your clear duty to evacuate as soon as possible. However, if you are in a building when a bomb goes off, seek shelter under a sturdy table or desk. Once the immediate danger has passed and you are able to do so, exit the building as quickly and safely as possible. There may have been damage to the building structure so you are advised to use the stairs and NOT the elevator (in some high-rise buildings, the elevator may be your only viable option).

- Do not stop to retrieve personal effects, make phone calls, etc.
- Assist others if needed.
- Once outside, move away to a safe area, and avoid secondary hazards such as loose lumps of masonry or glass falling on you.
- Keep moving until you reach emergency officials or a known safe area.
- In many cases, secondary explosions may have been planted; these are normally designed to disrupt the rescue services.
- While you will want to call home, your friends, or check on work colleagues, minimize your voice calls and use text. After a major disaster, the networks become over-loaded, which is why they are switched off.
- Cover your nose and mouth with anything you have on hand to limit inhalation of dust or other hazardous materials.

If you are trapped in a building, a room, or your escape route is blocked, remain calm. Avoid any unnecessary movement that will disturb the dust, letting it settle so you can see. Most buildings are made of concrete, so the risk of serious fire after a bombing is unlikely, but certain furniture, especially curtains, may be on fire. Water pipes may burst and parts of the building structure may be missing or fractured. If you are trapped, carry out the following:

- If there is a fire and it is too big for you to deal with, move away from it.
- Likewise, if you're current location is hazardous, can you move to a safer location?
- Ascertain if you are alone or if there are others nearby.
- Do you or anyone close require immediate medical attention?
- Signal your location to others: shout, use a flashlight, or whistle. Tap on radiators or pipe work, as this will echo through the building.
- Assess your situation before taking any action.
- Your goal is to clear the building by the safest means possible.

- If you are forced to wait for the rescue services, sit tight and do exactly what they tell you.

Terrorists have a nasty habit of picking targets where it is difficult for the rescue services to get to. The bombings in March 2004 at Atocha Station in Madrid killed 191 people and wounded 1,800 more. A year later, 52 people were killed and a further 700 were injured when the London underground was bombed. If you are on a train or in the subway and a bomb goes off:

Sometimes it's impossible to protect yourself against bombing. (DoD)

- Unless you are in immediate danger, you should remain in your train car until rescue services arrive.
- Open windows or doors if possible, and if it is safe to do so, because it can reduce the severity and number of injuries from a possible secondary explosion.
- Tend to any wounded and make them comfortable. Call for anyone with medical experience in the train car (see Chapter 12).
- If you are in danger and have to move, decide which route you should take to the nearest sub-ground station platform or above ground exit. Walking down the side of the track is not a good idea as there are many hazards, not least electricity, which may not be switched off.

HIJACKING

Hijackings started way back in the early 1970's and caught the world off guard. The concept of taking an aircraft full of people and then holding them ransom was a unique idea that quickly caught on with terrorist groups around the world. While the aircraft was in the air, the terrorists were in control, and while on land, they still had the hostages neatly contained and ready to use as bargaining chips. Add to the problem was the fact that many international flights contained people of several different nations.

Terrorist survivor after the hijack at Mogadishu, defiant to the end. (Barry Davies)

The initial format for a hijacking was to make demands; the release of captured terrorists from jail was a main one, that and the demand for a large amount of money. The early days of hijacking had a dramatic effect on the world, one which cumulated in the destruction of five aircraft at Dawson's field on September 12, 1970.

However, governments of the world were getting wise to this threat and soon organized specially trained anti-hijack teams. The first great result was the courageous assault by Israeli forces in Entebbe, Uganda. They mounted an operation that could have come direct from the pages of a modern thriller, and was a major turning point in stopping hijackers. A year later the PFLP hijacked a German Lufthansa 737 bound from Palma De Mallorca to Frankfurt. Once again, the German Special Forces tracked it down and successfully assaulted the aircraft.

During these days, several people were killed as a result of hijackings, but by and large the numbers were not high. But when hijacking returned in September 2001, it was to a

Author's Note: In mid-October 1977, I was in charge of a group of British SAS counter-terrorist soldiers, who had spent the previous week checking out aircraft layouts and entry points at Heathrow airport. I will not bore you with the details, but myself and Alistair Morrison were sent by the British Government to assist the German GSG9 (anti-terrorist team) and eventually finished up in Dubai where the hijacked 737 was now sitting. After a few days of chasing the hijacked aircraft around the Middle East, we finally had it pinned down in Mogadishu. We arrived in Mogadishu around midday to find the hijacked aircraft still sitting on the runway. Around midnight, we assaulted the aircraft, killing three of the four terrorists and putting seven bullets in the fourth. Although the pilot had been murdered two days earlier, all the remaining passengers were saved, with a few minor injuries. This nailed most of the hijacking for several years.

whole new ball game. Gone were the demands for freedom and money, as the terrorists had a new strategy: convert your hijacked aircraft into a flying bomb.

Early morning of September 11, 2001 saw two hijacked 767 aircrafts fly into the World Trade Center in New York City. The attacks were coordinated and well planned, and the resulting carnage claimed the lives of 2,752 people.

How to React in a Hijack Situation

I just know I am going to get into trouble for writing this, but it's what I would advise. At the height of hijacking in the 1970's, you stood a very good chance of staying alive. Plus, at the time, my advice would be to sit in your seat, don't make yourself obvious, and wait it out. But since the assault on America, I cannot say the same. The odds are that if you are on an aircraft that is hijacked, you will die.

Thankfully, airport security is much improved, and search techniques are carried out with due diligence. That said, if you really wanted to get a gun or bomb onboard an aircraft, it is not that difficult. It is possible to sneak a few innocent items onboard, and buy the rest in the Duty Free shop if you need to make a bomb. Knives are openly sold or can be obtained in many airport kitchens. So my advice, if you are caught up in a modern day hijack, would be to 'have a go.' Let's face it, if the terrorists are hijacking the aircraft to simply fly it into a major building, you are dead anyway, so what have you got to lose? Then, how do you go about retaking an hijacked aircraft? It's not as difficult as it might seem. Dangerous? Yes. Physically possible? Yes. There are a few rules you need to learn.

Rules

- Never do anything that will make the aircraft crash or lose control (the only exception is a last ditch stand to sacrifice everyone on-board to save hundreds on the ground).
- Know what you are facing. 'Knowledge Dispels Fear.' There is normally an average of four terrorists when a hijack occurs. Can you identify all of them and their positions?
- What weapons do they have? Guns / bombs / knives?
- Who can help you? (The average aircraft holds around 300 passengers, of which half are men.)

- Are you in a position to form an alliance with others, and develop a plan (do this without scaring anyone; some people will panic and scream to the terrorists)?

So you managed to talk several others into a plan, and to 'have a go' at overcoming the terrorists. What are your priorities? This will all depend on the terrorists and how they are armed. Basically, what are they threatening you with? It is difficult for terrorist to sneak explosives on board, and trying to conceal a grenade is just as impossible; guns and knives are much easier and are likely to be your main theat. But do you know how many guns or knives you have to face? The next thing is terrorist positions. Generally, they will split up in order to better control the passengers, but the leader will almost always be up front either in or close to the cockpit so he can control the whole operation via the pilot.

Once you have the answer to these questions, you can develop a plan. Again, in order to be successful, you need to have priorities. Here are a few tips:

- Always work in pairs. Two men can overcome a single man quite easily, and a three man team is even better. The lead guy may get shot or stabbed, but in general, you will be very unlucky to find yourself fatally wounded. Also, pistols fired, even at close range, are very inaccurate.
- Timing. Do it all together; each team attack one terrorist, but only after the main team has closed with the terrorist leader.
- Your priority is to take out the terrorist leader in or near the cockpit. Take control of the cockpit doorway and defend it with your life. Make sure that either the captain or co-pilot remains alive. Let the captain know you're the good guys.
- Start your attack with a diversion. For example, have one of the women scream and jump up and down as if she is having a fit. In many cases this will bring at least two of the terrorists close enough to see what's happening and re-establish control. Seize the moment!
- Move with speed and aggression. Together with your courage, these are the only weapons you have.

- Do not hesitate. Do not try to talk or argue with the terrorists. Simply have your team close as fast as possible, take whatever they throw at you and take them down. Kill if you have to.

Once again, this book is not large enough for me to teach you a lot about anti-hijacking, but there are a couple of things you should know. The first is that most handguns can be stopped from firing if you push back on the top slide. If you have to grab a gun, always push it downwards. Hits in legs will hurt, but rarely kill you. Same goes for a knife; take any thrust to the arms. Finally, it has been my experience that no matter how dedicated a terrorist is to their cause, at the point when another human is directly threatening their life, they will lose focus for a few moments— that is your time.

If you 'have a go', you will succeed. In the worst case scenario, the terrorists will remain in control, and you're all going to die. If you try and fail, at least die with the knowledge that you have saved hundreds of lives on the ground. Added to which you will deter further hijackings in the future.

Remember, of the four aircraft that were hijacked in September 2001, two were flown into the twin towers of the World Trade Center, causing nearly 3000 deaths. One was flown into the side of the Pentagon, causing another 189 deaths, but the fourth one is believed to have been brought down by the passengers. While all forty-four passengers and crew abroad were killed, no lives were lost on the ground.

Secretary of Defense Donald H. Rumsfeld lays a wreath at the crash site near Shanksville, Somerset County, Pennsylvania. The hijack was thwarted by passengers who tried to regain control—it cost them their lives, but saved countless others. (DoD)

Chapter 3

EARTHQUAKE AND TSUNAMI

Earthquakes can happen without a resulting tsunami, and a tsunami can be triggered by a falling meteor (but that is a rare occasion). Nevertheless, recent events have shown that both earthquakes and tsunamis are connected, and as such, have a tendency to cause numerous loss of life and incredible damage. Since the turn of the century, over one million people have died as a result of major disasters, the majority being from earthquakes and tsunamis.

Why earthquakes happen, without going into a lot of complicated detail, is fairly easy to explain. The earth is round and has a small inner core (center), an outer core, and a large mantle which makes up the bulk of the planet. Sitting on top of the mantle is the crust. By comparison to the rest of the planet, the crust is a thin layer that covers the surface. While the surface of our planet is fairly cool, the deeper you go towards the earth's core, the hotter it gets.

It is on this crust that we all live: you, me, and everything else. All the cities, towns, roads, forests, deserts, arctic tundra, and last but not least, the entire ocean. On land, the crust is about eighteen and one-half miles thick, but out in the oceans, it's much thinner, down to three miles in places. However, this crust is not one solid layer. If we could scrape away the topsoil down to the bare rock, it looks more like a jigsaw puzzle. The problem is that all these pieces are a different size and they move around bumping into each other. Each piece of the puzzle is called a tectonic plate and the edges of the plate where they bump and overlap are called faults. Beneath the earth's crust is the mantle, which is a lot of hot material heated by the earth's core, a process called convection, but in reality would more resemble a lava lamp. As the heated material rises to meet the crust and fill in the gaps, the flow helps drive the movement of the plates. Earthquakes occur around these faults. Sometimes two plate faults will join and stick together, yet they continue to move. As the pressure of movement forces them to unstick, the energy they release causes an earthquake.

The energy released is forced outward from the fault in all directions; this is known as a seismic wave. This wave simply shakes the surface of the earth. The range and strength of the wave will depend on the size of the fault and the amount of slip. Earthquakes are measured by a

Seismograph to determine the magnitude of the quake, i.e., how strong it is. The measurement is done on a scale known as the Moment Magnitude Scale (MMS). This is similar to the older, but well-known Richter scale, but much more precise. Each earthquake recorded by MMS results in a number, generally starting at 1.0 where an earthquake occurs but we do not feel them on the surface. At the other end of the scale an MMS reading of 9.0 will generally mean widespread damage and severe loss of life. The most powerful earthquake ever recorded using MMS was on May 22, 1960, when a quake hit the coast of Chile which registered 9.5.

Basically, earthquakes can be put into two different scenarios; inland and at sea. Inland earthquakes, such as the one in Haiti, cause damage through vibration and earth tremors. Earthquakes at sea, especially those near the coastline, cause both vibration damage and the possibility of a large tsunami wave; it is the latter of these that causes the most damage. As a race, humans have still not worked out when or how strong an earthquake will occur, but we are getting better at our predictions.

The power of an earthquake challenges most man-made objects. (Lance Cpl Brennan O'Lowney 31 MEU)

EARTHQUAKE DISASTER PLAN

It makes sense that if you live near an area which suffers from earthquakes, to take some precautions and prepare for a sudden disaster. You will need to sit down with your family, including the children, and talk about what you will all do in the event of an earthquake. As a starting point, do a little research on the internet about any previous earthquakes close to your home, and make a list of talking points.

- How frequent are the earthquakes?
- When did the last one happen?

- How strong was the largest earthquake, and what damage did it do?
- What warning systems, if any, have been implemented since; what are they?

The answers to these questions will make a good start to your family discussion. Talk about what you should do if an earthquake was to happen suddenly, and make sure to go through all the various scenarios. Who is responsible for what, and who checks on whom? How do you communicate? Earthquakes do not give notice. What happens if a massive shock wave hits around midday when dad is at work, mom is at home, and the children are at school? The process of your disaster plan will be much different to that of midnight when the whole family is at home asleep.

Most people never take precautions, and leave everything to the last minute. This may cost you and your loved ones their lives. For example, what do you do if you wake at 4:35 in the morning to find yourself in total darkness with no electricity and the house is rolling around like a drunken sailor? You can hear your children screaming, but you can't seem to be able to move. Suddenly, there is a mighty crash and you can see the night sky where your front wall used to be.

Evacuate to a safe zone, if at all possible. (Japan-source unknown—multi-usage)

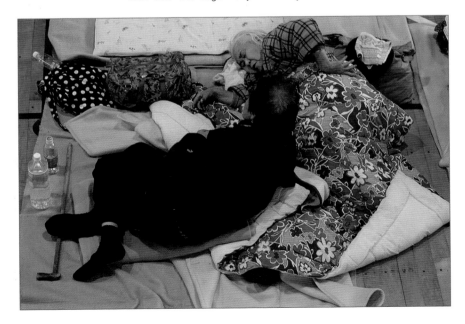

Sounds a bit far-fetched? Not exactly, as this is what happened to a family during the Christchurch earthquake in 2010.

Evacuate

In any disaster situation, if evacuation offers you safety, you must take it. Speed is always of the essence; the quicker you move, the better your chances are of survival. Many people were killed in Japan simply because they started to evacuate and then decided they needed something and returned home—there is no second chance. Once you leave, head by the quickest means to your contact point.

- Have a small but powerful battery-powered (or wind-up) radio with you and follow the instructions of local emergency officials.
- Make sure your dress is suitable, with warm clothing and sturdy footwear.
- Put your Disaster Grab Bag by the exit door so you don't forget it (see Disaster Grab Bag, Chapter 13).
- If ordered by the authorities to evacuate, you should do so immediately.
- Leave any pets at home. Do not waste time trying to catch them or put them in cages, etc.
- Lock and secure your home, only if you have time.
- Despite having your own evacuation route planned out, situations can change, so use travel routes identified by local authorities.
- When you reach your contact point, remember you may be the first to arrive, so give time to wait for others before you start to think the worst.

Author's Note: In the SAS, there is a system of contact drills which are used in very much the same way as those used in a disaster. If an SAS patrol (normally between four and six men) hit a large enemy force, they 'shoot and scoot.' Very often, in the confusion of the firefight, they will become separated, or get wounded. Their first objective is to reach the last appointed 'patrol rendezvous' (RV), which is normally only a few hundred meters away. This RV is open only for a short period of time. If anyone is missing they go to the emergency RV, which is some distance away and can be open for several hours, and so on. The principle is to provide a specified place and enough time for the patrol members to be reunited so they can continue their mission.

Your disaster plan should have similar guidelines to cover every combination of a disaster, and within given timelines.

In the first instance, the responsibility is to yourself and any one dependent on you, such as the very young or old and immobile within your immediate care. Whenever an earthquake hits, your immediate concern should be for your own safety, because you are no good to anyone dead. Protect others if possible, but do not place your own life in immediate danger. This is not self-preservation; it is staying alive in order so that you CAN help others. To a large degree, the shock waves produced by a major earthquake will determine your immediate reaction by forcing you to the floor and seeking shelter if indoors and moving away from falling debris if outdoors. Do not waste time trying to locate family pets or looking for the electricity or gas cut-off points; just get to safety.

Make contact

While self-preservation and finding a place of safety may be your first reaction, making contact should be your second. If you are not with your immediate family, you will need to know that they are alright, and the quickest way to do so is a simple text or phone call. If part of your disaster plan is to meet up, determine if this is feasible and safe to do so. Some points to remember for your disaster plan contacts:

- All family members should have each other's cell phone and landline numbers pre-set in their phone contacts. Better still, make a family group in your contact list and send a text message to everyone at the same time.
- If you are injured and immobile, pre-set a panic alarm with your coordinates and open a voice channel to a family member or neighbor outside the disaster area.
- If your whole family is expected to be within the disaster area, it is always a good idea to have a contact outside the earthquake zone. Once they know of your predicament, they can check calmly on others and notify the authorities of your predicament and location.

- As discussed in your disaster plan, make a contact point where you can meet up if possible; having your loved ones close by and safe is a major relief.
- In the event that one family member is trapped, you are also in a better position to provide help as a group.

When an Earthquake Happens

Trust me, when an earthquake of any disruptive size hits your location, you will know instantly what is happening. If you are standing, you will feel your first earthquake beneath your feet; if you are lying down and awake, you will see things moving of their own accord. When the tremor is slight and short, normally you can expect nothing more. However, if the tremor is strong enough to unbalance you, drop to the floor if inside a building, crawl to cover if possible, and hold on.

The main problem arising from a major earthquake is being caught in a collapsing building, in a car going over a bridge, or being hit by falling debris. Stay in one place until the tremor has passed. If the shock is severe, you will not be able to stand anyway. Aftershocks may be equally as strong and may come seconds or minutes after the first tremor.

As you move, avoid fallen power lines and stay away from buildings and bridges. Debris is easily seen from fallen buildings, but aftershocks may bring down more. Unless you are 100% sure the route you wish to take is open, do not use your car to escape. Many people in Japan died doing just this. The severity of the earthquake will almost certainly have destroyed some roads and bridges, causing traffic jams.

Once the initial shock is over, MOVE to a safe location.

Drop—Cover—Hold (the only exception to this rule is when you are in the street and in danger from falling debris)

When an earthquake strikes, Drop—Cover—Hold. (Barry Davies)

Author's Note: I was once in Jakarta, Indonesia, staying on the twentieth floor of the Shangri La Hotel. It was around 11:00 p.m. and normally I would head for Bat's Bar in the basement (great watering hole), but due to the amount of traveling I had done, decided instead to have an early night. I was just dropping off when I sensed something wrong and noticed the cushion on a chair by the window start to move; then suddenly it rolled forward and fell onto the floor. It was as if an invisible hand had moved it, so I sat upright. That's when I felt the shock waves hit me. They were rapid and extremely violent. I leapt out of bed and immediately was brutally thrown to the floor. I saw my wallet and mobile phone on the dresser and these prompted me to move. I grabbed both and made for the door. It was difficult to walk and stay on my feet; then the door would not open. In a panic, I pulled hard realizing too late that I had put on the safety chain. It came away and the door opened. Straightaway I was in a crowd of running people all heading in the same direction down the emergency stairs. It seemed to take forever. Around the tenth floor the second shock wave hit. A girl had stopped to take off her shoes and immediately people tried to climb over her. This only made the situation worse as people scared for their lives simply pushed the knot of fallen down to the ground and trampled over them. Eventually I made it to the ground floor and ran out into the gardens. Small pieces of debris had fallen and continued to fall, but the hotel staff directed everyone to safety. Half an hour later, the worst had passed and I returned to my room, but the impact of that earthquake will stay with me forever.

Coastal Earthquake

If you are on a coastline and you feel an earthquake for more than twenty seconds, you could be at risk from a tsunami. As with any earthquake, protect yourself first, unless you have young children in your charge.

Drop, Cover and Hold. (The only exception to this rule is when you are in the street and in danger from falling debris.)

If you are inside a building, stay put, as the worst danger is from falling masonry and glass on the outside. Crawl to whatever protection you can, like a table or a desk. If nothing is visible, stay in the center of the room away from anything heavy that might fall on you, such as bookcases, filing cabinets, glass pictures, etc. If you are in a high-rise and feel the need to evacuate, DO NOT USE THE ELEVATOR. Use the emergency stairs . . . ONLY after the tremors have stopped!

When the initial tremors stop and you feel it safe to do so, gather members of your family and make for higher ground free of the building. Do not seek shelter under structures such as freeway flyovers or under bridges. Stay in open ground. Apart from your emergency kit, DO NOT stop to gather things from your home—leave everything behind. A tsunami caused by an earthquake close to the coastline can produce a wave within minutes.

Natural Warning Signs

The time between an earthquake and a resulting tsunami can vary depending on how far from shore the earthquake struck. In 1960, when a 9.5 earthquake rocked Chile, people in Queule noticed a large change in water level in the local river. This prompted hundreds of people to head immediately for higher ground. Those that stayed behind simply died. Others reported seeing the sea recede, and again those that heeded the signs, survived. In some cases, Thailand in particular, people actually saw the tsunami wave approaching and stopped to take pictures—most are now dead. When an earthquake strikes, and you are near the coast, don't hesitate to make for higher ground.

When you get to higher ground, or high up in a strong structure, expect some company. Help others who arrive, especially mothers carrying children, the old and the immobile. Once safe, stay safe. Don't move until it's absolutely safe to do so.

Trapped Below Ground

To be trapped below ground, covered with tons of broken concrete and metal is a nightmare many would not wish to face—but it happens. For some, there will be hope; for others, simply the end. Most survivors that have been rescued say their time was spent between bouts of consciousness and sleeping. After several days had gone by many felt as if rescue would never come.

On January 27, 2009, in the city of Port-au-Prince, Haiti, Darlene Etienne found herself trapped below a mixture of smashed concrete and twisted steel. After fifteen days of

entombment, the seventeen-year-old girl gave up on any chance of rescue. Then, someone heard her cry for help. Shortly after, a French rescue team uncovered the chalky white face of Darlene—she had survived.

To understand how people can survive when trapped below ground, it is best to look at those people who work in the mining industry. While there are strict safety laws concerning mine workers, and how mines are worked, there always remains the threat of a mine collapsing. The story of the thirty-three men trapped in a Chilean mine and their successful rescue thrilled the world, and rightly so. They were trapped 700 m (2,300 ft) underground and survived for a record sixty-nine days before their rescue.

However, things in China are not so good. In 2010, some 2,845 accidents left 4,746 miners dead. That's around 75% of the world's total of mining disasters. On average, some fourteen miners die each day due to tunnel collapse, fires, flooding, or explosions. The stories of how the lucky ones survived varies from incident to incident.

The miners in Chile had a small amount of food with them in their safety pocket; this they rationed until contact with the surface was made and extra food and water could be dropped down to them. Their diet consisted of two spoonfuls of tuna, half a cookie, and a half-full glass of milk every forty-eight hours. On the other hand, there are reports that miners trapped in China have eaten their leather belts, boots, and even coal. To quench their thirst, many have drank their own urine or licked the moisture from the

> **Author's Note:** For anyone who gets trapped as the result of an earthquake, I restate the benefits of a cell phone. It is the one piece of modern hardware that you normally keep on yourself. Even without a signal, it can offer you immeasurable hope of being found, assist you with basic medical knowledge, provide light so you can see, and make a noise when you cannot call out any longer (see Annex B for more information).

rock face. In such a situation, anything that you think will provide you with nutrition or quench your thirst is fine. You may have little or no alternative.

Yet, when it comes to eating and drinking, being trapped in a mine is not the same as being trapped under a pile of rubble. Even if you can only move a little, there may be the odd insect that passes your way, the odd drip of water from a fracture pipe. THINK and use anything that will help support your life. The one thing to keep in mind is that there is always the hope of rescue.

TSUNAMI

Tsunamis are a natural part of the earth's process and development and they have been around since the planet first formed and most likely will remain with us for the foreseeable future.

A tsunami is a tidal wave, usually caused by an undersea earthquake or landslide. They can also be caused by a meteor or asteroid hitting the oceans, but this is a rare occurrence. The effect is a disruption in the water, which resounds outward like a shock wave or a stone in a pool. In the case of a tsunami, the wave is water, and as the wave moves from deep water in the open ocean to the shallower water near the coast, it transforms. This transformation is caused by the speed of the wave as it reaches shallow water. The wave slows, and the energy in the wave causes it to increase in size. For example, a tsunami several miles out to sea may be nothing more than a meter high, but moving fast (400 mph). By the time it reaches the shoreline it will have slowed, but have increased to several meters in height. As the wave encounters land, the underflow energy is dissipated somewhat; however, the top part of the wave will still contain a lot of energy. This wave energy is what causes the damage (remember that one cubic meter of

Band Aceh tsunami wave took the lives of so many people; the devastation is clear. (US Navy)

water has a mass of one ton). Beaches will be stripped of sand, trees, and coastal vegetation will be swept up, and beachfront property destroyed. The distance a wave runs inland will be directly proportional to the energy which caused the tsunami in the first place, plus the density of the shoreline. In the most extreme cases, vertical height of an onshore wave can be up to thirty meters. Moreover, a tsunami is not just a single wave, but a series of waves, the first one normally being the largest, as in Fukishima.

Tsunami Warning

There are two types of tsunami warnings: International and Regional. Most tsunamis are detected first by an earthquake triggering the seismic wave; this will indicate the location of the earthquake and its strength. If the earthquake is at sea, a tsunami wave will almost be expected to follow. The good thing is that the earthquake detection is very quick, as they travel much faster than a tsunami wave, giving time for a warning to be issued. The advancing tsunami can also be monitored by special early warning buoys that are placed out at sea. While this is fine in theory, when an underwater earthquake strikes close to the shore line, it inevitably means that the tsunami's wave will arrive quicker, and with more force. There are now early tsunami warning systems in place covering most of the world's oceans.

For some people, there will be no warning other than that of the earth shaking. Those that obey their basic instincts will survive, and those that do not will perish. This is reinforced by just one of the stories to come out of Japan.

A woman called Sachie lived on the coast of Japan near Minamisanriku, one of the hardest areas to be hit by the tsunami. Sachie is the mother of one-year-old baby and she told the Japanese media of her lucky escape.

"Kouka was having a nap in the house when the earthquake occurred. I immediately grabbed Kouka and ran outside, but the earth was still shaking. The ocean was overflowing and I was able to see the size of the tsunami, and instinctively realized I would not survive if I stayed inside the house. So I carried Kouka, and ran up the hill as fast as I could. When I reached the top of the hill, I looked back and saw my house was washed away by the tsunami."

Evacuation Plan

For those who live in an earthquake or tsunami high-risk area, your local emergency office will have made contingency plans. Find out what they are. Understand how your home, office, or workplace is affected by a tsunami. Know the best and nearest buildings that will withstand the worst tsunami wave. Where is, and how quick can you get you and your family to higher ground? Have a plan that will help the entire family, as you may be fragmented during the working day.

The ideal location should be at least two miles inland from the coastline, and at least 100 feet above sea level. You should be able to reach your place of safety in the minimum amount of time, less than fifteen minutes if possible. Your place of safety should be reachable both in darkness and in inclement weather conditions. Make sure that your emergency kit is ready and handy to grab.

Calculate how far your home and workplace are from the shoreline; calculate what reaction time you should have. Have the family carry out a practice drill: walk, run, or drive to the nearest place of safety. Calculate an escape route that will not be blocked by panic traffic. While these measures may seem a bit dramatic in the normal course of the day, if you practice just once, your chances of survival when a tsunami hits are greatly increased. Talk to your family. Make sure everyone in your family is aware of the emergency plan. Discuss what each of you will do during any emergency and what the individual responsibilities are. Make a safe point of reunification after the tsunami has subsided.

For anyone visiting a tsunami risk area, check with your lodgings to see if they have an evacuation plan, and again, know the designated escape route. Likewise, people who have no evacuation plan and remain in their homes, or close to the shore line, and who do not heed the warning sounds, will more than likely perish. Even in remote places where no alarm has been given or heard, the earthquake tremor itself should be enough to make you think—and act.

The first thing to remember is that if you can see the wave about to hit the shoreline, you cannot outrun it. Secondly, the wave will be weighted with rocks, trees, cars, and debris from buildings, all of which can kill or injure you. Your task is simply to stay away from the wave. Get as high as possible. This cannot be stressed enough. The moment a tsunami warning is given or sounded, you should leave whatever you are doing and make for higher ground. Local emergency management offices will advise you as to the best route to safety and likely shelter locations. In countries where tsunamis are prevalent, these are often marked.

Safety Events

- If you live in an earthquake area, always be prepared to move instantly. First off, if you feel an earth tremor, even if there is no tsunami warning, make your way to high ground or a safe distance from the shoreline. A large tsunami makes noise, like an express train or aircraft.
- On hearing a tsunami warning, do the same; but make sure you warn as many others that are nearby as possible, especially the very young and elderly. Move to an evacuation site if one has been designated and you have time.
- After a disaster warning, roads may become impassable or blocked by panic traffic. Do not wait in your car for the traffic jam to move; evacuate by foot if necessary. Remember, roads are generally built flat along the coastal areas, so use local footpaths to gain height.
- If you have no time to move to higher ground, enter the nearest strongest and highest building and go to the top

floor or the roof. (Most prefab-
ricated homes and industrial
factories will be swept away
by the wave.)

- As a last resort, climb a strong
tree, get as high as possible,
and hang on. Use your belt to
strap yourself securely. (Many
people in Thailand survived by
doing this.)

- Do not return to lower ground
until after everything is all
clear, as a tsunami is a series
of waves.

Caught in the Water

If you cannot outrun the tsunami wave and it is inevitable
you will be swept up, look around for anything that will float.
As the waters become calmer, look for a large floating
piece of debris to use as a raft. Anything that has a high
buoyancy factor and is easy to grip is ideal for the purpose.
Good swimmers will know that by relaxing, they will remain
floating in the sea. However, the waters of a tsunami are
very rough and a flotation aid is required quickly.

Caught in the
water, this man is
using a bag of
rubbish as a
floatation aid.
(Barry Davies)

If the waters push you near a strong structure or tree,
see if it's possible to grab hold and climb out of the water.
Staying in the water with no protection will mean that you
are subject to its wild movement and at risk for injury from
the floating debris. Your best chance is to get to firm land or
a strong standing structure as quickly as possible.

During the recent Tsunami in Japan, a journalist, Toya
Chiba, who worked for the Iwate Tokai newspaper, was
swept up in the raging water. He had been standing close to
the mouth of the Owatari River taking pictures when the
torrent swept him off his feet. Despite being surrounded by
cars and other debris, he managed to escape with minor
injuries.

Aftermath Recovery

Return home only after the official 'all clear' has sounded. Do not take it upon yourself to prematurely move to
lower ground, as tsunami waves can go on for hours. Like-

wise, some later waves are stronger and higher than the previous ones.

If you have a radio, listen to the emergency announcements and directed advice. This is important, as many places may be unsafe; fires may have broken out, bridges may be down, or as in the recent earthquake and tsunami in Japan, nuclear reactors could be damaged.

Search for other survivors, and give help to injured or trapped people, providing first aid where necessary. Help those who need special assistance, such as people in wheelchairs and old and young people who cannot help themselves. However, do not put yourself at further risk; if you cannot physically help, at least tell others or notify the rescue services. It may take some time before the emergency services arrive to take charge, so do what comes naturally to support yourself, family, friends, neighbors, and nearby strangers.

Searching your home after a disaster is a difficult task. (Lance Cpl Brennan O'Lowney 31 MEU)

Returning Home

In the worst case scenario, you may not have a home to go back to. In this case, you must seek a safe shelter by contacting the emergency services if onsite, or by yourself if not. You should not return home until it is perfectly safe to

do so, and in many cases, the emergency services may not let you enter the immediate disaster area. The area will need to be checked for survivors, people who are trapped, injured, or immobile (including those who are recently deceased).

The authorities may enforce security strict measures to avoid looting and for individual safety. Cards may be issued, allowing a homeowner to visit the site of their home, be it still standing or destroyed. In the case of the latter, it will be to retrieve any valuable documents or personal effects if they can be found. You may have a limited time with which to search before the area is quarantined off again.

You must obey the recognized authority and emergency services. Failure to do so could end in your arrest, or worst case, being shot as a looter. Remember, the emergency services are there to help as many people as possible to survive, not just you. They are professional and know what they're doing.

Enter buildings or your home with extreme care, as tsunami waters can damage foundations, weakening walls and structures and making them unsafe. Make sure that if

After the tsunami waters recede, what remains will quickly become contaminated and disease will swiftly follow. Move away if possible. (Band Aceh–source unknown)

you are moving around, that you have on really strong shoes or boots, as foot injuries are very common after tsunamis.

Check for electrical, gas damage, and leaks. Turn off both the main electrical system and the main gas valve if you have any reason to believe that there is a leak or damage. DO NOT reconnect them until it has been checked by a professional. Likewise, check for water and sewage damage, as a source of fresh water will be vital in the next few days. Listen to the emergency services' announcements regarding the usage of the local water supply. DO NOT be tempted to drink polluted water (see Chapter 11).

Lessons Survivors have Learned Following an Earthquake or Tsunami

The best place to learn something is from the very people who have survived this experience. In this case, people who have lived through a disaster. The list below, while not in any order, contains a summary of the comments, words, and advice given by those people who have survived an earthquake or tsunami. People always have an excuse for why they were not prepared, and many will claim that the expression is overrated; that is, until they are caught up in a disaster. 'BE PREPARED' is the main advice from all survivors.

- Put a good flashlight in your bedroom, together with spare batteries (or better still, a wind-up device).
- A well-built home can still disappear in less than ten seconds, so get out as soon as possible.
- Listen and understand what is going on. Get a radio, preferably a mechanical wind-up type or battery powered, and have a spare set of batteries in their pack taped to the radio.
- DO NOT rely on your television. In almost every major earthquake, the power goes OUT. Think about this for a moment: no lights, no TV, no freezer, no traffic lights; nothing electrical will work.
- While we all trust our emergency services, they are not always the knights in shining armor we'd like to think of them as. They rely on information just like you and I, and situations can be equally as confusing for them. Be patient, because the emergency services have to help a

lot of people, and they have a list of priorities which are aimed at serving the majority of the public.

- Trust the official emergency radio station for the best advice. Do not be forced into a decision by a rumor from Twitter or Facebook, even if it turns out to be true.
- Don't go jumping into your car and driving off to see if grandma is okay. No traffic lights means the intersections are blocked and dangerous. Cracks in the road caused by the quake, added to the fact that there is no street lighting, presents a dangerous situation.
- Expect hundreds, if not thousands, of people just like you to be walking the streets, many clutching bleeding wounds, or crying for a loved one.
- Always have some cash handy. The ATM machines will be down, and if they are working it's highly unlikely anyone will be refilling them for a few days.
- If your freezer is full and the power is off, use your barbecue to cook as much food as possible.

Chapter 4

FOREST & WILD FIRES

Forest fires are extremely
difficult and costly to bring
under control. (Fire Service-
Fort Bragg)

The cause of most wild fires can be put down to either man's negligence or the forces of nature, although the latter only accounts for a single percent of them. In the wilderness, it can be anything from a spark off the wheel of a locomotive passing through a forest area, or a simple lighting strike. In urban areas, fires can be started by earthquakes causing disrupted gas mains, or overturning any open flame.

Usually, it is poor behavior on behalf of humans that results in 99% of all wild fires, i.e., the dropped cigarette or the camp fire that was unattended. In some cases, it is the madness of a deliberate fire starter. Yes, incredible as it may seem, there are lots of people in the world who like to start fires, many of which simply rage out of control, killing innocent people and destroying homes and property.

Stupidity and bad habits are also one of the biggest causes of wild fire. Remember that matches and lighters are tools for adults and not children. Playing with matches, lighters, or fire is a NO for those too young to understand the danger, especially when you take them camping. In addition to understanding the uses of fire, also teach your children to respect fire.

In the bad habit department, this is mainly down to smokers. While it is illegal in many countries to throw a lighted cigarette butt out of a car window, it is also morally wrong. Nevertheless, you see this happening all the time. What the smoker does not realize is the speed of the car acts like the wind. As the dropped cigarette falls, the dying embers of it are rekindled and often drop into dry grass on the roadside verge. The result is usually a fire.

While fires can happen in cities, these are more isolated and are usually brought under control within a few hours. Most of the wild fires take place in forest areas, where they are not spotted until they have a good hold; added to which they can cover a large area, making it difficult to deal with.

Wild fires can happen all over the planet. Each year they destroy millions of acres of rich forest, destroy thousands of homes, and kill innocent people. In comparison to earthquakes, the death toll is relatively low, but the effect on nature and animal wildlife is atrocious.

One of the worst fires in American history happened in Wisconsin in 1873. The fire, fanned by high winds, eventually

Author's Note: In 2001, in the Valencia region of Spain, a man deliberately started a fire so that he could see a fireman's wife with which he was having an affair. The wild fire he started guaranteed the fireman would be away for some length of time. The fire in question got out of hand, eventually destroying some twenty homes and more than 60,000 acres of hillside woodland. The culprit would not have been caught had he not boasted about it joyfully to the fireman's wife. She, in turn, confessed her lover's arrogance to the police.

In 2009, a fire which was started deliberately cost the lives of two firemen, destroyed eleven homes, and caused millions of dollars in damage. The fire just to the north of Los Angeles burned for ten days before it was brought under control.

took over 1.2 million acres. The fire became so intense that it jumped entire natural barriers, such as the Peshtigo River. Whole communities were destroyed, and while there has never been an accurate death toll, it is estimated that some 2,500 people lost their lives. Peshtigo, prior to the fire, had a population of 1,700 residents; more than 350 bodies had to be buried in a mass grave simple because no one could recognize them. Many residents entered the river and while this helped protect many, cold water and drowning also took its toll.

Some fires are known to be deliberate, such as the 'slash and burn' policy adopted in Indonesia. In 2007, while

Wild fires often happen in remote places and require a large airborne force to bring them under control. (Sgt Karl Johnson)

traveling in Malaysia, I stayed in the capital Kuala Lumpur. It was as if the city was covered with fog, but it was actually thick smoke. Indonesia, mainly in the province of Sumatra, was destroying millions of hectares of forest and peat land; the clearance was to make way for palm oil production. The smoke from the fires was so dense it blocked out the sun in parts of Malaysia and Singapore. This 'slash and burn' policy produces 1.8 billion tons of emissions every year, accounting for four percent of global emissions.

UNDERSTANDING WILD FIRES

As with most things in life, it makes sense to gain some knowledge of the way in which a wild fire travels. This knowledge may help you keep away from the fire, or in the worst case scenario, at least help you avoid the worst of it by staying in advance of the flames. Always remember, fire moves very quickly, and if you are trapped, you will almost certainly perish.

Unless a person has witnessed a wild fire, it is impossible to realize the incredible speed at which it can travel. One of the most common mistakes made by those caught up in a wild fire is to try and outrun it. By having some knowledge of how a wild fire behaves, provides any potential survivor with a fighting chance. For example, fire travels quicker uphill than it does downhill. To a large degree, the direction of fire is controlled by the wind and the landscape. For example, fire will 'roll' around in a steep sided valley. On a flat plain, it will gust back and forth with the wind. Areas of good fuel, such as pine trees, will build the fire quickly, while areas of sparse vegetation will help calm the fire.

One of the first things to do is recognize if there is real danger from the wild fire. There are many signs, such as large clouds of smoke in the distance, the smell of burning vegetation, visible flames leaping over the forest, etc. Basically, if you see any of these signs, try to gauge what you are looking at.

- Is the fire above tree top level, for example can you see the flames (not just smoke)?
- Is the fire coming towards you, i.e., which way is the wind blowing? (Simply rip a handful of grass or light material such as sand and throw it in the air to find its direction.)

Author's Note: Having spent many nights sleeping in the forest, I know how easy it is to become complacent. Remember, if you are camping in the forest overnight, and you are asleep, many of these early warning signs may be missed. The first warning sign may be the crackle or glow of the fire. In this case, you could be in serious danger.

- If the fire is going away from you, then you are in no immediate danger. Contact the authorities and listen to their advice, as they may or may not know about the fire.
- If the fire is coming towards you, do you have the means of good escape?
- Do you have a vehicle, and is there a road leading directly away from the fire? Remember, **never attempt to drive through a fire!**
- If you are in a neighborhood of several homes, make sure that your neighbors are alerted.
- If no firefighters are present, or the wild fire has just been discovered, call the authorities immediately. Finally, quickly estimate the immediate danger to you and any others with you.

Once a fire has been detected, the first thing to do is determine your location and your position in relation to the

Preventing wild fires only requires a little common sense. Keep your fire small, always have a pail of water handy, and never leave fire unattended. (Barry Davies)

wild fire. Always take a moment to think and formulate a quick plan that will separate you from immediate danger.

- Determine your location and circumstance, i.e., are you on foot or in a vehicle or in a home?
- Are you alone or with others; do you have small children or elderly with you?
- Do you have a wild fire emergency plan?

PREVENTING WILD FIRES

If you live in an area prone to wild fire, it is advisable to carry out some protection of your property. This is done as a matter of course in many hot countries such as Spain, where fires break out on a weekly basis in the summer. Farmers and individuals who live in the 'campo' country-side, plant orange trees around their property, as they do not catch fire very easily. In addition to this, there is a whole series of simple things you can do that will help protect your home or property.

One farmer who had suffered through several fires has converted an old shower head on the side of his garage; this was fed by a 1000 liter water tank on the roof. He would stay to protect his property, and as he fought the fire, he would simply dash under the shower every few minutes to cool himself and remove the burning sparks. A simple idea, yes, but it's one that has been adopted by many people through-out this region.

Every home is different, as are the immediate surround-ings, and this makes it difficult to have a set plan for every-one. That said, there are many things you can do to protect your home from a fire. First and foremost, if you see a major fire, report it. Many countries have strict laws on burning trash. In many European areas, one must apply for a license to destroy by fire any agricultural surplus, and then it is only permitted on certain days and at certain times of the year. Fire watch is everyone's responsibility, so don't be afraid to call the authorities if you see a fire.

INSIDE YOUR HOME

While the inside of your home will contain all your valua-bles, if the outside of the house catches fire, there is a good chance that everything will be destroyed. It is, therefore, prudent to take precautions for both inside and outside of the home. Inside the home, you should:

- Cut off the gas supply. Move any bottled gas away from the home by at least thirty meters. Digging a pit and covering them is usually the best idea, or place them inside a concrete or brick building.
- Extinguish any open flames, open the fireplace damper and close any fireplace screens or doors.
- Close all apertures to the home, doors, and windows. Remove all combustible material, such as curtains, drapes, and plastic blinds.
- Move all flammable material and furniture to the center of the room.
- Have lots of cold drinks handy for the people fighting the fire outside. Have bowls or buckets of cold water and lots of wet cloths to wipe faces.

Check for combustible material close to your home and make sure you have a good emergency supply of water. (Barry Davies)

OUTSIDE YOUR HOME

- How close are the nearest trees and bushes? If so, can you clear an area free of combustible material? Brick and concrete will resist fire, while wooden decking will only add to the fuel. Treat all woodwork with flame retardant chemicals. Wooden shingles on a house should also be treated.
- Do you have a wall surrounding your property? Will this stop the flames reaching your home? Remember, if your home is on a slope, the flames of any fire will sweep up towards you very quickly, and you may need to extend your area of protection around the house.
- If your home has a log stove or open log fireplace, put fuel in a safe place, or make sure any heating oil or gas tank is well-protected.

- Make sure any electricity cables are protected and put them underground, if possible. At the same time, be aware of any overhead electricity cables that are supported by wooden poles—these are likely to fall in a fire.
- Turn your swimming pool into a safety zone, if you have one. As a last resort, or when your clothing is on fire (and after you have rolled on the ground), immerse yourself in the pool. Place any valuables that will not be damaged by water in a plastic container and sink these into your swimming pool.
- Look around to see if any items are made of combustible material and dispose of it or place them in a secure place (garden furniture and sun shade umbrellas, for example).
- Make sure that fire engines can get to your property and they know where you are. Always have fire tools handy (buckets, spade shovel, rake, axe, saw, or chain saw) if you want to fight the fire before the fire services arrive.
- Know who to contact and have their details handy.
- Always have an escape route, no matter which way the fire arrives from.
- Discuss wild fires with your family and work out a plan with your neighbors.
- Have enough large fire extinguishers, placed in the best locations, both inside and outside the home. Set up a sprinkler system. Have a supply at hand and ensure your delivery system, hose, etc., will reach way beyond your boundaries. Have a petrol engine pump just in case the electricity is cut off. Have a ladder handy in case you need to wet down the roof.
- Improvise, for instance, a simple lawn sprinkler fixed to your roof to spray the home with constant water. Do the same for any combustible areas or volatile material by keeping it wet.
- Have a proper evacuation plan. Don't leave it to the last minute, and get out while you can!
- Back your car into your garage so that you're ready for a quick escape. Leave the keys in the ignition, check that you have enough gas, and close all the windows. Make sure, however, that you leave the doors open.

- Have your family pack enough items to last them about three days, just in case you decide to leave.
- Confine pets to a safe place. It's not always possible to round up all your livestock or animals. Decide if it is best to free them or leave them behind so that they are in the safest possible place.
- Pre-arrange temporary housing outside of the danger area. Friends and family will be better than a public shelter.
- Inform others outside of the danger zone that you are moving.

A good wall and the removal of close proximity vegetation will help secure your home. (Barry Davies)

If you intend to stay and protect your property, you must take into account the risk you are taking, not just for yourself, but for any other family and friends. It is always best to send the very young and the elderly to a safe place before the fire reaches your property. They will be of no assistance in fighting the fire and their lives will be put in harm's way.

Likewise, those that do decide to stay should prepare to fight the fire on the best terms possible. You must make sure that the proper duties are assigned to each individual and equipment should be in place and functional. Make up a firefighting set of clothing that will protect you from the flames, falling sparks, and smoke. Use material that will not burn easily to cover you head and hands and wear strong leather footwear. If your live in an isolated area where fires are prevalent, you might consider investing in a full fireproof suit (you will find a lot of them on the internet).

Author's Note: Better still for those who live in an area prone to fire, purchase special clothing that is designed to be fire resistant. Special Forces are issued a coverall that is specifically made to resist fire. These can sometimes be purchased from local military traders. They are easy to slip into and will provide some protection.

WHAT TO DO IF CAUGHT IN THE FLAMES

If you should be unlucky enough to get caught in the flames and your clothes are on fire, the first thing that you should do is put your hands over your face, drop to the ground (dirt ground is best, but lawn will suffice), and roll back and forth until the flames are extinguished. DO NOT ATTEMPT TO RUN, as running will only increase the flames. If you have a hose or a water supply nearby, wet yourself from head to foot. For most people, remember what you were taught as a child: 'Stop, Drop, and Roll.'

If you are near a pool or river, get in it. If you cannot find water, look for a place that cannot be burned, such as rocks or concrete. Lie as flat as possible and breathe the air close to the ground. Breathe though a handkerchief or piece of cloth to avoid scorching your lungs or inhaling smoke.

Keep in mind that the fire will move very fast, and you will not have to endure the heat for very long. Once the flames have passed, roll to extinguish any flames and remove burned clothing.

RETURNING TO YOUR HOME

The first thing you should do when returning to your home is to check the utilities, such as gas and water, as these may well have been disrupted by the fire. Undamaged homes with the water system intact should be safe to drink. Always check with your supplier before using propane or heating oil, and get someone to check the tank and make sure the valves are turned off until it has the all-clear. The tank may have moved, or bulged from the heat, or the fuel pipes make have cracked or broken. DO NOT RISK IT!

Search the entire home, starting at the roof, and inside the attic. Work your way down and around your home. Examine the garden area for any remaining signs of smoke wisps. Continue to check for at least four to five hours after the fire has past. Wild fire winds can blow burning embers anywhere, which can remain dormant for hours before bursting into flames once more. If there is fire damage, be careful cleaning your property as there may be health risks from exposed or damaged hazardous material.

Any burnt or smoldering debris should be wet down immediately. Always use a mask, if possible, to prevent inhalation of dust or hazardous fumes. Beware of fire-damaged items, such as cleaning products, paint, batteries, and fuel. Wear protective clothing, strong boots, and thick gloves (rubber gloves when clearing sewage pipes, etc.) when clearing burnt debris.

As soon as possible, cut down any burnt trees, as these can become unstable. Sadly, very few can be saved after a major fire. Pine trees suffer the most, but some deciduous trees are resilient and may produce new branches and leaves. Similarly, evergreen trees may survive when only moderately scorched.

FIRES IN THE OUTBACK

Many people seek adventure in the great outdoors, myself included. We live in a wonderful world, and some areas are just breathtaking. Personally, I love the rocky mountains of Canada, the beautiful peaks and valleys of Southern Germany, and the magnificent fjords and moun-tains of Norway. Here I have walked, camped, and felt that lifting of spirit that only such views can offer. At the same time, I have seen vast areas of natural beauty stripped bare, leaving nothing but the blackened earth.

If, like me, you like to camp in the forest, please keep in mind the risk of starting a fire, as well as the risk of fire should it start in your vicinity. When you arrive at your wilderness campsite, it will most probably be daylight, so take a few minutes to observe your location and the surrounding scenery.

- Are you in a valley or the side of a mountain?
- Is the valley or mountain covered with trees? If so, what type of trees?
- Is there water nearby, like a lake or river? Do you have a safe and direct path to the water?
- Which direction is the prevailing wind blowing?
- What have the weather conditions been like in the area? When did it last rain?

If you are alone and start or encounter a fire that has become out of control, always make an attempt to put it out. One of the first rules of lighting a fire in the wilderness or in your own backyard is to make sure that you have a source of water handy. A bucket or hose pipe will help in the initial stages to bring a fire under control. If no water is available, then use any form of blanket, such as your jacket to beat out the flames. Do not hesitate; seconds can mean the difference between getting a fire under control or it getting away from you.

If the fire is out of control, raise the alarm by any means possible; don't let others suffer for your mistake. Look for any source of water nearby, a river or lake, and see if it is within reach and if so, make for it. Providing you can swim, get as close to the middle as you can, keeping your body below the surface with just your face, showing enough to breathe. Wet a handkerchief or some other material and cover your mouth and nose.

If you decide to move, always keep a watchful eye on the fire, especially any change in wind direction, as this will help determine your escape route. Always head downhill if at all possible, but don't get trapped. Remember if you must cross a river, make sure everyone can swim proficiently or make a quick flotation aid.

NO ESCAPE

If you are trapped with no escape, do not attempt to outrun the fire. In certain circumstances, there may be a gap in the fire wall, especially where vegetation is skimpy. Do not be tempted to run through it unless there is no other alternative. The heat on the other side of the fire is extremely hot. Additionally, fire will roll back on itself and you'll end up engulfed in flames.

Should the situation arise and you are forced to run through the fire, select the lowest point of flame, and run downhill. Cover your face and hair with a wet cloth (urinate if that's all you have). Make sure the minimum amount of flesh is exposed and run as fast as you safely can. Travel as far through the flames as possible, and keep going until you feel you are on safe ground and at least 300 meters behind the fire wall. Should your clothing catch fire, roll on the ground to extinguish the flames.

If you cannot move and do not have a chance to run through the flames, dig or find yourself a shallow ditch and cover yourself if possible with wet clothing. If no wet clothing is available, use dirt.

If a man-made or natural fire break, such as a road or an area free of vegetation, is close by and you can safely reach it, do so. Large vegetation-free areas of rock are good, yet a largely cultivated area is better. The larger the area, the less smoke you will have to inhale. Be careful of falling branches from burning trees, even after the fire has passed. Old dead wood and evergreen trees will catch fire quicker than deciduous trees and will burn with more ferocity. Trees whose tops are very close together, and with lots of low undergrowth, are places to avoid, as they offer too much in the way of fuel for the fire. An open area with sparse vegetation will offer a better chance of survival.

Assuming the flame front has passed you by and you have survived, move, keeping the wind on your face and the fire away from you.

Author's Note: Some time ago while doing some research on the internet, I came across this homeowner's story, 'Surviving a Wildfire.' It highlights the need for preparedness, and courage when battling the elements of fire.

Jeffe Aronson and his family live near the Victorian Alpine National Park near the Snowy River, about twenty miles northeast of Omeo in Victoria, Australia, in a remote area home to about 300 people.

"On the day the fire reached our area, January 26, 2003, my mother-in-law and niece were visiting us from America and bore witness to the approaching fire. I knew my family would kill me if either of them were hurt, which is assuming the fire didn't get me first. Of course, all lent a hand during the most intense part of fighting the fire.

We felt as though we were well-prepared to take shelter on our property as the fire advanced towards us. Leading to this decision was the fact we had spent the previous three years preparing our home and landscape for such a day. Listening to public awareness campaigns, we knew that with landscape and construction preparations, we would have an area of safe refuge and also be able to put out spot fires afterwards that often consume homes. Although located deep in the forest, we generate our own hydro-electrical power, have reserves of water and fuel, and have a trailer-mounted fire pump and water tank.

Some of our preparations included tin-covered windows, gutters cleaned then filled with water, but most importantly, the clearing of brush on our twelve acres of land near our home and structures. A neighbor remarked that we were creating a 'moonscape'. This same neighbor was frantic in the days before the fire, preparing his property like ours as best he could. Most everyone in the valley came closer together in the lead-up to it all, yet we all also knew that when the fire approached, we'd all be on our own—too busy saving our properties to help others. We were lucky, too, as the fire slowly moved towards our area providing everyone fair warning of up to three weeks to prepare or evacuate.

The evening before the fire struck our property, embers and flying fire-brands filled the red sky over the ridges to the east. A sound like when you're camped upstream of Lava Falls in the Grand Canyon: throaty, rumbling, sublime, but somehow also threatening, could be heard. Rusty flames could be seen along the horizons and filling the valleys, but strange-ly no wind as it crawled in front of us for seven hours while we waited. We stood fast, waiting to jump into action if the fire came close to the house, but this night it didn't.

The next morning we could see spot fires in the valley, but the wind was surprisingly absent. Driving in the valley around my home, I found half-dozen trucks, a dozer, and most of the valley's residents, leaning on their vehicles lined up along the crest of a ridge. Most were jawboning and watch-ing the spot fires across the valley discussing where it would burn next. It wasn't long before we got our answer. Things began to heat up, literally and figuratively, as I met my neighbor who watched a spot fire right across from his home quickly grow in size. Spot fires also began multiplying across the river, and crawling towards the Bundara River's banks towards farmhouses and horses. The wind, now picking up, began whipping grass fires like ocean breakers in a storm across the slopes and towards my home. Graham, the owner of a local pub, reported that the fire had quickly grown in size and jumped the river. My vehicle, towing a trailer with a make-shift fire pump and water tank with hose and tools, was perfect for helping to put out small grass fires threatening a seasonal home; but when the radio in my truck crackled, I was told to head back home quickly as the fire was heading in the direction of the house.

In the short drive to my house, I could see fire in the back of the property with the forest now ablaze. Thick red smoke was billowing from our gully just upstream, the one we burned in the spring, as I took the video camera to the ridge to overlook the scene. The flame front was only 100 meters away, as flames burning along the river, looking as if someone had poured grease along its sides, cornered our back barn and approached my property at a gallop. Returning back to the house, I yelled to my family, "This is it!" We put the last of the tin on the windows, got mom inside, detached my makeshift pump and water tank from the truck, and stored the truck inside a shed. Within minutes, we could see spot fires appear across the river, first one, then twenty, as if by magic. In less than sixty seconds, several hundred acres of mountain, the entire bloody mountain, was aflame. We tried to call and warn our neighbors downwind, but the advance was so swift they, too, were surrounded by the firestorm. Fire everywhere! We were running around like maniacs trying to put out nearby spot fires and prevent the house and shed from igniting. Mom stayed inside, wetting rags to cover openings below the doors, as our niece helped where she could, dragging hoses around corners, bringing water, and using a camera to film the event. Smoke, heat, and cinders surrounded us in a whirlwind, preventing us from determining in which direction the front was coming.

Fire approached and engulfed our 600 liter fuel tank only sixty meters away and our 22,000 liter plastic water tank, but we had done our best to remove ground fuel around both tanks days before. We were yelling to each other, but the sounds from the roaring fire were deafening, preventing us from hearing one another. I worried that if we lost the water tank, we would have only 1,000 liters of water in reserve. Trees exploded into flames as smoke choked us, but we persevered. I thought, 'They say that when the front is upon you, to shelter inside until it's passed. But how do you know when the front is passing, when fire is everywhere?' I answered my own question as we fought on, pulling hoses this way and that way, choking, eyes smarting, me stupidly calling out to my niece to film this or that, then to grab a hose to help me. It was insane and chaotic. To top it all off, the bloody smoke alarms in the house were screaming out to us during all this mayhem. Then, as I tried to stop flames from consuming firewood and timber piles and from spreading to our shed, I realized that it was time to retreat. Breathing was difficult and I could barely see. My skin was staring to really feel the heat and I realized it was time to take shelter. Watering down the fire pump as my last act, I sprinted into the house with the others. When I realized that my wife was not in the house, I exited through the back door in the lee of the tempest, rounded the shed, and found her with a trusty water backpack sprayer, attacking a burning tree. Together we went back inside, coughing and rubbing our eyes and asking if everyone was okay. Conditions inside were better but still challenging. Wind-driven firebrands were coming inside under and over the doors as my wife took her sprayer to put them out. I was kneeling on the cement floor, spitting thick mucus and guzzling some juice, trying to get hydrated. We heard a large explosion in the distance and thought it may be a neighbor's fuel tank or ours. Hurricane force winds battered the house, but the tin-covered windows and skylights held. Peeking out the door, we saw fire everywhere. A firebreak we prepared around the shed seemed to be holding. Sounds of trees falling to the ground in rapid succession piqued my curiosity to look outside every couple of minutes. The wind tried to rip the doors from my hands. This went on for another fifteen minutes or so, making the whole battle last for maybe forty-five minutes.

Then, as if the universe had audibly sighed, it calmed enough to feel like we just might beat this thing. I exited our home, and, able to see and breathe again, grabbed a hose and started putting out small fires, which were everywhere I looked: in drip lines, garden plants, trees, grass, and bushes. We used a chainsaw to cut up two fallen trees off our driveway. Power to the house went out, as I checked on the hydroelectric generator near the river. Heat and fire had damaged some wiring and also melted some plastic piping coming from our water and fuel tanks. Utilizing a backup generator, we maintained power and were able sustain ourselves. Our home was relatively unscathed once the spot fires were extinguished, and I hooked my trailer and water tank to my truck and set off to help put out other fires. Park Rangers who drove down our gravel lane after the front had passed said they'd expected smoking corpses after they'd seen the fire engulf the woods around us. Our neighbors, who live in a home in that same pasture, said that when they saw the fireball explode from the edge of our forest, it sounded like an airliner taking off. Upstream, our neighbor's house fared worse than ours. His home was burnt to a crisp, as was another neighbor's cabin downstream. Just over the ridge, still another neighbor's timber shed was burnt, but all were otherwise well. We wave to one neighbor as he and his family sat on their veranda, and it seemed to me that they were soaking up precious life with renewed appreciation while surveying the ruin about them. The mule and the ponies were fine, as were the chickens, despite seeing dead kangaroos and birds littering their paddock.

I think back to my neighbor's comment. 'Moonscape' indeed. Thankfully, unbelievably, most trees on our property remained standing. Though they're burnt and some crashing to the ground, we can only hope they come back next spring. Our home and outbuildings were scorched but only slightly damaged. More importantly, all of us are alive and well, surviving the firestorm. So here I sit, pounding out my first impressions, having gone through one of those famous Australian Bushfires. My wife and I have hugged and kissed, and we've all given each other a high five. We sit back and listen to the warnings they're giving on the radio to other people in other towns and valleys, as this unknowable power wends its way towards the only thing that's going to stop it—the ocean. We silently wish them well for their lives and belongings.

But we survived and now that night has fallen, the mountain across from us had a million small fires, brilliantly glowing like the stars we've so sorely missed of late. We stand there in the cool evening, watching the fire-stars, my wife wrapped in my arms, exhausted but victorious. Just after midnight we hear the patter of rain on the roof, the first in weeks and sorely missed."

Chapter 5

MAJOR FLOODING

Flooding is normally
slow, which gives you a
little time to prepare.

117

In 1931, China suffered a series of floods which are considered the worst in history. In terms of human deaths, these where estimated to be in the millions. Much later in 1975, the Banqiao Dam was overwhelmed by floodwaters caused by continuous rainfall. The Dam burst, killing an estimated 170,000 people and destroyed thousands of homes. In 2008, many states in India were affected by flooding during the monsoon season which took the lives of 2,500 people and left many starving and without homes.

There are two types of flooding: one where the water rises gradually, and one where a great volume of water suddenly appears, the latter being called a flash flood, or storm surge. While flooding does take lives, it does so because people are caught, trapped, or ill-prepared. Flooding from heavy rainfall is unlike that of a tsunami, which is caused by the force of an earthquake or meteor striking the earth.

Heavy continuous rain over a long period of time will cause flooding. Rivers will be unable to hold the extra water and will spill over onto already waterlogged ground. This type of flooding is normally slow and takes place over a number of days.

Many areas of the world are prone to this type of flooding on an annual basis. The waters rise to a predicable level for several days before slowly receding. The debris left behind by normal flooding, while messy, is unlike the devastating flotsam of a tsunami. Buildings and other structures are not normally damaged, other than water saturation and mud deposits.

Hurricanes can also bring heavy flooding, as was seen in New Orleans with Hurricane Katrina. Winds gusting up to 140 miles per hour pushed the waters to a height of six meters, thus flooding over the inadequate levees. With much of the city below sea level, a major disaster was inevitable, resulting in an area of 90,000 square miles being affected. Some 80% of New Orleans was under water; in some places this was twenty feet deep. The cost in lives reached 1,836, and cost an estimated seventy-five billion dollars in damage.

Storm surges can produce extensive coastal flooding up to twenty-five miles from the coastline. Flooding affects both cities and the countryside, with the severest damage being caused where the population is high.

HOUSE PRECAUTIONS AND PREPAREDNESS

If you live in a known flood area you, will have some time to protect your family, property, and belongings. You will know from previous experience how high and how fast the floodwaters will rise and roughly how long they will last.

If you live in a coastal area, you will know the damage that can be caused by a hurricane; you will also know what defenses are in place.

FLOOD WARNING

In the Western World and many other countries, flood warnings are issued either by TV, radio, or by a telephone call to a local person who will them disseminate the warning by telephone. If you have lived in a flood area for several years, you will be used to and understand the local warning system. If you are not, you should seek advice from a close neighbor. In more remote areas, a radio warning is generally broadcast. If you get neither of these warnings and you live close to a river, then you should pay heed to the water levels and the weather conditions. Constant rain is a good indicator, but it is often the case that the rainfall further up river, especially from mountainous areas, will flood the river several miles away.

Being in a flood area can mean that if you choose to remain in your home, you may be cut off for days. Although you are most likely to have the opportunity before the flood arrives to leave your home, make sure to stay with family or friends unaffected by the floodwaters. As previously stated, floodwaters generally rise slowly, giving you time to make a decision.

FLOOD PRECAUTIONS

If you live in an area which is prone to annual flooding, then your property should have been built accordingly. The foundation should have been built higher out of the ground and then filled with heavy gravel prior to construction of the plan of the house. In the United Kingdom, this is now a statutory requirement for all new housing within a possible flood area. This basically means that the house and its contents will sit above any floodwater.

Where flood levels are known and seasonal warnings are sent out, it makes sense to move any furniture to higher floors, if possible. Bring in a professional electrician to advise on the position of your electrical system, paying particular attention to the location of low sockets and the placement of the fuse box. In essence, make sure there is NO electrical socket or any connected electrical unit, such as refrigerators or washing machines that can come into contact with the floodwater. Water and electricity are a dangerous combination.

Install a backflow valve into your sewer system to prevent the backflow of sewage, which can be forced to the surface by floodwater.

In many cases, the level of water need only be a few inches higher than normal to enter your home. You can prevent this by using sand bags to block all apertures, such as doors or low cellar windows. Do not overfill the sandbags; around two-thirds full is best. Lay them in a dropping motion so that they flatten out. Stack as you

Flood defenses are now getting highly sophisticated and save millions of dollars' worth of damage. (Blobel Germany)

would lay bricks in a herring-bone fashion.

If the state or local community does not supply sandbags, then you can normally buy them from garden centers or army surplus shops. Fine sand is best as this will absorb more water and help make your barrier watertight.

Where an attempt to build up the riverbank proves to be a better answer, then a lot of sandbags will be needed in a hurry, so consider using a sandbag filler. This ingenious device, originally developed for rapid use in providing quick protection in isolated defensive positions in Afghanistan, has proved to be a real winner with the local councils in the United Kingdom. The sandbag filler is man-portable and is designed for either a one or two-man operation. Two men can fill over 200 bags an hour, while the same two men doing this by hand could only fill around forty, and it would be harder work.

A sandbag filler which will fill four times as many sandbags in the same time as two men filling by hand in the traditional method. (BCB Int. Ltd.)

In addition to the above, you can also protect your home by doing some of the following:

- Make sure the drains are free of leaves.
- Clear the outdoor areas of summer furniture, garden tools, and other moveable objects that might be blown or washed away.
- Keep a good stock of non-perishable food and water, along with a torch, batteries, and a radio (wind-up, if possible).
- Important documentation and items should be kept at the highest part of the house, preferably in a waterproof lock box.

Flash floods are very dangerous, and just because you are in a large city, do not think you are safe. A British couple has recently been killed in a flash flood following torrential rain in Spain. The elderly holidaymakers, aged seventy-two and seventy, where sitting outside a market street café enjoying their in the quiet seaside resort of Cala Fine-strat on the Costa Blanca. The flash flood drove through the market washing all the market stalls before it, as it hit the café, it took the two British vacationers and the café owner with it.

It transpired that the local town council had asphalted the bed of the ravine (where the market took place) without permission and had been fined some 83,000 Euros by the Spanish Ministry of Environment and was told it would have to pay damages for any incidents that occurred. Just a few months later, the rains came and several people died. Many people were injured trying to gather items from the flood waters only to be hit by cars and larger objects. Spanish emergency alerts were usually set off when forty liters of water fell to the square meter—but this flash flood was caused by just seven-point-two liters per square meter, so no alarm was raised.

During August 2011, major flooding hit Thailand and other parts of Asia, causing vast damage and over 500 deaths, mostly from drowning. In addition, some 110,000 people have been displaced nationwide. As Thailand's worst flood in more than half a century continued to move steadily into Bangkok, the city's drains and canals flooded onto the streets. As the streets became impassable, the Bangkok traffic, which on a good day is chaotic, became gridlocked. The drivers had little choice other than to abandon their vehicles or risk drowning.

The problem is the waters had not receded quickly enough. They have remained high for some weeks. Given the amount of plastic bags, rotting food, and sewage overflowing, there is a very high risk of disease. Raw sewage and animal carcasses can be seen floating in the water. Many submerged homes no longer have running water or working toilets, forcing remaining residents to bathe and defecate in the open, often in waters surrounding their homes. That waste can be spread into water where chil-

dren play. Yet, people still wade through the waters as they go about daily life, and children think the water is great for swimming in, most unaware of the risk they are taking.

"There's a lot of danger around it," says Mark Thomas, a spokesman for UNICEF, which is assisting with sanitation issues. "You need to keep kids out of the water, and everybody should stay out of the water as much as possible."

Mosquito-borne diseases, such as dengue fever, are a concern as well as eye infections and waterborne ailments that can lead to diarrhea and severe dehydration. As the flood waters remained, a new threat came to the city: crocodiles and snakes could be seen swimming in the water.

A crocodile captured swimming on the streets of Bangkok during the recent flooding.

PREPARING FOR A HURRICANE

A hurricane is a storm system within itself that forms when a low pressure system develops, generally over the tropics and near the equator. The ocean water must be at a certain temperature (26.5°C) and with sufficient depth (fifty meters); the combination of which causes the atmosphere in the area to become unstable enough to create and sustain

Category	Winds	Effects
One	74-95 mph	No real damage to building structures. Damage primarily to unanchored mobile homes, shrubbery, and trees. Also, some coastal road flooding and minor pier damage.
Two	96-110 mph	Some roofing material, door, and window damage to buildings. Considerable damage to vegetation, mobile homes, and piers. Coastal and low-lying escape routes flood two to four hours before arrival of center. Small craft in unprotected anchorages break moorings.
Three	111-130 mph	Some structural damage to small residences and utility buildings with a minor amount of curtain wall failures. Mobile homes are destroyed. Flooding near the coast destroys smaller structures with larger structures damaged by floating debris. Terrain continuously lower than five feet above sea level (ASL) may be flooded inland eight miles or more.
Four	131-155 mph	More extensive curtain wall failures with some complete roof structure failure on small residences. Major erosion of beach. Major damage to lower floors of structures near the shore. Terrain continuously lower than ten feet ASL may be flooded requiring massive evacuation of residential areas inland as far as six miles.
Five	greater than 155 mph	Complete roof failure on many residences and industrial buildings. Some complete building failures with small utility buildings blown over or away. Major damage to lower floors of all structures located less than fifteen feet ASL and within 500 yards of the shoreline. Massive evacuation of residential areas on low ground within five to ten miles of the shoreline may be required.

Hurricane Katrina as seen from space. (NASA - FEMA)

thunderstorm and convection activity. The hurricane's clouds begin to cool rapidly as they rise. This rapid cooling produces a massive amount of energy. The humidity levels and wind shear all contribute to its characteristic rotational configuration. Virtually, all hurricanes need to mature within five degrees from the equator in order to cause a circulation around the eye of the storm due to the Coriolis force. The strength of a hurricane is measured on the Saffir-Simpson scale.

Those people that live in a coastal area prone to hurricanes will know of the dangers, and should be prepared for hurricane season. In many cases, the news and weather reports will highlight any major problems way in advance. Knowing the potential threat to your home and preparing for it early is one of the best ways of dealing with a hurricane. But if you live in a mobile home, trailer, or you KNOW your home is in a low area and will flood, you should leave . . . and quickly.

If you are sure your home will take what the best of a hurricane has to offer, and you intend to stay put, then at least take some basic precautions, and do them early.

- Start collecting material and tools that you will need to protect your home, such as wood for the windows and doors. Make sure that they are cut to the correct size, as you will not have time during the storm to fiddle with them. Mark each board with a number so you know what fits where. Have a good supply of ply-lock clips handy and a nail gun and make sure everything is handy and that you're ready to rock. Test your generator and make sure that it's located well above any storm water level. Do all this before the storm starts.
- If things are not looking good, secure your home and leave. Have an evacuation plan, one that does not rely on leaving everything to the last minute. Know where you will move to, i.e., relatives, friends or hotel, etc., and how you will get there. Remember that you will need to move before the roads become flooded, which can happen sooner than you think.
- Stay tuned into the hurricane reports, as the storm path can change both in direction and intensity. Be advised and take note of government recommendations and orders—it's what you pay them for, so heed their advice. Note the location of any local shelters. If you are forced to move to a local shelter, take your own sleeping bags, blankets, food, and water. Do not expect to be treated as if you're in a five star hotel.

DURING THE FLOOD

There is very little you can do while the floodwaters continue to rise; however, you can prepare for this. As with any disaster situation, you should prepare an emergency pack. If you have not abandoned your home, you will be trapped for several days, sometimes even weeks.

If you know from past experience how long the waters normally last, then you might consider purchasing a small inflatable boat to get around in. This should only be used for emergencies where you are forced or desperately need to leave your home (for instance, when a person is very sick). You should not treat this as a toy for children to use, because when the time comes to use it, you don't want there to be any rips or tears. Likewise, many people treat a small flood as fun. FLOODWATERS can be very dangerous, particularly for children.

Plan for the electricity to go off and find alternative means of light and heat. Make sure your cabinets are well-stocked with foods that can be heated on a camping gas stove or something similar. Have a supply of alternative entertainment for children and make sure you've stocked up on batteries so they can continue to play their games, etc. Once inside your home and the floodwaters are high, stay inside.

There are times when you may be in for the long haul, such as with Hurricane Katrina. You will need to be prepared for this.

- Stock up on food and water. You will need about one gallon for each person per day. Flooding does not always affect the main water supply, but it can, so make sure you have the proper reserves available. Stock up on canned and non-perishable foods. You should be able to survive for at least two weeks. Don't forget any infants, as they will need special food, and make sure to have a good supply on hand. Make sure you have a non-electric can opener and any other special supplies you may need for the children and elderly.
- Check to make sure that your medicine cabinet is well-stocked and that any required medication is in good supply. Also, check out items such as toilet paper and baby diapers, if needed.
- Turn off the electricity at the main switch. Use camping gas for light and when you're cooking. Make sure you have enough fuel stored in a safe place. Have at least one flashlight, plus a lot of spare batteries, for each person.
- Provide entertainment for the children. Remember, if you are running a battery-powered TV, its main function should be information and not entertainment. Double check that your TV is digital and not analog, as the older models will not work.
- Make food provisions and amenities for household pets, as going to the toilet in the garden will not be possible.

- Listen to local radio news, but avoid using the phone, except in an emergency.
- Make up a grab bag, should you have to move suddenly.
- Use a waterproof pouch and place all your important documents in it, such as passports, insurance documents, house deeds, medical records, etc. If you don't have a waterproof pouch, a large food container with suffice.
- Be prepared to leave the house and go to a safe place if ordered by the authorities.

DRIVING DURING A FLOOD

Driving in any flood is dangerous. It's not just the water, but also it's the debris the waters carry. (Adam DuBrowa - FEMA)

Many people will often drive into a flood area, unaware of the dangers. Recognizable objects disappear below the water and there is no line to follow. Many roads fall off at the edge, and here the water will be very deep. If you drive into this, your car may tumble and turn over, trapping you inside below water. Driving into a tunnel which descends is also a very bad thing, as floodwaters gather and can easily swamp your car.

> **Author's Note:** Some years ago while driving in the countryside close to where I was living, I spotted a car upturned in a ditch. A week earlier the road had been impassable due to heavy flooding. I learned later that the car had driven through the floodwaters, come off the road, and overturned and went into the small drainage ditch. The car rolled upside down, and both the doors and roof were impossible to open. The water seeped in and drowned the driver and his wife. They were a local couple who knew the area well.

- Do not drive in a flooded area during the hours of darkness.
- Never attempt to cross a flooded area in your car.
- Watch out for fallen electricity lines.
- Do not drive into an underpass, as they are water catchment areas, some deep enough to cover your car.
- Stay on the main roads where you can visibly see the road markings and barrier.
- Try to tune in to the local radio channel.
- Prepare to drive towards higher ground.
- Prepare to abandon the car and head to higher ground if the water levels begin to rise or if the car is stuck or disabled.
- If the car is about to be submerged in water, and it's difficult to open the door, exit through the window without losing any time. Get out while you can!

CLEANING UP AFTER A FLOOD

Flooding is very messy, and there is no other way to say it. You will have your work cut out for you cleaning up. The amount of cleaning up depends on what caused the flooding and the area you live in.

> **Author's Note:** I live in Spain, a county renowned for its brilliant sunshine. But I can tell you, it rains in Spain, and rains heavily. These storms, known as 'gotafria,' can take you by surprise unless you know what to expect and are prepared. This type of flooding is caused by heavy rain after a very dry period. To experience a gotafria is an awesome sight: extremely heavy rain instantly floods everywhere, high winds drive the floodwaters, and within minutes all the lower streams, streets, and water courses are flooded with boiling water. While very few lives are lost, the damage and clean-up required is enormous.

The waters gather, and move at tremendous speed carrying cars, trees, and earth in their path, in a very similar way as that of a tsunami. Walls fall, underground garages fill quickly, and homes are invaded with meters of water—and all this can happen within less than two hours. Then comes the clean-up.

Experience has shown that the quicker you clean-up, the better and faster you will recover. If you leave the mud and debris until it gets hard, you will find it difficult to clean. The ideal time is immediately after the water has receded.

- First, remove any large debris or objects that have been swept into your home.
- Work out a clean-up plan, which rooms you will do first.
- Next, remove as much of the mud that has settled on the floor.
- Then using a power washer, wash down the walls with clean water. Use a small amount of bleach in the water if your machine allows this. If not, follow up with a bucket of water and bleach to clean off any remaining dirt.
- Once you have removed and cleaned the room, allow it to dry.
- Finally, clean the walls and floor using a light bleach solution to stop fungus growth and to thoroughly sanitize the room.

FLASH FLOODS

While flash floods do not claim many lives, they do appear suddenly and cause a great deal of damage. A flash flood is a sudden flood event caused by a hydrologic response of the drainage basin. Flash floods are normally strongly localized and are caused when heavy rain falls over a small catchment basin. The terrain may channel the extreme run-off to produce a flood peak that reaches its maximum in just a few hours, even minutes.

Flash floods happen in the oddest of places and with such force that a mere foot high wall can sweep you off your feet. Moreover, flash floods are increasingly observed in urban areas where the surface is unable to absorb large amounts of water in a short period. Often, the push and speed of floodwater are much more important than the

water levels in terms of potential impact on population and structures.

Flash floods happen in barren areas of the Middle East, and are caused by heavy rainfall in the upper mountains, normally along the coastline where evaporated sea water is blown inland in the form of clouds. As these are forced to rise by the mountains, the vapor cools and turns to rain. The water falls quickly through the gullies until it forms one large body of water trapped in the lower valleys. The rushing water is rarely more than a meter high, but it moves with great force, carrying with it a large amount of rocks, sand, and gravel swept up from the valley floor. The force of the water and the debris it contains will kill anyone trapped in its path. The water usually dissipates as it reaches the flat open terrain, quickly evaporating into the earth. Flash floods take place in the same area, normally leaving behind such tell-tale signs of water-swept debris.

Flash floods arrive very quickly and will wash away all within its path. Get to higher ground for safety.

GET OUT OF ITS PATH

If you are experiencing abnormally heavy rain in your area, you would be advised to move to higher ground. If a flash flood warning is given, you should make your way to a safe location until the danger has passed. Should you be unlucky enough to be standing in the path of a flash flood, make every effort to get out of its way. It may look as if it is only a few inches high, but the power and force of the water will knock you off your feet. Flash floods are dangerous, even small localized ones. If you are in a car and not in the path of the floodwater, you should exit and make your way to higher ground. If your car is caught up in the flash flood, you will have little choice other than to stay in your car and hope that it is eventually washed to one side, or trapped in such a position as to allow you to exit.

In late August 2011, Hurricane Irene hit the east coast of the United States; one of the first victims was a young woman from New Jersey who was found dead in her car. She had called the police earlier, after the car had been washed away by the flash flood. "She left her house, went in her car and was swept away," said New Jersey Governor Chris Christie.

Chapter 6

EXTREMES OF WEATHER—HOT & COLD

Extreme cold is very
treacherous; don't sit down
and wait to die – move.
(Barry Davies)

While the deaths from earthquakes, tsunamis, and hurricanes count into millions, there is no predictability to the numbers. However, records show that there is steady number of deaths each year from the effects of extreme weather. These deaths are nowhere more apparent than in my native United Kingdom. In January 2010, the weather was the worst in thirty years. People in the north of Scotland suffered for weeks as the snows fell and the temperatures stayed well below freezing for weeks. 1,506 deaths were registered in Scotland in the first week of January, many from the cold. The most vulnerable were the elderly, many of whom simply died in their homes. Social services were severely hampered by the cold and depth of snow, which made roads impassable, and the normal flow of fuel and food came to a grinding holt.

Man is a tropical animal, and in most parts of the world, needs clothes to protect him against the elements. In a survival situation, maintenance of the body temperature and prevention of injury are equally as important as finding food and water. The body temperature functions best between 96-102 degrees Fahrenheit, so preventing heat loss or heat gain is of primary concern to the survivor. Factors which cause changes in the body temperature include climatic temperature, wind, moisture loss, and illness. Heat gain or loss is transferred by conduction, convection, radiation, and exacerbated by evaporation, respiration, and wind.

Extreme cold weather conditions occur in both the Northern and Southern Hemisphere. From 1999-2000, the United Kingdom saw one of the heaviest snowfalls of the century upon which temperatures fell and remained well below freezing for almost two weeks. The roads were impassable, cars would not start, and people were housebound.

You will be surprised at the number of people who died from the cold, when the means to stay alive were within reach. Most people will simply dress the same as they always do, but add an extra coat for warmth during the winter. The best method of dress in extreme cold weather is the 'layer system.'

The principle of using a layer system in order to trap warm air has proved itself to offer the most benefit in cold conditions. Thin cotton underclothes, covered with one or more layers of warm wear made from wool, fiber pile, or fleece is ideal. The outer garment should be windproof, and preferably waterproof. It could be made from tightly woven cotton, polycotton, fiber-pile material, or nylon. The most important factors to remember are:

- Keep clothes clean.
- Avoid overheating and sweating.
- Keep clothing dry.
- Repair defects immediately.
- Improvise.

Clothing should not be worn so tight that it restricts the flow of blood, which distributes the body heat and helps prevent frostbite. If you are wearing more than one pair of socks or gloves, make sure that the outer pair is larger and fits comfortably over the other. Loosen any clothing at the neck, wrists, and waist during excessive exercise. If the body is still overheating, take off the outer layers of clothing, one layer at a time. When work stops, you should put the clothing on again to prevent chilling.

It may look cold on the outside, but staying inside this makeshift shelter will prevent heat loss and frostbite. (Barry Davies)

Author's Note: While in the SAS, I was involved in a winter exercise. My patrol parachuted onto the island of Senya, in the far frozen reaches of Northern Norway. In the middle of winter, the only daylight we saw would sneak under the canopy of darkness for an hour at midday. As we dropped into a blinding snow storm, it soon became obvious that survival would take precedence over the exercise. For four days, we walked (our skis were useless) knee-deep in a blinding snowstorm in temperatures that fell below minus thirty degrees. Our sledge containing all our fuel and rations had been launched by parachute moments before we jumped into the darkness—it was never recovered. Living on what we could carry in our rucksacks, the patrol faced a test of human endurance. We made shelter, built a fire, and waited to be rescued. As the days went on, we found ourselves making 'stone stew,' a mixture of water and anything we could find in our rucksacks and pockets, which included boiled sweets, biscuits, and a chocolate bar. On day five, we had made a hole in the ice of a nearby lake from which we pulled three large fish with relative ease. On day six, the weather eventually abated and we were rescued.

During World War II, a number of American servicemen became marooned in the arctic wasteland—with most of them dying. They did so because few ventured far from their crash site. They made no attempt to catch fish, hunt game, or even attempt to travel south. None that were later found had prepared a rescue signal, and most had died; not from the cold, but from starvation.

The one governing factor in extreme cold weather is warmth, and so, maintaining a fire is essential. However, there are fires and then there are fires. Believe it or not, the most common cause of accidental death in the arctic is not freezing to death but fire!

However, fire remains the single most important element needed by man surviving under arctic conditions.

FIRE IN THE HOME

During winter, we all like to come home to a nice fire. Many people today have central heating to warm their home, while some retain an open fireplace for coal or wood. In either case, before the winter arrives, make sure you have an ample supply of fuel. You will need enough fuel in reserve to last you at least one month. Do not rely on your fuel being delivered, as during extreme cold weather, it is unlikely that the fuel trucks will be able to reach you.

If you have a coal or wood burning fire, make sure your reserves are stored in a handy position and are readily accessible. The good thing about an open fire is that you can burn almost any kind of fuel to produce heat (my advice is to stick to those items that do not produce toxic fumes). In an emergency you can use any of the following:

- Old wooden furniture.
- Old unwanted books.
- Rolled up newspapers or magazines.
- Barbecue fuel.

Warning: Make sure that any room you burn a fire in is well-ventilated to prevent carbon monoxide poisoning.

Surviving Extreme Cold Weather Outdoors

It may be the case that you are trapped away from your home or in an earthquake disaster area when extreme cold weather hits. In such a case, you must seek shelter where there is a fire or it is possible to light a fire.

If you are leaving your shelter for any length of time and your fire is unattended, it will eventually burn out. Always make sure that there is dry tinder handy for your return and a reasonable supply of fuel. Even if you are traveling, and it is not your intention to return, you may, for unforeseeable reasons, be forced to return to your shelter.

Lighting a fire in the open during extreme weather conditions is at best, difficult. True, there are many modern forms of firelights available, from matches to gas lighters. However, under such conditions, you will require a form of wind break and a permanent flame in order to achieve any success with fire lighting. It is best

Learn how to light a fire in extreme cold; be prepared as you will only have minutes before you freeze to death. (Barry Davies)

to use a candle placed inside a tin in such a way that it is easy to light, easy to get a light from, and provides light in order to see what you are doing. Place a small amount of combustible material over the can and let the candle heat it until it catches fire. The governing factor here is 'heat,' as the fire will not burn unless you can build the heat to a degree higher than the prevailing temperature.

If you are planning to stay in one place for longer than twenty-four hours, and given that the materials are available, you should seriously consider constructing a Yukon Stove. It is one of the best ways to use fire for cooking and other purposes. It is also fairly safe and can withstand a certain amount of bad weather, even when built in the open.

A Yukon Stove is made from rocks, stones, and mud, in the shape of a tortoise shell. A hole is left on the windward side (best offset a little in extreme winds) for fuel and ventilation and there is also a hole at the top, acting as a chimney. If you have a metal box or can available, this can be built into the back wall to make an oven. Before any food can be cooked in it, though, a layer of twigs must be put down first, otherwise the food will burn on the hot metal. These twigs will eventually turn into charcoal, which can be saved and used to deodorize purified water and for medicinal uses. A large flat rock should cover half the chimney outlet and be used as a griddle. If you wish to use your Yukon Stove inside your shelter, make sure that you have adequate ventilation, as the Stove will produce carbon monoxide gas. The Yukon Stove has many advantages:

- It can burn unattended.
- Heat will be retained.
- Fuel consumption can be controlled.
- Will safely dry wet clothing.
- Is able to provide safe heat.
- Can be used inside a large shelter.

If you are outdoors, waiting in the cold can be made easier by lying on some form of an insulation mat. This can be made with any material, such as cardboard, old clothing, or anything that will keep you off the ground. Protection from the wind can be achieved by simply covering the body with a plastic survival bag (a strong garbage bag will suffice). A

small tin converted into a candle or oil lamp will help provide a little heat for your hands, and provide light during the hours of darkness.

Ensure a Good Night's Sleep

We normally spend a third of our day sleeping; but during a survival situation, particularly in extreme cold, you should increase this to twelve to fourteen hours. This applies to both indoor and outdoor survival conditions. While waiting for the weather to moderate or to be rescued, sleep will prevent fatigue and exhaustion. However, if conditions allow, and there are no limiting factors, exercise daily in the form of making your home secure or if outdoors, foraging for fuel and food.

If you are outdoors, shared body heat with other survivors is comforting. Forget the inhibitions and huddle together, placing older people and children in the middle. There are also a few things you can do to make your sleep period more comfortable.

- Eat your biggest meal just before you go to bed.
- Exercise to warm your muscles, but do not perspire.
- If you cannot shower, strip and rub your body with a dry towel, if possible.
- Put on extra clothes and socks.
- Wear a hat to bed.
- Go to the bathroom just before you go to sleep.
- Four hours of sleep before midnight is better than four hours of sleep after midnight
- If outdoors, make sure your shelter is windproof.

If you are forced to sleep in the cold, always use insulation and waterproofing. Two simple plastic sacks filled with grass will save your life. (Barry Davies)

- Make your bed as comfortable as possible; if outdoors, use insulating material.
- If reliant on an open fire, have a plentiful supply of fuel handy.
- If you cannot sleep, plan what you will do the next day, but do not disturb others.

Water in Extreme Cold

Even for those people lucky enough to be in their homes, water can still be a problem. Water is taken for granted; but when the water supply is terminated due to pipes freezing or bursting, you have a problem. The toilets will not flush and there is no water for drinking or cooking.

Finding water is not a problem, as the surfaces outdoors will be covered with either snow or ice. The problem is converting these to obtain a daily supply of water, as this can only be done by heating. Avoid eating loose snow or ice, as it can cause damage to the delicate membranes inside your mouth, as well as causing dehydration. If you really need to drink, and snow is the only thing available, crush it into a snowball with your hands. Continued compression will cause the snow to melt and you can let the water drip into your mouth. Ice is much easier to melt than snow due to the lack of air between the water particles. Breaking the ice into smaller pieces, or crushing it will speed this process further and you won't need as much fuel to melt it. If you do need to collect water from ice and snow, always boil the water. Don't waste valuable fuel, melt only what you need and drink the water while it's still warm.

THE EFFECT OF COLD ON THE HUMAN BODY

If you have no heat to warm you up, then arctic temperatures present several problems, the main one being hypothermia. The old, in particular, are prone to hypothermia during periods of extreme cold. Many living in well-protected homes have sat in a chair while the central heating has broken down and suffered from excessive heat loss from the body.

If caught outdoors, wind and rain will accelerate the cooling of the body because its movement decreases air temperature. Being wet increases this risk, as water will conduct the heat away from the body, therefore cooling it rapidly. Garments that are wet or damp, either through water or sweat, will lose their insulating properties, beginning to drain heat from the body.

Hypothermia occurs when the body temperature falls below 35°C (95°F) and body heat is being lost faster than it can be replaced. At this stage, body functions start to slow down and may stop altogether if the condition is not treated. It is important to be aware of the symptoms, especially if you are subject to any of the conditions described below:

- Uncontrollable shivering.
- Skin is pale and dry and sub-normally cold to the touch.

Author's Note: I have seen some of the fittest soldiers in the world succumb to hypothermia, mainly through being injured while operating in extreme cold conditions, or stupidity by not being properly prepared. Hypothermia is a real killer.

A good protection against hypothermia is to wear a pair of women's tights. Many SAS soldiers do this when working in Arctic conditions. (Barry Davies)

- Muscular weakness and tiredness, lethargy.
- Irrational behavior.
- Change in personality, for example, an extrovert may become an introvert; a quiet person may become aggressive.
- Dimming of sight and needing to sleep.
- Slow, weak pulse.
- Slow, shallow breathing.
- Eventual collapse and unconsciousness.
- Possible cardiac arrest.

As soon as hypothermia is suspected, it must be treated by restoring lost body heat. This means getting the casualty out of the wet and cold and into shelter as soon as possible. Use dry clothing/covering to replace any wet clothing. If the victim has been totally submerged in water, remove all the garments as they will reduce body temperature faster than naked flesh. If you have a metalized (silver foil) survival blanket, use this to reflect any radiated body heat back to the body. Hot food and drinks are a good method if the casualty is conscious. If another healthy survivor is present, they will be able to share their body heat with the casualty.

The casualty may become unconscious with no signs of breathing or of a pulse, so proceed immediately with assisted ventilation and chest compression. The casualty will still need to be warmed. Even if the casualty's body temperature has fallen to 26° C (79°F), do not automatically presume that they are dead. Carry on with resuscitation techniques until he has reached normal body temperature; if he cannot then be revived, death can be assumed. Remember if one person is suffering from hypothermia, there maybe others, so check everyone in your party.

Hands and feet are at the extremes of the body's circulation and so need extra attention if they are to maintain heat. Make sure that any fastenings at the wrists, ankles, neck, and waist are snug enough to prevent heat loss, but not so tight that they cut off circulation to the extremities. Keep the hands covered as much as possible. If they become cold, warm them either between the thighs or under the armpits. Wear warm slippers if indoors with a thick pair of bed socks. Moving the feet and wiggling the toes can warm frost-nipped toes, and warming them against a companion's body is also very effective. Pay attention to your footwear and try to keep your feet as dry as possible. If you are forced outdoors, then overboots are also a great aid in protecting the feet against the cold and wet. If you do not have any overboots, try and improvise by putting a spare sock and a plastic grocery bag over each boot. If you are not moving around, take off your shoes or boots and give your feet a good ten minute rub every few hours.

Caught Outdoors

If you are caught outdoors for any length of time and immediate shelter is not available to you, try to maintain your body temperature. When the body becomes cold, it puts priority on retaining the core heat rather than warming the extremities. Therefore, it shuts down the blood vessels in the skin. In extreme cold weather, the parts of the body at the limits of the circulation may actually freeze and cause tissue damage. This is the condition known as frostbite. Frostbite can creep up on a person so gradually that they are not aware that they have it until the last minute. You will need to be on guard against this dangerous condition; if it becomes serious, it can lead to gangrene and loss of the affected part. The first symptoms to be noticed will be a feeling of 'pins and needles' in the affected part. It may also become stiff and numb. Later, the skin of the area will turn pale, then white, before becoming a mottled blue and eventually black as tissue death occurs.

As exposed skin is most prone to frostbite, check uncovered areas frequently, especially the nose, fingers, and toes; other areas that need to be checked regularly are the ankles and wrists. If you are with someone else, make sure that you check each other frequently for any warning signs that frostbite is occurring. Any frostbitten areas that are discovered should be slowly warmed by some natural means. Skin to skin contact provides the best method of slow warming. If warm water is available, use that, but make sure that it isn't too warm (do a 'baby-bath' test). Any frostbitten casualty should be moved to

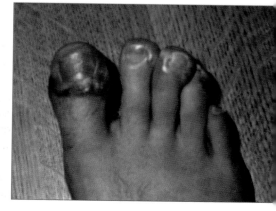

Frostbite will almost certainly mean amputation – protect against it. (Barry Davies)

a shelter as soon as is practical and they should be insulated against further heat loss with blankets and extra clothing. Hot drinks and food should be given to the casualty as soon as possible.

If you discover frostbite:

- DO NOT rub or massage the affected area (except in the very early stages).
- DO NOT apply snow or ice; this will only serve to make the condition worse.
- DO NOT use direct or strong heat such as hot stones or a fire to warm an area.
- DO NOT give alcohol to drink as this can lower body temperature further.
- DO NOT allow a casualty with a recently frostbitten foot to walk.
- DO NOT break open any blisters which may occur.

Travel During Extreme Cold Weather

If you are trapped in your home for several days and the weather shows no sign of letting up, you may, for any number of reasons, risk going outdoors. If you are already outdoors, you may wish to move in order to find better shelter or help.

The decision to travel or not to travel must be made on a day-to-day basis, bearing in mind all your reasons for traveling in the first place. However, once committed to traveling, you should continue your journey in an endeavor to reach your goal. Unfortunately, the weather conditions are unpredictable and getting caught in a snowstorm in the middle of winter represents a serious threat to life. One military solution is to adopt the 'time to shelter principle.' This simply means that if you are surprised by storm or have an accident en-route, you must estimate the time it will take to construct a shelter given what's available in your immediate surroundings. If this time is greater

When traveling in extreme cold, make sure you are prepared. It's too late once you are exposed to the elements. Note the improvised snow goggles. (Barry Davies)

than returning to your last overnight camp, then always go back; if it is less, build a new camp. The early American trappers had a similar system going from cabin to cabin. If they could not make it to the next cabin, they would turn back.

Always make sure that you have the means to light a fire packed in a waterproof container before venturing on your travels. Even if you are making good progress you are advised to stop while there is enough daylight to construct a shelter and build a fire. Do not venture into a snowstorm at night, as it will almost certainly mean your death.

Even if you are native to the area, it is easy to get lost or disorientated in a winter snowstorm. The name 'white out,' refers to a heavy snowstorm, when the wind whips the ground snow above head height. In any event, visibility is reduced to zero and your only option is to remain in your shelter. Fresh and driven snow hides a multitude of risks into which it is easy to step, so make sure to take care where you walk. Try to travel with the wind on your back, as this will protect you and speed up your walking.

NEVER TRUST ICE

Frozen lakes and rivers provide the traveler with a flat and easy-going terrain to move across, but they are fraught with danger. No matter how cold the temperature is, ice can **never** be considered safe. Always avoid dark colored or clear ice and make sure that if you have to walk over ice, walk on white ice, which is a lot safer. If you must cross ice, check that it is solid and thick; the time of year and air temperature is also a good indicator of ice walking safety. Do not venture too far from the shore line, and as a basic safeguard, always carry a long pole, one that is capable of supporting your weight. Carry by holding it with both hands in the center, this will provide a bridge and extraction hold should you fall through the ice. The pole can also be used to test suspicious

Never trust ice. It is extremely difficult to get out of an ice hole once you have fallen through – and you only have a few seconds before it's too late. (Cpl Laviolette, courtesy of the Canadian Department of National Defence)

patches of ice. Be ready to drop your pack should you fall through ice.

Partly frozen rivers and streams can be crossed, providing you are aware of the water depth at its deepest point and it is safe to wade across. If you do this, remove your socks (not your boots) and trousers before crossing, using your pole as a staff in the water. Replace your dry socks and trousers once safely across.

Surviving in extreme cold conditions is harsh enough, but falling through the ice will almost certainly kill you, even if you do manage to crawl out. Falling through the ice will knock the breath out of you—you will ball-up with muscle contractions and there is also the possibility that you can die from a heart attack. You must do everything within your power to resurface through the entry hole and pull yourself free. Turn towards the shore, as the ice is generally thicker on this side. Extend and drop both arms out onto the ice; if it breaks free, keep trying until you have a solid purchase. If your pole stopped you falling in completely, or you can use it to get a secure hold, use it to pull yourself from the water. Grip on your pole and pull your body forward towards the shoreline—spread your legs to gain side or rear purchase on the ice around the hole. Remain prone at all times, even when out of the water; try to lay flat and roll across ice until you reach the shore.

If you go under the ice, you have little chance of survival, but there are several cases where people have come out alive. The best method is to kick the ice above with your feet until you can make a hole in which to surface through, and then follow the procedure above. If you remain clinging to the ice, exposed parts will freeze in less than five minutes.

Author's Note: You can never be sure of ice. It may look and feel solid, but there can be weak spots that will crack and drop you into the water. It has been my experience, when forced to cross ice, that it is worthwhile building the makings of a substantial fire with some fine kindling ready to light before you step foot on the ice. This way should you fall through and manage to get out, you at least have a chance of survival as your fire is already prepared. Although it adds to your weight, a long pole carried across your chest like a tightrope walker will not only stop you from falling into the freezing water, but will be a tremendous help when trying to get out.

Rolling in fresh snow will act a blotter, but this is only a temporary reprieve, as you need to make a fire and provide shelter from the wind—without either, you will die. If you do not take immediate action, you will start to become unconscious in seven to ten minutes, with death following quickly.

Build a fire before your hands, mind, and body become immobile.

Take off wet clothing and remove as much water as possible by twisting and squeezing before they freeze.

Put on any extra clothing and exercise for a few minutes.

If there are several people in the party, share some of your outer clothes temporarily.

It is better to be naked for a short while, and you will survive longer, than staying in wet clothes.

Once you have fire and shelter, avoid panic! You must dry and warm your body first before your clothes.

SURVIVING SEVERE HOT WEATHER

For some reason, heat waves are welcomed by the majority of people and are rarely seen as a problem. Believe me, hot weather is a real killer, a silent killer which rarely makes the headlines. Every year, thousands die from heat exhaustion; the elderly, the sick, the very young, and, believe it or not, many fit athletes. To put a severe heat wave into perspective, they claim more lives each year than hurricanes, tornadoes and flooding all put together.

In August 2003, a record-breaking heat wave baked Europe, causing some 35,000 deaths. France alone suffered 14,800 deaths as a direct result of the heat wave, where temperatures rocketed to 104°F (40°C) and remained at this level for almost two weeks.

This was not the only problem: severe heat causes other environmental and civil problems, such as the rivers and lakes to dry up. France has some fifty-eight nuclear power stations which provide 70% of her power requirement . . . and guess what? They use river water as an essential part of the cooling system, and no water means they have to shut the reactors down, resulting in no electricity. No power for the air-conditioning, fans, or

To survive in hot weather, you need to wear loose, light clothing; white will resist the sun, while dark material will heat up. (Barry Davies)

Author's Note: On October 27, 2006, Corporal Peter Armor (264 SAS Signals) died during a routine training session. He had been with another SAS friend and both had spent an hour in an air conditioned gym before going on a distance run. The temperature topped 40°C (104°F) as they set off along a beachfront on a run that would normally take them about an hour. Corporal Armor had missed a few days training because of diarrhea, but felt fit enough for the run. On the return journey, he felt ill and slowed down. His SAS colleague realized something was wrong and left to fetch their transport. When he returned, he found that Corporal Armor had collapsed. He was rushed to hospital, but died from organ failure nine days later. Corporal Armor was at the peak of physical fitness when he collapsed.

refrigeration will just make a bad situation far worse. A heat wave combined with long periods of no rain will cause a drought—a very dangerous situation.

Our bodies operate at around 98.6°F, but when we are subjected to extreme heat, our bodies try to compensate by varying blood circulation and sweating. If the body heat continues to climb to around 104 degrees and is not brought under control, we risk death by failing vital organs. Naturally, some people deal with increased body heat better than others, but severe heat will kill not just the old and weak but also the very fit.

Severe heat is not the only element that affects our body; the environment in which we reside also adds to the risk. For example, the sun will heat up a city or large town with the heat being retained within the concrete structures such as building and roads. These areas can be higher than the surrounding countryside by as much as ten degrees. In 1995, Chicago suffered from extreme heat which took the lives of 739 people in just a few days.

The common factor is the failure to recognize the problems relating to severe heat and the slow response by authorities to respond. A warning about a predicted heat wave is more often than not seen as a good thing rather than a danger. People bask in the heat, while heat-related deaths go unreported. The lack of public recognition as to the dangers of high temperatures simply adds to the lethality of a heat wave, which I might add is not recognized as a major disaster.

Heat Exhaustion

Surviving in the heat does not mean you have to be in a dry, arid climate such as the desert. Records show that the majority of people that die from severe heat are located in cites. One of the main priorities is water, both preventing its loss from your body and the acquisition of a water supply, i.e., **drink lots of water when it's hot**. Dehydration and heat exhaustion have the effect of weakening the individual to a state of total collapse, no matter how fit or strong the individual may be. Remember, as you sweat, you also lose salt and other body minerals. While salt tablets will help, they are not the only answer. There are many sports beverages on the market which are designed specifically to replace lost minerals.

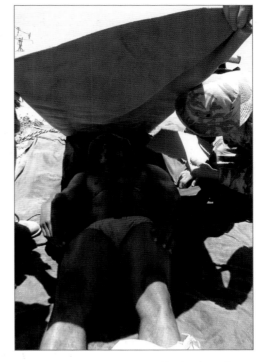

Heat exhaustion requires immediate cooling of the body. (Barry Davies)

- Make sure you have a good supply of clean fresh water handy.
- Drink at least two glasses of cool water per hour during the day.
- If you are doing manual work or sweating, consider taking salt tablets. (If you are old or sick, consult your doctor before taking salt tablets.)
- Do not drink alcohol or large amounts of sugar as these will cause you to lose body fluids.
- Do not drink ice cold drinks as you may suffer from stomach cramps.
- Avoid eating heavy meals as these will simply heat up your body.
- Wear light colored and loose clothing. (Dark colors absorb more heat.)
- A wide brimmed hat will help protect your head, but don't forget to protect your neck.

- Sunglasses will protect your eyes and apply a good sunblock cream to any exposed skin.

Signs and Symptoms of Heat Exhaustion

The onset of heat exhaustion normally comes quickly with the lack of energy and the inability to do even the most simple of tasks, such as walking a few steps without feeling totally exhausted. The onset of these symptoms can be accelerated if you have just come from a cold environment, such as an air-conditioned room. The first signs are as follows, more or less in order, but not always.

- Weakness.
- Dizziness.
- The inability to walk more than a few steps.
- Nausea.
- Headache.
- Pale, cool and moist skin.
- Fast and weak pulse.
- Disorientation.
- Tiredness.

In any environment where it is excessively hot and you have to work outdoors, start slowly and maintain a steady pace. If you feel any of the above symptoms, you must stop immediately. Likewise, if exertion makes your heart pound and you find breathing difficult or are gasping for air, STOP immediately.

Treatment

First and foremost, recognize the symptoms of heat exhaustion both in yourself and others. Stop what you are doing and rest in the shade if available. Drink cool, not cold water; do not drink alcohol. If you are at home or near a place of work, take a cool shower or sit in a cool bath. Move to an air-conditioned room, but do not have the temperature set too low. If you do not have air-conditioning, look for a public location that does, such as a library.

If you are outside or unable to carry out any of the above, rest anyway. Shelter from the sun is vital, even a small covering for your head will help. Remove any extra clothing and use this to shelter your body. If you have water, drink even if it's warm; wet a handkerchief and hold this to the back of your neck just where the skull joins the spine. Stay quiet and focused until the sun has gone down before attempting to move.

Heat-related deaths are preventable; the factors that govern the body's ability to cool itself are dependent on the individual. Age, dehydration, heart disease, obesity, poor circulation, and alcohol can all have a detrimental effect. Additionally, high humidity prevents the sweat from evaporating, thus preventing the body from releasing its excess heat.

Many people must venture out during the day, even in an excessive heat wave. If you have to go outdoors, particularly, if you are about to do manual labor, see if it's possible to work during the early morning and late evening.

In severe cases of heat exhaustion intravenous fluids and salt are necessary. (Barry Davies)

Looking Out for Each Other

Most military units have a Buddy-Buddy system: basically, you have a friend with whom you operate. During military operations, especially when fighting in a war, your buddy looks out for you—and you for him. This same system is a good one to adopt during a severe heat wave. Daughter watch mom, mom watches the kids, and dad watches everyone. If possible, visit family members during a heat wave to

Author's Note: The temperatures in Spain during the month of August are particularly high and the sun beats down relentlessly. Temperatures have reached 42°C (107°F) in some places and overnight lows will not fall below 24°C (75°F) in others. Very few people work during the month of August, and all construction and manual work simply comes to a halt. Even in a normal working day, the Spanish worker will stop around 2:00 p.m. and rest until around 6:00 p.m., when they will commence working. In this way, the Spanish have learned to overcome extreme heat and avoid its dangers.

check on them. When you go shopping, do not leave infants, young children, or animals inside your car, even if you are only going for a few minutes. In very hot temperatures around the 40°C (104°F) mark, both children and animals could be dead in less than twenty minutes. It's the simple things and common sense that really count.

- Young children need to be told when to drink.
- Old people do not sense the change in temperature quickly.
- People who are overweight will retain more body heat.

Cooling Systems

Strange as it might sound, there have been some advances in 'cooling systems' for soldiers who have to work in very hot climates, given that over the past decade, America, Britain, and many other countries have been fighting, and continue to fight in the Middle East. Despite efforts to reduce their burden, these soldiers, carry an ever-increasing weight upon their bodies: excessive weight and high temperatures are not a good combination. Below are some of the innovative ideas that have been developed. Many of these are cheap and now available to the general public.

Dehydrated Water

I know this is a misconception, but as a hydration supplement, it achieves the same as if you could have "dehydrated water." It dramatically improves the body's natural absorption of water. Basically, this is a clear liquid electrolyte which is added to water. Use one sachet per three liters of water and shake well. I tried it and it was extremely beneficial.

Neck Cooling Scarf / Hat

This is a simple, yet effective body cooling product that works by evaporation. You simply need to immerse the scarf in clean water for approximately ten minutes. This allows the poly crystals contained within the scarf or hat to absorb and retain a large volume of water. When worn, the retained water evaporates and draws away body heat, creating a cooling effect.

Both hat and scarf can be re-soaked once it has dried out or lost its effect. The hat has mesh netting, which helps ventilate the head, and a Legionnaire flap to protect the neck. The poly-crystal chamber is in the top of the hat, and like the scarf, can be immersed in water to provide extra cooling to the head.

"Chilly"

Most soldiers now carry their water in a hydration pack which fits on their back. The pack has a tube which comes over the shoulder and allows the soldier to drink without having to use his hands. These packs are commonly referred to as a 'Camelbak,' after the popular brand. In hot conditions, water in a hydration pack can reach temperatures well above the core temperature of the body. Drinking warm water is totally ineffective to cool the body. Two years ago, a British company made a personal water cooler which sat on top of the hydration pack and inter-rupted the flow of water. The device (called Chilly) works simply by evap-oration alone and requires no batteries; yet, it will significantly help to reduce heat stress injuries and dehydration. The Chilly provides a continuous supply of cool, palata-ble water. It, therefore, encourages frequent sipping and so improves hydration. It also lowers the core temperature of the body.

The neck cooling scarf is a simple device which works wonders. (BCB Int. Ltd.)

Most soldiers carry a hydration pack to prevent dehydration. The Chilly interrupts the flow of the water, reducing the temperature and making the water cool and more palatable. (BCB Int. Ltd.)

Chapter 7

TORNADOES

Tornado, beautiful
nature, but so
destructive. (FEMA)

Tornadoes are spectacular, and when in close proximity to people and buildings, very dangerous. While they are to be found in many parts of the world, the largest number are concentrated in the United States, Europe and South East Asia.

Many people assume that tornadoes and hurricanes are very similar; yet the only similarity is the damage they cause. While it is possible to see more than one tornado at a time, each tornado is an isolated storm which always forms ahead of a front. They can form quickly and disappear just as quickly; at other times a tornado can stay on the ground and leave a large area of devastation. They can generate wind speeds in excess of 250 miles per hour and cause vast damage.

A rotating column of air will form within a cumulonimbus cloud and extend towards the ground. This is the classic funnel we are all familiar with. It is only a 'tornado' when it actually touches the ground. The funnel will whip up dust and debris that can be seen spinning directly upwards from the ground; this is the most dangerous stage and is known as 'maturity.' It can, during full maturity, destroy homes, vehicles, and humans as it sweeps through its path. As the tornado loses strength, it starts to shrink and the funnel becomes narrow and sways a lot more; likewise the amount of destruction reduces. As the tornado continues to decay, it narrows to what is known as the 'rope stage,' before finally dispersing.

A tornado can form when warm air moves upward into an area of cold air; as this happens, instabilities begin to form. The top cold air will eventually give way, causing the storm winds to begin spinning. This, in turn, will create a funnel shaped cloud. If that funnel cloud touches the ground, it becomes a tornado.

The severity of a tornado is ranked by the Fujita Scale. This scale is an indicator of the damage we can expect, depending on the speed of the tornado.

The deadliest tornado happened on April 26, 1989 in Bangladesh, claiming the lives of 1,418 people. In 2011 (as I write this book), America is suffering the worst tornado death toll since 1950, which so far has reached 520. The insurance cost for this same year paid out for tornado damage is estimated at around six billion. While the loss of

The Fujita Scale

F-Scale Number	Intensity Phase	Wind Speed	Type of Damage Done
F0	Gale tornado	40-72 mph	Some damage to chimneys; breaks branches off trees; pushes over shallow-rooted trees; damages sign boards.
F1	Moderate tornado	73-112 mph	The lower limit is the beginning of hurricane wind speed; peels surface off roofs; mobile homes pushed off foundations or overturned; moving autos pushed off the roads; attached garages may be destroyed.
F2	Significant tornado	113-157 mph	Considerable damage. Roofs torn off frame houses; mobile homes demolished; boxcars pushed over; large trees snapped or uprooted; light object missiles generated.
F3	Severe tornado	158-206 mph	Roof and some walls torn off well-constructed houses; trains overturned; most trees in forests uprooted.
F4	Devastating tornado	207-260 mph	Well-constructed houses leveled; structures with weak foundations blown off some distance; cars thrown and large missiles generated.
F5	Incredible tornado	261-318 mph	Strong frame houses lifted off foundations and carried considerable distances to disintegrate; automobile-sized missiles fly through the air in excess of 100 meters; trees debarked; steel reinforced concrete structures badly damaged.
F6	Inconceivable tornado	319-379 mph	These winds are very unlikely. The small area of damage they might produce would probably not be recognizable along with the mess produced by F4 and F5 wind that would surround the F6 winds. Missiles, such as cars and refrigerators would do serious secondary damage that could not be directly identified as F6 damage. If this level is ever achieved, evidence for it might only be found in some manner of ground swirl pattern, for it may never be.identifiable through engineering studies.

life caused by a tornado is not normally as great as for other disasters, they are a natural phenomenon that keep occurring.

In March 1925, the deadliest tornado in American history killed 695 in Missouri, Southern Illinois and Southwest Indiana. On Sunday, May 22, 2011, Joplin, Missouri felt the full zlast of an F5 that claimed the lives of 143 people. Again, it was one of the most lethal tornadoes to strike American soil.

TORNADO FORECAST

Many people believe that tornadoes will strike at more or less the same time and in the same area as they have done previously. However, in truth, there is no simple answer when it comes to forecasting a tornado. It requires a very good weather prediction, usually one or two days in advance. The temperature and wind flow patterns in the atmosphere, which can cause enough moisture, instability, lift, and wind shear required for tornado thunderstorms can all be acquired, but even then it's not certain a tornado will form. For the purpose of this book, we will rely on the fact that if you live in an area prone to tornadoes, you should plan to deal with one, or better yet, several.

TORNADO WARNINGS AND SIGNS

People who live in tornado-prone areas should always listen out for both radio and television warnings. There are two key alerts related specifically to tornado conditions. The first is a tornado watch and the second is a tornado warning.

Tornado Watch—This is when weather and atmospheric conditions are conducive to the development of tornadoes in the warning area.

Tornado Warning—A tornado has actually been sighted by spotters or indicated on radar and is occurring or imminent in the warning area.

- If you're not within hearing distance of a radio (i.e.; lone worker), and you receive no warning from others, look for these warning signs:

- Hail is a good indicator that possible tornado activity is on the way. Advancing hail can cause the sky to have a greenish tint to it.
- Likewise, orange skies generally mean that high winds are blowing dust around in the air.
- Trust your instincts; most people can tell when a storm is coming and the air sometimes has a smell like a burning electric component.

When you seriously suspect a tornado, or have received a warning, you should warn everyone else in your immediate vicinity and then make sure people move to the tornado shelter. If you do not have a tornado shelter, you should move to the lowest part of the house; the basement or cellar is best. If time permits, dress in a large coat and give each person a blanket so as to protect them from flying debris and broken glass.

Tornadoes have no respect for light structures such as mobile homes which are easily destroyed. (Marilee Caliendo - FEMA)

MOBILE HOMES

Those who live in mobile homes should evacuate to a stronger dwelling. Mobile homes offer little to no protection against a strong tornado. Many people put their trust in straps and secure ties, but in evidence these are no match for the high wind speeds produced by the tornado. While many homes are extremely heavy, their construction and size make them easy to rip apart.

Many mobile home parks in tornado zones will have a dedicated tornado shelter, if not, locate the nearest strong concrete structure. As a last resort, find a deep ditch, as this will offer you a better chance than staying in your mobile home.

YOUR HOME

For those people who live close to a known tornado zone, make sure you have a designated room as a tornado shelter. A basement, or below ground level rooms will offer the most protection. If your home is on ground level foundations, a small room, such as a bathroom or closet on the lower floor will suffice. If feasible, always have a pile of blankets and cushions situated within the designated tornado room.

OUT AND ABOUT

If you are away from home, at school, or shopping, for example, you should seek shelter in the lowest part of the nearest strong building. Most schools in a tornado area will have an emergency plan whereby the teachers will lead the pupils to dedicated shelters.

The structure of the building is important; those made from lightweight timber cladding can be easily destroyed by the tornado. Likewise, brick buildings, especially brick-built walls, can also be easily toppled. Building and structures made from reinforced concrete offer the best protection.

OPEN LAND

An approaching severe weather front is not difficult to miss. Your natural instinct is to seek shelter, which you should do without delay. If no shelter is available, lie down in a ditch or depression in the ground and cover yourself

with a strong waterproof sheet or blanket. Before you make yourself comfortable, check the surrounding area to make sure you are not exposed to falling trees. If it's raining, will the ditch start to fill with water to the point where you are forced to move?

DRIVING OR IN THE CAR

If you are driving and there is no protective building close by, you should stop and remain in your car. Apply the handbrake and put your seatbelt on. Cover your face and hands with a coat or blanket if you have one, as flying debris may smash your windows. While those in mobile homes are safer in a ditch this is NOT true of vehicles unless it is a large box shaped truck. It is true that large trucks have been lifted up by a tornado; this is generally due to its large surface area. While a few tornadoes have been known to lift or turn over cars, the latest advice is that you will be safer in your car than exposed out in the open. A study of torna-

A tornado that swept through Catoosa County destroying a complete forest area. What chance would a human have?
(Judith Grafe – FEMA)

Taking your chances inside a car during a tornado storm might be marginally better than being caught outside. (Marilee Caliendo – FEMA)

does measuring F1 and F2 on the Fujita scale, found that 96% of cars don't get turned over or thrown around.

Park under a road bridge to avoid flying debris, but be aware that if the underpass is more than a few meters in length, excessive winds can be further accelerated in that space. In such as case, it could be hazardous. Avoid parking in such as position as to block or hinder emergency vehicles.

TORNADO SHELTER

Building a tornado or storm shelter is a very good idea, as they will help protect you and your family. It is possible to build your own shelter, or you can opt to buy a ready-made one. If you do decide to build a shelter, opt for one that will provide protection for most natural disasters. The first thing you need to do is choose whether you want it inside or outside of the house. Next, you need to estimate how large your shelter will be. Don't forget that you might end up being in it for several hours or even overnight. The good thing about having a shelter is that it will alleviate some of the anxiety created by the threat of an incoming tornado or hurricane.

Once your shelter is complete, make sure you have sufficient equipment inside to see you through the worst of the storm. Make sure that your shelter has some form of lighting system separate from that connected to the grid. You will need several gallons of water stored in clean, clear containers, each one being easy enough to lift. You will need some form of chemical toilet or toilet bucket arrangement, and it is best if this is screened off with a blanket (no one wants to see granny going to the bathroom!). Have some emergency food, but keep this down to cold tinned foods or granola bars. You are advised NOT TO COOK in your shelter, as you may well suffer from carbon monoxide poisoning in a confined space. If you

Tornado shelter – this old storm shelter helped save the lives of a local family in Shawnee, as their home was destroyed.
(Win Henderson – FEMA)

have children, it is a good idea to have some form of entertainment, as this will reduce the boredom and relieve their anxiety. If you intend to take animals into the shelter with you, make sure they are also catered for with regards to toilet and food.

Finally, don't forget your Disaster Grab Bag. In this you should have anything you might need should your home be destroyed by the storm or tornado. Have your cell phone handy, a battery-powered radio, flashlight, blankets, a first-aid kit, and important documents such as deeds and insurance papers (see Disaster Grab Bag).

Do not waste time and get in your shelter as swiftly as possible. If your shelter is outdoors do not keep running back to the house for some last minute item. The largest amount of deaths from a tornado is caused by people being hit by debris. Blunt force trauma injuries account for some 92% of all tornado injuries and deaths. Avoid being caught out in the open close to a tornado.

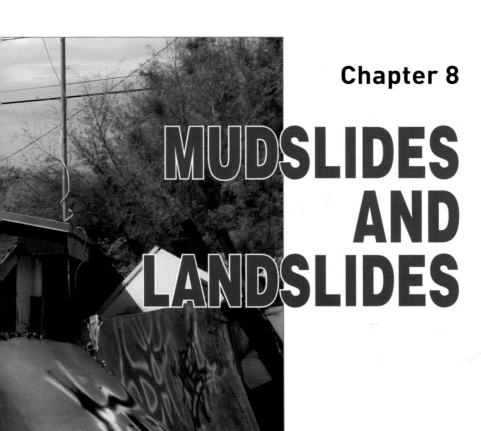

Chapter 8

MUDSLIDES AND LANDSLIDES

Mudslides may be localized but they arrive quickly and with deadly force. (Robert J. Alvey – FEMA)

Landslides and mudslides happen all over the world, and by comparison to earthquakes and tsunamis, they do not cause massive destruction or loss of life. That said, for those who have suffered at the hands of a mudslide, the experience is traumatic. Mudslides are normally localized, and in many cases hit the poor people of our planet: those who cannot afford substantial housing. But there have been many cases where human error is to blame, and where stupidly has cost the lives of many people.

Worldwide, landslides cause billions of dollars in damage and thousands of deaths and injuries each year. As mud and landslides are isolated incidents and the number of deaths is usually low when compared to other disasters, they rarely receive much news coverage.

While people can take steps to reduce their personal risk, it is best to understand the hazards of a mud or land-slide and prepare an emergency plan.

Highland Towers, Malaysia.

Author's Note: I was in Malaysia on December 11, 1993, visiting friends who had an apartment in block three of Highland Towers. The three blocks of apartments had been built between 1977 and 1982 at the bottom of a large hill on the outskirts of Kuala Lumpur. Behind the Highland Towers, there exists a small stream of water, known as East Creek. Before construction of the towers was started, a pipe system was built to divert the stream to bypass the Towers.

In 1991, on the hilltop above the apartments, a new housing estate was in progress and as such, a lot of trees and vegetation had been removed from the hillside, exposing the soil and allowing it to absorb more water. Additionally, the excess water used from the building site was fed into the same pipe that diverted the waters of East Creek. The monsoon rains, which had been exceptionally heavy for several days, literally broke the pipe in several places, allowing water to escape. The water turned to mud and subsequently, a mudslide moved down the hill with massive force. It destroyed retaining walls in its path and eventually hit block one. The block moved forward before breaking into two, and crumbling to the ground.

The official death toll released by the authorities was forty-eight. However, Highland Towers was notorious for a place in which to accommodate mistresses and girlfriends, and many put the number of those killed much higher.

My friend and his family had an apartment in block three, which was evacuated; but we were in the apartment at the time. The remaining blocks remained empty and under a security watch. However, with the passage of time and a reduction in security, the two remaining blocks were looted and stripped of everything. The remaining blocks on Highland Towers have since been demolished as unsafe.

Landslides can be caused by storms, earthquakes, volcanic eruptions, construction blasting, and the abrupt change of slopes by erosion due to human modification. There is very little difference between a mudslide and a landslide, as they both produce a flow of debris or soil, rocks and vegetation downhill. Landslides are at the drier end of the spectrum and tend to creep downhill slower than a mudslide. Landsides can occur naturally: wind pushing again trees on a slope will loosen the roots; rainfall may cut itself a river bed on its way downhill or, the natural movement of the earth. Landslides are activated by a whole host of elements.

While there are lots of reasons why landslides occur, more often than not, they occur when man has cut into the earth to make way for a new road or housing project. Cutting through a hillside to allow a motorway to pass through will weaken the walls of the mountain. Removing the bottom of the mountain to flatten it for housing estates can also undermine the structure. Both of these cases are not helped by heavy rain, which will carry soil particles downhill. At the same time it will saturate the ground and weaken the roots of vegetation. All these pressures go towards creating a massive mudslide.

Heavy rainfall, combined with gravity, is a powerful force in moving earth. Although mudslides carry more water than landslides, they also contain a lot of solid material such as rocks and trees. Mudslides move fast—faster than most people can run. Because of their high water content, they flow like mud cement being poured.

Areas of mudslides and landslides are mostly determined by the soil composition and bedrock it sits on. The looser the soil, the more likely it is to react when saturated with water. Clay soil will move sluggishly as the clay particles absorb water at a slower rate and stick together more,

Areas of potential mud or landslide are not the place to build a home. This house sits at the bottom of a levee in the path of a potential mudslide. (Patsy Lynch – FEMA)

while organic soils covering areas of vegetation will absorb water like a sponge.

The type of bedrock also makes a difference; if it is porous, such as sandstone, it will drain the water rapidly, while granite will keep the water in the soil. Where the bedrock is fragmented, the water will act as a lubricant which in turn moves the soil. Where the cracks in the bedrock are mainly horizontal, they will offer little resistance to the flow of water. Vertical cracks in the bedrock will actually help keep an area stable by absorbing and distributing water over a wider area.

While landsides can occur on very gentle slopes, in practice, the steeper the slope, the more likelihood of a land or mudslide occurring. The amount and type of vegetation on a slope is also a major factor. Forest areas will intercept the rainfall before it hits the ground; this helps disperse and weaken the effect of water falling on dry soil, as exposed soil will simply be washed away. The roots also play a major part as they hold the soil in place, the deeper the roots, the less chance of a landslide. Excessive logging kills the roots and their ability to hold the soil in place. The only problem with forests is that the trees are prone to wind, which can destabilize the base of the tree, especially on a slope. The chance of a landslide is dependent on the vegetation, the soil, and type and structure of the bedrock. Add rain to this equation and we have a mudslide.

As rain continues to fall, the soil and rock layers become inundated with water. The water table, the point at which the ground below is wholly saturated with water, moves towards the soil surface. A muddy, wet cement-like mass is formed, which will then move downhill to the lowest point it can find. As this moves downhill, it picks up vegetation, rocks and anything in its way. The mudslide will generally take the path of least resistance until it is stopped or runs out of momentum.

WARNING

One clear indication of mud or landslides is to see if they have occurred before in your area. However, recent movement or alteration to any steep-sided ground mass close to your home may give cause for concern. During and after a major storm, with high winds and heavy rainfall, observe the surrounding area for any rift or break in the uniformity of the slope. If your home is located on ground that has not moved in the past, is relatively flat, and is not dominated by any steep, sloping ground, you will generally be safe.

Land and mudslides are normally unexpected and happen with almost no warning; nevertheless, there are two things that can be done: Prepare, and read the Warning Signs.

- Look at the position of your home. Is it sitting directly below a hillside?
- When it rains, what path does the water take?
- In heavy rain, is there a lot of soil mixed with the water?
- Has the vegetation on the slope above your home been modified?

If the answer to any of the above applies to you, make sure you take some precautions.

- Take note of the weather reports. Keep a wary eye on the local weather.
- If it has been raining for several days, and you suddenly get intervals of heavy rain, the waterlogged soil may give way.
- If water is running down the hillside, watch the course it is taking. Be alert to any rise in water levels in natural streams and water courses.
- Look at the consistency of the flow and any soil or debris it contains.
- Listen for any unusual noise, such as trees cracking.
- **If you have any doubts, evacuate. Move to a safe location.**
- Inform neighbors of your doubts; help the old and the young.
- If you cannot leave, or the mudslide is upon you, move to higher ground or to the highest room in the house.
- If you are able, move out of the slide path to a stable area.
- If you are caught out in the open, curl into a ball, hands over your face, try to move with the flow—literally float!

AFTER THE LAND OR MUDSLIDE

After a while, the slide will eventually stop, or simply run out of energy. If you are safe, first check to see that your immediate friends and family are safe. Ask if anyone actually saw anyone being drowned by the slide. Is anyone missing? Report the incident to the authorities by the quickest and easiest means possible. Land and mudslides are normally localized and the authorities may not know about it until well after it has happened. Contact the relevant rescue services and report the location if possible. Take control.

After a large mudslide, there is little chance of survival.

- Stay away from the slide area. There may be danger of additional slides.
- Check the weather and keep a close eye on the hillside.
- Gather your family and neighbors. Check who is missing and where they were last seen.
- Without putting yourself or others in danger, help those who can be rescued immediately, i.e., those trapped in homes untouched by the slide. (Do NOT go near the mudslide.)
- Listen to local radio for the latest emergency information.

- Watch for flooding, which may occur after a landslide or debris flow. Floods sometimes follow landslides and debris flows, because they may both be started by the same event.
- Check for injuries; check the elderly and young children.
- Locate safe and dry shelter.
- Be aware there may be broken gas pipes or electricity poles down.

PLAN FOR A LANDSLIDE

As with any other disasters, it is always prudent to have an evacuation plan. However, when talking about a mud or landslide, the parameters are slightly different. There will normally be some warning signs to watch out for. At the start of any intense storm, watch for the drainage pattern and see how the water is running off and where it is settling. Watch the hillsides around your home for any signs of movement. If there are trees on the slope, look to see if any are starting to tilt. Any small changes in the landscape could be your only warning. If you live in an area prone to land and mudslides and you are experiencing a storm, stay awake and alert. The majority of people that have died in mudslides were asleep in their homes. Be particularly cautious after a really heavy bout of rain during a storm. Make a simple plan, and have cut-off signs which should trigger your actions.

- Your plan should be based on the following: if in doubt, move out. If you do not leave, at least move everyone to a second floor or higher.
- If you intend to escape by car, be very careful until you reach an open road. Watch out for road or collapsed pavement after erosion, fallen rocks, and possible debris flows on embankments.

When your home is destroyed by a mud or landslide, you will be forced to consider finding alternative accommodations, food, warm clothing, and a host of other items. Think ahead and plan for the eventuality while hoping it will never happen. Finally, don't forget your Disaster Grab Bag, as you are going to need it if your home is gone.

Plan for a mudslide. This municipality has constructed deflection barriers to deflect the mud flow. (Robert J. Alvey, FEMA)

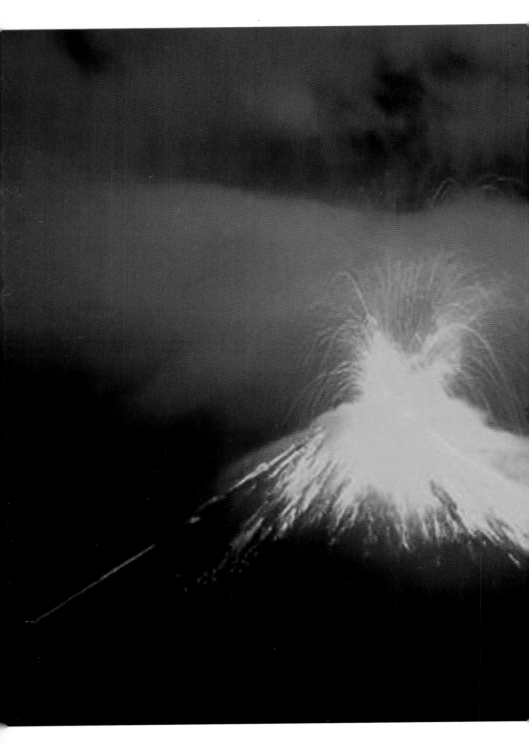

Chapter 9

ADDITIONAL
DISASTERS

Active volcano.

It is worth mentioning other types of disaster that affect civilization from time to time; these include volcanoes, famine, communicable disease, and avalanches. The only good thing about these disasters is the fact that they are isolated, or for the most part, correctable; yet they are disasters and, as such, take the lives of millions of people each year. While there are many other types of disaster and communicable diseases, I have outlined some of the most serious ones below.

VOLCANOES

There are about 1,500 potentially active volcanoes in the world, of which about fifty to sixty blow each year. In addition to this, an estimated five million people live within the danger zone of an active volcano. What most of us know about volcanoes is that they erupt and spew out molten lava and always seem to happen far away, so we are not really bothered. However, did you know that thousands die during a major eruption? Additionally, the cost of the clean-up or disruption can run into the billions.

In March 2010, a small eruption in Iceland rated 1 on the Volcanic Explosivity Index (VEI). By May, the volcano was pushing out 150,000 tons of ash a day, blocking many of the European air routes and causing massive disruption which echoed around the world. All flights in and out of the United Kingdom were cancelled for over six days, bringing air transport to its knees. With passengers stuck in airports around the world, unable to get home, hotel rooms and rates came at a premium —the overall cost running into billions.

Author's Note: I was sitting happily in my hotel in Kuala Lumpur, Malaysia at the time of the 'Ash problem' where the occupancy rate was around 70%. Two days into the cancellation of flights to the UK and other European airports, the hotel was filled to capacity. Individuals who had been on vacation and had not taken out full insurance were trapped with escalating costs; many who had been in either Singapore or Thailand moved to Malaysia where hotel rates were kept at a reasonable rate. What struck me was the fact that Mother Nature could create a scenario whose implications stretched around the world.

What is a Volcano?

A volcano is a gap in the earth's surface which allows magma (molten rock) to get through. When pressure forces the magma up, it erupts, sending out lava, ash, gases, and pieces of rock. Over the centuries, this has built up on the earth's surface to look like a conical-shaped mountain. In most cases, the mountain has a vent at its center from which the lava, ash, and gasses erupt when it is active.

When a volcano is active and the eruption begins, the lava may simply roll down the side of the mountain, or it may shoot fiercely into the air. The ash can be forced high into the atmosphere and carried on the wind for thousands of miles. Mudslides can occur and the earth around the volcano can crack. All in all, a pretty destructive force of nature!

Can a Volcano Eruption be Detected?

As with earthquakes, we use seismographs to detect a volcano as it, too, emulates from a trembling of the earth. Modern technology means that in the past twenty years we have created instruments that can detect and measure magnetism while inclinometers can detect movement caused by a volcano starting to bulge with the pressure. Most basic signs, such as the warming of springs and lakes are a more traditional method.

However, while studies continue and technology improves, at this moment in time, we still cannot precisely predict when a volcano will become active, as even a quiet volcano can erupt without any warning. How big a volcanic eruption is can be measured, but again there is no one structure of table for this. The most common is the Volcanic Explosivity Index (VEI) developed jointly by the U.S. Geological Survey and the University of Hawaii.

What to Expect when a Volcano Erupts

If you live in an area which has a volcano close by (say around thirty miles), you will need to take some precautions. The good news is that according to the VEI scale, really massive eruptions don't happen very often.

VEI	Description	Plume Height	Volume	Classification	How often	Example
0	non-explosive	← 100 m	←10,000 m³	Hawaiian	constant	Kilauea
1	gentle	100-1000 m	→10,000 m³	Hawaiian/Strombolian	daily	Stromboli
2	explosive	1-5 km	→1,000,000 m³	Strombolian/Vulcanian	weekly	Galeras, 1992
3	severe	3-15 km	→10,000,000 m³	Vulcanian/Pelean	few months	Ruiz, 1985
4	cataclysmic	10-25 km	→0.1 km³	Pelean/Plinian	→1 year	Galunggung, 1982
5	paroxysmal	20-35 km	1 km³	Plinian	→10 years	St. Helens, 1980
6	colossal	→30 km	→10 km³	Plinian/Ultra-Plinian	→100 years	Krakatau, 1883
7	super-colossal	→40 km	→100 km³	Ultra-Plinian	→1000 years	Tambora, 1815
8	mega-colossal	→50 km	→1,000 km³	Super volcanic	→10,000 years	Yellowstone, 2 Ma

In the worst case scenario, when a volcano does erupt, you can expect the full works: blasts or flows of molten rock, hot ash, earthquakes, avalanches, mudslides, flash floods, tsunamis, and wildfires. While all these are unlikely to come at once, you can normally expect a whole lot of ash. While this might not seem like a big deal, trust me, once you have suffered the fallout of an ash cloud, you don't want to go through it again.

Volcanic ash is made up of crushed powdered rocks and hard gritty fragments from a whole range of minerals and glass. Be warned, the ash from a volcano is very dangerous. The closer someone is to the volcano, the hotter the ash will be when it falls. It will irritate your eyes and skin and, in combination with burning gasses, it will enter your lungs and cause serious damage. Volcanic ash does not dissolve in water, is extremely abrasive and mildly to severely corrosive; the ash also conducts electricity when wet.

When the eruption starts, you need to know how powerful it is, i.e., are there great pieces of hot rock raining down on you? You will need to know how much ash is being pumped out and in what direction the wind is taking it. The answer to these two questions will dictate whether or not you stay put or move.

You will know when a volcano eruption is about to take place. Move to safe distance – it's your best chance of survival.

Staying Put during a Volcano Eruption

If you deem it safe enough and intend to stay put, then you need to be prepared for the worst. You will have taken this decision either because you feel the eruption is far enough away or because the authorities have made this recommendation. You will still need to make an evacuation plan and communicate this to your family. Likewise, you will need to protect your home from any ash fallout.

Personal-protection equipment

You will need some form of protection before venturing outdoors during or after an ash fall, as you will be exposed to high concentrations of airborne and settled ash particles. You need to prevent any inhalation of ash particles or damage to the eyes. Your protective equipment should comprise of:

The best personal protection is distance, but if you are caught, gain the high ground and remain under a solid structure – watch out for fires.

- Filter face mask (best to use a surplus military respirator).
- Goggles (a tight fitting ski type, with no vents is best).
- Coveralls.

- Headwear (a hard hat is best).
- Gloves.
- Extremely strong boots.

Essentials you will Need in your Home

- Personal protection equipment.
- Drinking water to last you at least three days. (Calculated on around one gallon per person, per day.)
- Food for all occupants for at least three days.
- Flashlights and lanterns (the power often fails when there is heavy ash fall).
- Battery or dynamo operated radio to receive instruction and warnings.
- If reliant on electric heating, extra blankets and alternative heating system.
- First Aid pack.
- Cleaning supplies, vacuum cleaner, brooms, shovels and lots of cling film (wrap all your electronics and valuables up with cling film for protection).
- Cash, since ATMs will be down.

Volcanic fallout produces a massive ash cloud that causes untold damage and disruption. The 2010 eruptions of Eyjafjallajokull caused air travel to come to a standstill across Europe.

Actions when Volcanic Ash Fall is Expected

- Make sure you have the essentials in your home.
- Bring everything possible indoors.
- Disconnect, if possible, all downpipes from the guttering.
- Garage your car and seal the doors and windows.
- Close and seal all doors and windows to your home. Put damp towels at the base of each door.
- Shut down all vents into the house.
- Those suffering from lung ailments, such as chronic bronchitis or asthma should move to the best sealed room in the house. Remove contact lenses, as the ash will damage your eyes.
- Don't forget your pets.
- When the ash falls, remain indoors and stay calm.

Caught out in the Open Close to a Volcano Eruption

Normally, there will be some warning that a volcano is about to erupt. At this point, you should distance yourself and head with others in your care to a safe location. Do not panic; simply move by the safest and quickest means. In the unlikely event that you are caught out close to an erupting volcano, take the following precautions.

- If you are able, move away from the volcano as quickly as possible.
- If large lumps of lava rock are falling, seek some form of shelter in a building or car. Wait until the worst has passed.
- If ash starts to fall, use a wet handkerchief or cloth over your nose and mouth. Try to stay upwind of the ash cloud.
- If you have a radio, listen to the emergency warnings and advice.
- Do not wear contact lenses as these will result in corneal abrasion.
- Depending on your location and proximity to the volcano, watch out for mudflows and landslides, lava flows, or fires. If any of the above are close, move away or get to higher ground.

- If you are in a vehicle, and the road is clear, proceed to distance yourself from the volcano. Travel at a slow pace and be aware of falling objects or possible mud or lava flows when crossing bridges; look upstream to see what's happening.

One of the worst things about a volcanic eruption is the ash and the mess it makes. Volcanic ash is not like your normal ash from a fire; it's really harsh. The clean-up can take months and if it rains, then the problem is only impacted. The scope of this book does not call for me to go into the cleaning procedure of volcanic ash, but for those that need to, you have my sympathy.

AVALANCHES

Avalanches do not cause a great deal of death, with the average being around 150 per year. Nevertheless, in the past, there have been some major death tolls when earthquakes have caused massive and multiple avalanches in an area. It is almost impossible to predict when an avalanche is going to occur. Even in Europe, where scientists have studied the phenomenon for years, it is still difficult to forecast a precise time and place. However, slopes which have an angle of between 30° and 45°, and where the depth of snow is more than thirty centimeters (one foot), are those which are most at risk from avalanches. It is, therefore, important to recognize the factors which cause avalanches.

The ground may have been previously covered with a layer of old snow, which has deteriorated through fluctuations in temperature to form a smooth, hard, flat surface. A thicker layer of soft snow may well have built up on top of this base. The angle of slope, gravity, and the speed and direction of the wind will all contribute to

This avalanche destroyed homes, buildings, and roads. (Dave Saville – FEMA)

making the top layer of snow move, causing an avalanche. This sort of avalanche is known as a soft slab avalanche and is the most common type.

Avalanche Assessment

Knowledge of snowfalls in the previous week, the temperature, and the wind strength will all help in an assessment of what lies beneath any fresh snow fall. Asking local guides about high-risk areas and adjusting your route accordingly is also a good idea. Continue to adjust your assessment during your walk by taking note of how the snow is reacting to your weight on it. Is the snow crisp and firm beneath your feet or is it loose and rolling away down the slope? If you see snow breaking up and falling away, even in a small area, you should consider yourself at risk and move if at all possible to level ground.

Moving Through an Avalanche Area

Moving through an avalanche area is dangerous. A dog is being trained to assist in avalanche rescue operations. (Andrea Booher – FEMA)

It is highly unlikely that many people will simply move into an area and get swallowed up by an avalanche. It does happen but only when the avalanche is triggered by an earthquake and releases massive amounts of snow and rock, as in Peru when 18,000 people died on May 31, 1970.

If you are walking during the winter, the chances are that at some point you will have to climb a steep, snow-covered slope. An ice axe is an advisable item of equipment to carry. This is a mountaineering tool which has a blade-shaped adze and a curved serrated pick attached to a spiked shaft. Ice axes come in a variety of lengths, but for hill-walking, an axe with a handle seventy centimeters (two feet) long is recommended. A sling should also be attached to the axe so that it can be put round the wrist and not lost in the event of a fall.

When walking uphill, the shaft is best pushed into the snow for support, while you make steps in the snow with your boots. On steeper slopes or while traversing, you may find it easier to use a two-handed grip on the axe.

When descending a steep slope, it is best to face inwards towards the slope, using both hands on the ice axe for support and making steps with the toes of your boots. On gently-sloping downhill slopes, it is safe to walk forwards, using the axe as a walking stick and by digging in the heels of your boots for support. Have a check list for traveling in an area prone to avalanches.

- Check the weather forecast before setting off.
- Consult a local guide or expert about the route you intend to follow.
- Plan your route with care and leave a copy of it with a responsible person.
- Have a cut-off time for your return.
- Do not walk alone.
- Dress using the layer principle. Salopettes (ski pants) are warmer than trousers for winter walking. You should protect your hands and head with thermal gloves, a neck-over and a balaclava (ski mask).
- Wear comfortable walking boots which are appropriate for winter use.
- Wear gaiters to protect your boots and lower legs.
- Carry an ice axe, but learn how to use it beforehand.
- Watch where you walk. Keep a lookout for signs of avalanches.
- Keep a careful watch on the weather.
- If you get into trouble, retrace your steps or walk towards the nearest point of known safety.

If you are caught in an Avalanche

One quick note: avalanches are very rarely caused by noise (this is more of a myth). An avalanche can start at any time, but in many cases it is triggered by people walking across a snow slope, and the snow will simply slide from underneath their feet. When it gets going, it will feel like the earth is being ripped from under you. As the snow starts to wash you downhill, it will also start to cover you. How

My dear friend, Andy Baxter, died along with another person, as a result of an avalanche. (Barry Davies)

badly you are hurt will depend on how large the avalanche was when it first hit you, and how deep you get buried will depend on how long you spend in the fall. On average, of all those people caught up in avalanches, around 5% die immediately from being crushed or hitting hard debris or rocks, etc. If you are buried, than the sooner rescue workers get to you, the better. If they can pull you out within the first fifteen minutes, you have a 95% chance of survival. If they don't get to you before an hour or so, your chances are pretty grim. Here are a few tips on what to do should you find yourself in an avalanche.

- The moment you feel movement below your feet, move up or to the side for safety, but chances are you will not be quick enough.
- Stay on your feet as long as possible. (You will most likely end up tumbling like a rag doll.)
- Try a flailing action with your arms, to stay on top of the snow. Try to stay loose; do not ball, as this will push you lower in the snow.
- When it stops, and if you are alive, you will be in one of two situations: on the surface half buried, or completely buried in the snow.
  - In the first case, simply crawl out onto the surface and head immediately to the edge of the avalanche (if you are injured, stay where people can see you).

- If you are buried, you have a problem. If you can, push the snow away from in front of your face. Next, spit to determine which way up you are. If you think you can make it, try to dig your way to the surface.
  - Here you need to make a decision: work to dig yourself out, or conserve air and wait to be rescued. That question will be answered by where you are and how many other people were in your area. Don't bother shouting, as this simply wastes good air.

There are several new devices for people who venture close to an avalanche area. These include beacons and inflatable life vests. A beacon is fine if someone is looking for you. The life vest known as an Avalanche Airbag System (ABS) is a set of airbags in the rucksack which inflate when an emergency cord is pulled. The system has radically reduced the numbers of deaths caused by avalanches, but be warned, it is not a 100% guarantee.

FAMINE

Famine is one of the greatest killers of all time. There are many recorded cases of famine going back through the centuries, and famine is still with us. The Great Leap Forward in China, between 1958 to 1961, when Chairman Mao introduced a policy whereby the rural farms would become collectives and private farming was prohibited as counter-revolutionary, caused the largest deaths from famine in recent times, with a minimum of sixteen million people dying. Some put the death toll as high as forty-six million.

Even today, an estimated one billion people in the world will not get enough to eat. Basically, famine means a shortage of food; this can be localized or widespread. Famine can be caused by several different factors:

- Lack of food due to climatic change.
- Political disruption by an oppressive government.
- War.
- Breakdown in the distribution process.
- Poverty and price.

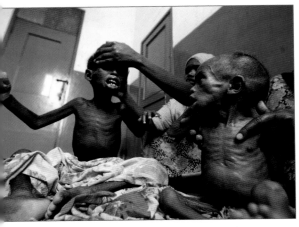

Whatever the reason, famine causes starvation, malnutrition, disease, and death. The 1973 Ethiopian famine took place with no abnormal reduction in food output, and consumption of food per head at the height of the famine was fairly normal by Ethiopian standards. The problem lay in the purchasing power of the hungry people; they had no money or barter power, so they had no food. This famine was generated by financial restrictions.

In 1847, during the Irish famine, some 400,000 people died; in that same year almost half a million cattle were shipped from Ireland to the United Kingdom and over a million gallons of butter. There was enough food to feed the Irish population, but most of it was shipped to England. This famine was caused by an oppressive government.

There is no real excuse for famine in today's world, yet it continues. (source unknown – multi-usage)

The Answers to Famine

There is no easy answer to famine. From time to time it raises its ugly head, mainly in Africa, and the television will show several 'tearfund' campaigns to raise money for the

Author's Note: I have long pondered the problem of starvation. Having traveled this planet, I have seen few places where food is not available in abundance. In many countries such as Spain, so much food simply stays on the trees until it rots and falls; enough I would say to feed a third world country several times over. The problem then, is one of preservation and distribution.

The argument is that the people live in an area where there has been no rainfall for a year, and they are unable to grow their own food. They have no money to buy food, so no one wants to transport food to them, other than government aid and the non-governmental organizations (NGOs). Even with food aid, their situation will not improve if they don't get rain, or even water. Even with the best will, without water, there can be no agricultural enlightenment. Would not the best answer to be to move them? But what government wants a load of half-starved, penniless people?

Food wastes in Spain as tons of fruit and vegetables are simply dumped each year because it's not commercially viable to sell them. (Barry Davies)

starving. In the meantime, we will just pop down to our local supermarket and stock up for the week.

In the short term, those suffering from famine need to be fed, and provided with supplements to help them recover to the point where they can help themselves. This is normally done through government and massive intervention by NGOs.

Long-term measures involve investment in agriculture alertness using modern techniques and providing an ample supply of water for irrigation. Another alternative is a total change of habitat, moving the people to an area which is richer in growing crops.

COMMUNICABLE DISEASES

There have been many fatal diseases over the past centuries, which, slowly but surely, man has overcome. Smallpox, a highly contagious disease, once ravaged millions of people, killing some sixty million in Europe alone in the 18th century. Today, it has been eradicated from nature. Cholera, Ebola, AIDs, and Malaria still remain, and all take a heavy toll even today.

Malaria

Malaria accounts for over one million deaths each year and is second only to AIDs as one of the leading killers. If you are bitten by a malaria, carrying mosquito, the parasite it injects into your bloodstream will reach your liver within less than an hour. While some of the parasites can remain dormant for years, others will invade your red blood cells causing them to rupture, with the spillage affecting even more blood cells. This repeated cycle robs the body of oxygen-carrying red blood cells and causes fever. The infected cells also start to block up the circulation system affecting the brain and kidneys. If you do not receive treatment quickly, you could very well die.

Mosquitoes, possibly one of the most dangerous insects on the planet. (Barry Davies)

Mosquitoes

As mosquitoes breed in stagnant, sluggish water or swampy ground, you would be well-advised to avoid camping near any of these, aiming for higher ground where possible. They more frequently bite during the late evening and nighttime hours. Make sure that exposed skin is covered as much as possible. Tuck clothing in, i.e., trouser legs into socks, and sleeves into gloves. Cover your body with mosquito netting, curtain netting or parachute (for consistency) material, handkerchiefs, or anything else that may be improvised. Smearing mud over any exposed areas of skin will deter the amount of mosquito bites.

Any insect bite has the potential to introduce infection, but tropical mosquitoes are the carriers of several dangerous diseases that can be fatal. Diseases and parasites such as malaria, filariasis, yellow fever, and dengue fever, as well as various forms of encephalitis are all carried by the mosquito. Therefore, it is wise to do as much as is within your power to protect yourself from their bites.

- Mosquitoes breed in stagnant/sluggish water or swampy ground, so make sure that you do not make your camp near any of these. Aim for higher ground instead.
- Make sure that any anti-malarial drugs are taken as prescribed for as long as you have a supply.
- Use insect repellent continually and make sure that exposed skin is covered.

- Suitable coverings include mosquito netting, curtain netting or parachute material, handkerchiefs, or anything else that may be improvised.
- Nighttime is when most mosquito bites occur.
- Tuck clothing in. For example, trouser legs into socks and sleeves into gloves.
- Mud smeared over any exposed areas of skin may deter mosquitoes.
- Slow burning, smoky fires will drive insects away.

Prevention

The best prevention is to take anti-malarial tablets and protect your skin while in an area infested with mosquitoes. There is a wide range of anti-malarial tablets around and you should ask advice before purchasing. In most cases, you will need to start taking the tablets before you travel and continue to take them for several weeks after your return.

As with anti-malarial tablets, there is also a wide range of skin protection that will stop the mosquitoes from biting you. The main compound of many is DEET, which is a very good mosquito repellent. These come in stick, aerosol, or liquid form, and are applied by smearing them over the exposed skin.

Given that mosquitoes attack mainly in the late evening, a large mosquito net would come in handy. Once again, you can get these at most camping stores.

Warning: No malaria tablet, insect repellent, or net is 100% effective.

Author's Note: I am not sure how effective they are, but it is possible to download various applications for your mobile phone or iPad that claim to keep mosquitoes at bay. But there is a problem: it is difficult to ascertain if the applications actually work due to the fact that most produce a noise to deter the mosquito. That noise is in the 16 KHz to 20 KHz range, and humans cannot hear it.

Chapter 10

RESCUE AND NGOs AND TECHNOLOGY

The Red River Valley Water rescue team carrying home-owner who needed rescuing due to rising water. (Patsy Lynch – FEMA)

197

After every disaster there will be survivors, but the surrounding environment will most likely have changed dramatically. Where villages and towns once stood, will be nothing but barren land covered with debris. The very nature of the disaster will define how this debris is scattered. For example, after an earthquake, some of the buildings and houses will have collapsed, but within the area of these ruins, there will be usable material and food.

On the other hand, following a tsunami, the wreckage will be little more than a sea of broken humanity; everything that once stood will be mashed into an accumulation of debris. A combination of both earthquake and tsunami will only serve to exacerbate the situation further.

Survivors of any disaster must take heart that the earth will NOT stop moving beneath their feet and the waters will recede. For those still alive, this is the time for you to bear the unbearable and start over.

Disaster relief means you should be rescued, taken to a place of safety, given food and clean water, and a warm place to sleep. When safe to do so, many men and women will go out into the disaster area and try to find those that are missing.

If you live in a heavily populated area when the disaster strikes and you managed to survive, the chances are the civil authority will leap into action and start a rescue operation. Most major cities and towns now have a disaster plan already drawn up. These plans are designed around management, i.e., prevention, preparedness, response, and recovery. Each division of the authority, i.e., medical, police, fire, civil engineering, and military, will all have their own plan based on an overall strategy. This was clearly shown in Japan, which was prepared for a major earthquake. The Prime Minister took personal charge of the

Author's note: The shock of surviving any major disaster and finding yourself surrounded by the remains of your home is, to say the least, traumatic. Add to this the fact that your loved ones may be dead or missing, or that you have suffered an injury, or even have been trapped below a collapsed building, and you start to see what the human brain has to put up with. The thing you must keep in mind is that 'you are alive.' Life breeds hope, and with hope comes salvation. That said, sometimes salvation can use a little shove!

emergency plan; aid was rushed in from over 100 countries, yet over 9199 are dead, and 13786 are missing. The cost of the disaster ran over three hundred billion and it will take at least five years to recover. If this same disaster had taken place in a less prepared country, the damage and loss of life would have been catastrophic.

While we have the reassurance that central government will do all it can to help before and after a major disaster, we must also help ourselves. So where do we start?

LEADERSHIP

The chance of being a lone survivor is rare, especially in a well-populated area. In civilian matters, the senior government representative or senior police officer should take charge, as they will have prior knowledge of what to do. However, this is not a hard and fast rule, as leadership may be delegated to someone who has qualifications best suited to the situation. This point may sound trivial, but it is of vital importance. Studies have shown that group decisions are not popular and are likely to split the party rather than unite it. An appointed leader should be strong enough to listen and evaluate all advice, yet implement decisions that will benefit the whole group. A group of survivors, split by differences of opinion, is in serious danger. Dividing your group means dividing your resources and lessening your chances of survival.

Never be afraid to take charge. If there is someone better who can do the job, they will soon come to the forefront. Don't fight, accept and work together, as good leadership does not simply mean one person is in charge.

Governments rely on NGOs to deliver food and emergency shelter, as well as medical assistance. (SAR Brunei)

NON-GOVERNMENT ORGANIZATIONS (NGOs)

It is likely that at some stage after a disaster, the rescue services will come looking for survivors. In many cases, this is done by road with NGOs arriving with government troops and medical aid.

Over the past twenty years, the growth of NGOs have been rapid, and today they are a visible, respected, and an entrenched part of society. The accomplishments of NGOs in providing healthcare, education, economic opportunities, and disaster relief is recognized around the world. Their help in the latter has shown to be invaluable, as after a major disaster, few countries, including the United States or China, are able to manage effectively without outside help.

One of the great things about an NGO is that it is free from bureaucratic structures and systems, thus making them highly effective. They are also flexible in their approach and response, and can adapt quickly to changing circumstance. The purpose of NGOs are not to supplant the governmental relief agencies, but to act as a coordinating mechanism between the government apparatus and the affected populace.

Funding to support many of the NGOs comes from private donations, much of which is collected through 'tear-fund' advertising. We have all seen these, the woman holding the skeleton of a baby, the arid backdrop, the flies, the child drinking dirty water, and the statistics. Let's face it, 'tearfunding' works, and for the most part, the money is used for a good cause.

NGOs will respond to a disaster no matter where it is; but one of the problems they face is government bureaucracy. After the tsunami in Asia, many of the NGOs were held up from delivering emergency aid through a complex government bureaucracy, costing the lives of many people. So, if the aid you are expecting is delayed, don't blame the rescuers, as it's normally due to some petty clerk holding everything up.

SEARCH AND RESCUE (SAR)

Search and rescue comes in many forms, but most have the same aim, which is to locate, extract, and provide emer-

SAR team arriving at Banda Aceh shortly after the tsunami. (SAR Brunei)

gency medical aid to victims trapped after a natural disaster. The military also use SAR units, but these are mainly aimed at recovering downed pilots or Special Forces operating behind enemy lines. In the context of disaster, the SAR team can be from your local fire service, or it may be from several other countries.

For large natural disasters, teams will be sent from all over the world. In general, these teams will be highly professional and drawn from the fire, police, and other government organizations. The SAR team brings together highly trained personnel with engineering skills or medical knowledge, communication experts, and search dog handlers.

Most will be trained in multi-hazard disasters, from technological accidents and terrorist damage, to earthquakes and floods. In the United Kingdom, the New Dimension Programme provides training and equipment to the Search and Rescue force. Both training and equipment are held at the government facility near Morton-in-Marsh in central England, where almost a hundred dedicated Marshal trucks, laden with equipment, stand ready 24/7. When a disaster happens, the role of SAR teams is to respond in order to rescue the maximum number of people in the shortest time, while minimizing the risk to themselves.

How they Search

Depending on the size of the disaster will dictate how many SAR teams are on the ground. In essence, most are

SAR team
arriving in Banda
Aceh, Indonesia.
(SAR Brunei)

allocated a specific area to search for survivors. The first
thing the teams will do is identify any possible locations
were victims could be trapped. These are generally referred
to as 'voids.' There are different types of voids, such as a
lean-to void, where a wall has collapsed diagonally against
another, or pancake voids, where multiple floors of a block
of flats has fallen. Voids can also be small spaces which
have offered victims protection, such as under a table or
beneath a stairway.

The search team will normally work in pairs, just like the
military buddy system. They can either start at the bottom
of allocation and work up, or will do so in reverse. Whatever
they do, it will be done in a methodical and systematic
pattern. From time to time, they will stop and listen, or
make noise in an effort to communicate with trapped
victims.

To cut down on duplication, such as which buildings have
already been searched, and to indicate the possibility of
further collapse, buildings are marked. There are several
marking types, but for the illustration of this book I will use
the United Nations International Search & Rescue Advisory
Group (UN INSARAG) marking system.

Once Search and Rescue have cleared an area, the debris will be cleared. (Lance Cpl. Brennan O'Lawney 31st)

- A one meter by one meter square is marked with day-glo orange where it can be clearly seen. The box has an X through it from corner to corner.
- It will have a G for Go or N for No-Go, plus the date/time when the search was completed.
- The number of live victims pulled from the building will be written to the left while the number of dead to the right.
- Any additional hazards will also be marked in the square with reference to which floor, etc.

All trapped victims that are alive will receive direct medical care based on a triage system to prioritize those needing immediate attention. Where the void is in an unstable position, the SAR team may well remove any dangerous debris or stabilize it until all victims have been rescued. Removing a victim is not always easy and requires the use of dragging or carries by the rescue workers. In some cases, the victim will have to self-extract. The main concern is to avoid any further injury.

Rescue Helicopters

If you are in a remote or cut-off area, it is possible that helicopters will be used to locate survivors and provide

Rescue helicopters may see you but are not able to land, or they have more pressing orders. (Jocelyn Augustino - FEMA)

assistance. In such a case, it is beneficial if you make your presence known. Make yourself as obvious as possible. Bright colors and movement are the best combination, or anything that can be seen easily from the air. Depending on your situation and the type of disaster, you must make yourself visible accordingly. For example, if you are in a flood area and trapped on a roof, there is little chance of building a signal fire. Likewise, if you are surviving an earthquake, there may be numerous fires caused by gas leaks and fallen power lines, etc. This is a good time to have a colored smoke grenade handy.

At night, shine a flashlight. But if a helicopter approaches, direct the beam at the ground. This is because the crew will be using night vision goggles to improve safety and even small external light sources shone directly at them can seriously reduce their efficiency or stop them working altogether.

DO NOT expect the first helicopter you see to come swooping down to rescue you.

After any disaster, one of the quickest ways to assess the damage and start the rescue operation is by air. The government will dispatch numerous aircrafts, both fixed wing and helicopters. Remember, these pilots have a mission to fulfill; they will take note of your location and predicament and providing they have orders to do so, may attempt a rescue or drop food and water.

In flood areas, or where it is impossible for them to land, they may simply acknowledge your presence. Likewise, helicopter crews can take a considerable amount of time assessing the possible problems that may be encountered at a rescue site. It is not uncommon on very windy days for a pilot to have several attempts at establishing and hovering close enough to the casualty to be able to get a winch man or rescue team to your position. The following priorities normally govern the decision making:

- Aircraft safety.
- Winch man safety.
- Survivor safety.

It may seem odd to place the casualty at the bottom of the priority list, but there is little justification for endangering the lives of several rescuers unless the situation calls for it. Rescue attempts are, therefore, all about risk assessment.

Should a helicopter approach your location, make sure that you secure any loose items before the helicopter arrives in the hover. The wash from the rotors cannot be avoided and they generate violent winds of up to seventy miles per hour or more. If the helicopter looks like it is going to land on flat ground close to you, make sure everyone stays away until the loadmaster or pilot calls you forward. Always approach a helicopter from the front heading or side, making sure you are in plain view of the pilot. Crouch down as you approach the blades.

Be careful when approaching a helicopter. Be guided by the rescue staff. (Jocelyn Augustino - FEMA)

- Never walk downhill towards a helicopter; you risk losing your head.
- Never approach a helicopter from the rear; the pilot might not see you and move.
- Wait until you are called forward or the blades have stopped turning.

TECHNOLOGY IN A DISASTER

I have always voiced the opinion that man is such a clever beast, infinitely capable of developing technology far beyond our wildest dreams. Man is also stupid; we start wars, waste food while there is famine, and squander water while others go thirsty.

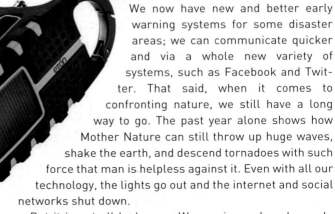

Combined
Wind-Up and
Solar-Powered
Radio / Flashlight
/ Cell Phone
Charger.
(Barry Davies)

Even so, technology steams ahead and in most cases, it is for the better. We now have new and better early warning systems for some disaster areas; we can communicate quicker and via a whole new variety of systems, such as Facebook and Twitter. That said, when it comes to confronting nature, we still have a long way to go. The past year alone shows how Mother Nature can still throw up huge waves, shake the earth, and descend tornadoes with such force that man is helpless against it. Even with all our technology, the lights go out and the internet and social networks shut down.

But it is not all bad news. We survive and we learn. In today's world, we do have new technology that will help, and at the forefront is personal communications. It is estimated that there are some five billion cell phones on the planet, and that, on average, America alone sends out some two and one-half billion text messages every day. Disasters happen and within minutes most of the world knows about it—within days, rescue teams assemble and are dispatched.

Given that my background is military and my lifelong interest is in technology, I have highlighted a few items below that will serve to help during any disaster. The humble cell phone has been covered already, but there are also many new innovations.

Combined Wind-Up Radio / Flashlight / Cell Phone Charger

While it has been around for about twenty years, the latest release of the Eton Scorpion offers an excellent combined radio, flashlight, and cell phone battery charger. More importantly, the radio's ability to access the NOAA radio stations and alerts is a major plus; these stations broadcast local and national weather news. This useful little wind-up radio not only has the great functionality of using hand power, but it includes a solar panel, bottle opener, and flashlight. By cranking 500 times, (roughly a minute and a half), you get a full two hours of play time on the radio.

When the device is fully charged, the flashlight will last longer than the radio's two-hour play time.

Another nice feature is the ability to charge your cell phone. However, be warned that charging a cell phone battery is not as easy as charging the Eton's own battery. You will need to crank the handle for around twenty minutes before your cell phone has enough power to operate efficiently, but in an emergency, it is still a good choice. Secondly, always double check that your cell phone battery is suitable for this type of charging.

Unmanned Aerial Vehicle

While it might seem a little futuristic, the modern Unmanned Aerial Vehicle (UAV) is a wonderful addition to the Search and Rescue teams after any disaster. Once thought of as little more than a toy, the UAV has come of age. The military now fly thousands of UAV missions each week, all over the world, especially in war zones.

A UAV is an aircraft that is flown without a pilot actually sitting in the cockpit. That said, most UAVs are too small to actually hold a real pilot, so the pilot remains on the ground and in control of the UAV. These pilots are more of a Navigator or Combat Systems Officer as the military call them. In the past ten years, there has been a huge growth in both

Small UAVs like this one will soon be used to search for survivors after a disaster. They can fly out several miles and send back live video to the operator. (BCB Int. Ltd.)

numbers and differing size of UAVs, added to which the larger military units can be armed; these are known as UCAVs.

However, it is the smaller and more user-friendly UAVs that are best suited to helping out in a disaster. These fall into the category of Mini, Micro, and Nano. Significantly, these can be launched and operated by a single person. They have a range, depending on type of several kilometers and can all transmit live video images back to the controller. Many Fire and Rescue servicers employ these small UAVs as part of their equipment.

How useful are they? Well, take the recent Tsunami in Japan for instance, where after the sea had receded, there was nothing but areas of mass debris and collapsed buildings, all of which had to be searched. This means that Search and Rescue would have to climb over every square meter, looking and shouting for any survivors trapped below. A swarm, (yes some UAVs will swarm like bees) of UAVs could cover a wide area very quickly. If there was any likelihood or sight of a human being, any one of the UAVs could drop down to within a few feet of the specified spot. If unsure, the UAV can ask in a loud voice, "Is there anyone there?" It will then listen for a response, a response that the controller would hear. By such means, Search and Rescue teams could be directed quickly to any survivor position. A few of the larger UAVs are fitted with heat sensors, which can detect body heat, while others can deliver urgently needed medical supplies to inaccessible places.

In addition, just think how useful it would have been for the teams working to contain the leak at the nuclear reactors at Fukishima. There would be no need to put the lives of people in danger when a small UAV could go in and investigate. Sensors to detect radiation could quickly be fitted with the results beamed directly to the UAV controller.

UAVs are new, but it is likely that they will be present after any major disaster in the near future. A small silent flying machine, with eyes, ears, and sensors to help find you and assess the damage would be very useful.

Solar Power

One of the first things needed after any disaster is power. Power to light up darkness, power to maintain the hospitals' operability; power is needed for everything. Yet, after earthquakes, tsunamis, tornadoes, floods, and wildfires, the first thing to usually fail is the power. It is traditional for governments, medical, and Search and Rescue organizations to use generator back-up systems which are hopefully placed in a position where the disaster will not affect them. There were backup generator facilities at the nuclear reactors in Japan, but the tidal water swept over them, hindering them useless (since they were placed below sea level).

We are all aware that solar power has progressed, and it will be a great day for the planet when Photovoltaic (PV)-generated power replaces fossil fuels. Today, there are several companies producing the ideal back-up system, designed again for the military, but so useful in many of the

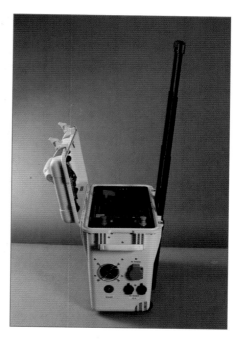

disaster areas, especially where there are long periods of sunshine.

In its basic form, a hand-pulled trolley that contains a battery and one or two other items to provide you with a stable power supply. The battery can be charged by using any form of input power: solar panel, generator, even the national grid when it is on.

On average, the system will run a normal light (based on eight hours per day) for around a week without its external top up. It is also possible to run items such as fans, laptops, and fridges from the system. When a solar panel is connected, the life of the system is extended to several weeks and even indefinitely.

The 'CellCube' is a much larger version and is capable of powering small hospitals, command centers, and shelter buildings used for disaster relief. This is basically a large steel container, similar to those used by shipping companies, and again, packed full of deep cell batteries.

The larger of the CellCube energy storage solutions provides 200 kWh of average output and 400 kWh of storage capacity. This can be charged via the electrical grid, as well

Solar power is now very efficient. This small trolley can be charged by just about any input and supply a constant flow of electricity. (Meeco)

Flexible solar sheets and solar tents are now becoming available, which will ease the plight of survivors and refugees. (source-Orange)

as by solar, wind, or hydro power. Due to its flow technology, the CellCube maintains full storage capacity even after unlimited cycles of deep (100%) discharge. Both systems provide an integrated all-in-one solution in a waterproof housing. All that is required is for the user to plug into the power.

Today it is possible to purchase flexible solar panels that will simply fold and fit into a small rucksack. These can be unfolded and used even on a campsite. One of the good things about flexible solar panels is that they do not damage easily; even if some of the panels become cut or seriously damaged, the rest will still work. While they can be clipped directly to a device needing power, they are best used via a storage battery. The system here is a simple 12 volt system. This can power a 12 volt bulb continuously and even run a small fan for several hours during the day.

While the larger solar sheets are quite expensive, it is possible for a few dollars to purchase a small one that will at least charge your mobile phone and run a small night-light, very handy when you have nothing else!

Chapter 11

WATER AND FOOD

Water is so important to life, but it has to be safe. If you are not sure, purify it. (Barry Davies)

Throughout this book you have read that water is life, and next to the air we breathe, it is top of the survival tree. Water is nature's most precious gift, and as we have already learned, it is essential to life. However, the water we consume must be clean and free of contaminates and parasites. When it comes to sustaining life, water and food is the very core of long-term survival.

Our bodies run on water. Like a car engine low on oil, our bodies are greatly affected when we become dehydrated. Dehydration and heat exhaustion have the effect of weakening the individual to a state of total collapse. Dizziness, severe headaches, and the inability to walk are signs that emergency measures are needed. The first priority is to cover the body and avoid sweating, as this will reduce water loss. Signs of severe dehydration consist of:

- Fatigue.
- Weakness, unable to go more than a few steps without resting.
- Dry mouth.
- Tingling sensation at your fingertips.
- Dizziness and headaches.
- Collapse.

A normal healthy person can live for about twenty-five days without food, but ten days is the best you can hope for without water. Surprisingly, a human being can survive on as little as four ounces of water a day, so if clean drinking

Author's Note: When I was about twenty-five years old, I was in Aden (capital of Yemen) in the Middle East. There had been an uprising in the town and many British people had been killed. I was dropped by helicopter onto a nearby mountain, together with a small group of snipers. The walk from the drop-off to the point where we would set up our base was not more than 1,000 meters away, yet I struggled to make it. At first, I wondered what was wrong with me, as I was young and very fit. True, this was mid-afternoon and extremely hot, with no shade. About halfway, I had to stop and sit down, as did two others—we had heatstroke. The problem was that we had just come directly from air-conditioned rooms into the sizzling heat of the dry mountain. It happened so quickly. I finally rested, had a good drink, and placed a wet scarf around my neck and after a couple of hours, I was OK.

water is scarce, it must be rationed. Always skip the first day, as your body will have retained a certain amount of water. Depending on your supply, start off with about ten ounces each, per day. Keep this up, if possible, for the first four or five days, then slowly reduce the daily intake to around four ounces. Always moisten the lips and mouth before swallowing.

If you are in a group, the priority for the rationing of drinking water must be given to those doing any strenuous physical work at the disaster site, with young children and older people coming a close second on the priority list. In addition to drinking, all food preparation and hygiene (cleaning your teeth) should also be carried out with good clean water. If good clean drinking water is readily available, drink at least four liters per day.

SOURCES OF CLEAN WATER

As for natural sources, the most obvious is rainwater. Be prepared for rainwater collection and storage; gather every clean item that can be pressed into service: buckets, bowls, and even strong plastic bags. Always make sure that anything you use to hold water is checked for cleanliness. In the extreme, any clean cloth can be used to mop up water so that it can be wrung into a container —or even sucked

Catching rainwater is simple, and it will normally be clean enough to drink; however, not during an ash cloud from a volcano. Simply get the largest waterproof shoot you can find and hold or stake it out. (Barry Davies)

dry. Have a dry run of your collection set-up, don't wait until it starts raining. It is imperative not to lose any water you could have collected. If all storage space is full, drink all you can, for your body is also a storage vessel.

If you are close to the sea, do NOT attempt to drink sea water (although it can be purified with the right equipment). Likewise, consider all surface water touched by tsunami waters to be contaminated. Use common sense and do not drink water that has an unusual odor or color, or that you know or suspect might be contaminated with fuel or toxic chemicals. While in certain circumstances this may seem to make collecting water difficult, remember that muddy water is not necessarily contaminated. Although some water you find will need treatment, the following list will provide you with some idea of where to look for safe drinking water. Alternative sources of clean water can be found inside and outside the home:

- Rivers or lakes NOT contaminated by flood or tsunami waters.
- Reserve tank of home hot water boilers.
- Swimming pools, but make sure to dilute with fresh water.
- Local stores and supermarkets normally have lots of bottled water.

There are also many ways to collect clean water which does not involve moving too far. Below are a few basic survival methods of collecting or producing water. Believe it or not, you can collect good drinking water from the ground or from plants and trees.

The Survival Still

If no water can be found in any of these locations, or if any water found is impure, a drinkable supply can be obtained by the use of a Survival Solar Still. This is a simple device which will produce water almost anywhere. To make it, a clear plastic sheet about two meters square is required, together with a water container. A plastic drinking tube about one and a half meters long is desirable.

Dig or scoop out a hole in the ground, about one meter across and some seventy-five centimeters deep in the cent-

As an alternative the to traditional Survival Solar Still, I tried urinating into a plastic bottle and then sealing it to another empty bottle until it was about quarter full. You have to be careful not to contaminate the empty bottle by keeping the bottle with the urine in it on the bottom. Next just lay the two bottles in the sun with the empty bottle slight raised so that the urine does not enter. The evaporation does the rest. Be careful when separating.
(Barry Davies)

er, where the container is placed. Fasten one end of the tube into the container. Spread the plastic sheet over the hole, bringing the other end of the tube out under its edge and secure the edges of the sheet with spaced stones. Put a rock or weight onto the center of the sheet so that it sags into an inverted cone. The center should be allowed to drop about thirty-five centimeters below horizontal. Now put soil or sand all around the edge of the hole to secure the sheet and seal the hole off from the atmosphere.

What will happen is that the sun's rays will pass through the sheet, warm the ground underneath, and evaporate any water present. This will result in the air trapped below the sheet becoming saturated. The water vapor will begin to condense out onto the underside of the plastic. The droplets will run down along the sheet and fall into the container. The still will usually produce at least half a liter in twenty-four hours, though very dry desert conditions may yield less than this. In better conditions, one and a half liters may be expected.

There are some points which must be carefully observed during construction:

- Make sure that the sheet does not touch the sides of the hole at any point, or the water will be lost back into the ground.

- Make sure that the sheet is clear of the container also, or some water will be sure to run down its outside and be lost.
- Check that the seal around the edge of the hole is complete and airtight.

Production can also be increased if any fleshy plant material can be sliced or broken and used to line the hole. Daily output can be increased in this way to two liters—even in the desert.

However, a single still is unlikely to provide enough water to sustain one person indefinitely.

Dew Traps

A simple plastic survival bag can be employed to construct a dew trap. Cover a suitable green plant with a bag with the neck being tied around the plant base. Dig a small depression near the plant and press the plastic down into it. This will form a collecting point for the moisture transpired by the plant.

All vegetation draws water from the earth and distributes it to the foliage. It is a simple matter of sealing off a section of this foliage to produce moisture condensation. Make sure that you choose healthy looking foliage to cover.

Simply tie a large clear plastic bag over any living vegetation to get a small amount of clean water. Always use safe recognizable plants or trees. (Barry Davies)

It is also possible to gather fresh foliage and seal it in a polythene bag; this will also produce a small amount of water. Likewise, a plastic bag can be put on the branch of a tree covering the fresh new leaves. Once the moisture starts, it will form its own reservoir.

Water Purification

There are many ways to purify water so that it can be safely consumed, including sea water. Water purification tablets provide a quick and convenient way of sterilizing water. Each tablet will purify one liter of water in about ten minutes. The tablets will kill bacteria, but they do not remove any dirt present in the water. The treated water will taste of chlorine. In addition to using chlorine tablets, you can also use iodine. If you do, always follow the manufacturer's instructions. If there are none, use two drops per liter at maximum. In my humble opinion, the use of household chlorine bleach and iodine are best reserved for cleaning the water storage utensils and other products, such as food, that have been rescued from the tsunami or floodwaters.

LifeSaver

The world's first all-in-one, ultra-filtration water bottle called the LifeSaver, uses a highly advanced ultra-filtration system. It will remove bacteria, viruses, cysts, parasites, fungi, and all other microbiological waterborne pathogens. It does this without the aid of any foul-tasting chemicals like iodine or chlorine. It uses failsafe technology, so that when the cartridge has expired, it shuts off, preventing the user from drinking contaminated water. Just change the cartridge and continue to use. LifeSaver creates safe, fresh drinking water instantly; you simple fill the bottle at one end, give it a few pumps, and then drink clean water from the other end.

Water Purification Pump

In addition to the LifeSaver, many new filters have emerged. In general, these all have a ceramic filter which removes all suspended matter and pathogens, including E. Coli, cryptosporidium, cholera, and amoebae. The system works by placing one tube into the water source, which is

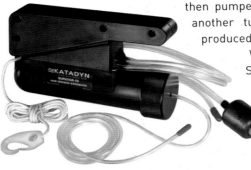

then pumped by a small hand mechanism to another tube from which clean water is produced.

Water filtration pumps, such as the Survivor 06, are designed to provide potable water from seawater in an emergency. It is a simple hand pump which is approved for desalting, as defined by SOLAS 1974; it also carries USCG approval. While designed to be carried on life rafts, it would come in very handy after a tsunami has contaminated all the local water.

Desalination pump will convert sea water to drinking water. (BCB Int. Ltd.)

Traditional Methods

IMPORTANT: Water contaminated with fuel or toxic chemicals will not be made safe by boiling or disinfecting. Use a different source of water if you know or suspect that water might be contaminated with fuel or toxic chemicals.

While excellent water filtration devices are available, I doubt if anyone will purchase such a device prior to any disaster. So, we will have to rely on the more traditional methods of purifying water. Water can be made safe to drink by boiling, or adding disinfectants. Before you attempt to do this, it is always best to remove as many large particles as possible. For this, you will need to set up a simple water filtration system. It just takes a little imagination, but what you are doing is sieving the water though as fine a filter as possible. Filter materials can be anything that will let the water pass while holding back the larger lumps. Spare clothing, sand and grass, are all acceptable, but ground charcoal is the best. Below is a simple water filter:

Boiling

Once your water is looking a bit cleaner, the next thing to do is to kill off all the disease-causing organisms, including viruses, bacteria, and parasites. Basically, boil the water so that it bubbles rapidly; continue to boil it for at least three minutes. Let the water cool before drinking!

Boiled water is fine to drink, but if you are making enough to store, make sure the bottles or containers are also sterilized. An old trick with boiled water is to tip it from one container to another; this will cool the water and also add air, and improve the taste. If it is available, add a little fruit juice to sweeten it to encourage children to drink more. It is also good to add a little salt if available.

Carrying Water

As any Special Forces soldier will tell you, a condom is an item of survival equipment with a wide range of use. When held in a sock or shirt sleeve, it becomes a water carrier. It cannot be filled by simply dipping into a water supply. To use its storage capacity adequately, water must be poured in with a bouncing motion to extend the length. If filled correctly, it will contain approximately one and a half liters when extended to a length of thirty centimeters. In addition to being a better carrier, it can be used as a water-proof container for small and medium sized items which need protection from becoming damp (e.g., dry fire tinder or matches). Two condoms together can be used as a very effective slingshot. The condoms chosen should be the inexpensive variety, non-lubricated and heavy duty. Your kit should include a minimum of three.

Salt

We lose a lot of salt from our bodies, and on average we require about six grams each day to maintain a healthy balance (half the population consumes over twice this

Condoms - the perfect light-weight water bottle. All military pilots carry a survival kit which contains two condoms. Fill them with water and use a sock or shirt sleeve for easy carry. (Barry Davies)

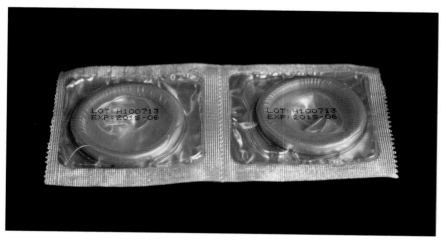

amount). Sweat and urine contains salt, as well as water, and this loss of salt and water must be turned to your advantage. If it isn't, then you will suffer from heat-stroke, heat exhaustion, and muscular cramps. The first sign of salt deficiency is a feeling of sudden weakness and a hot dry sensation to the body. Resting and a small pinch of salt added to a mug of water will eliminate the feeling very quickly. Under normal conditions, a small amount of salt to all your fluid intake, or food will suffice.

Remember, water is very important, and your chances of survival will be greatly increased if you understand fully the human body's need for water when it is in short supply. Conserve and protect your existing body fluids from the start and right through the disaster. Assess your supplies and initiate a planned and disciplined use of what you have. Consider possible sources of water and make plans or take action to obtain it. Check the purity of water from any source and take adequate measures to make supplies safe. Finally, while thirst can kill quickly, drinking contaminated water will mean a certain and a slow death!

FOOD

Once you have settled into a safe shelter and have located a source of acceptable drinking water, it's time to think about food. Food is not a priority in the days following a disaster, as most of us can easily miss eating for two or three days; in many cases it will be beneficial. As soon as the more urgent aspects of the situation have been dealt with, start to plan your food supplies. The prospects of early rescue may seem good, but remember: the survivor is the one who hopes for the best, but plans for the worst. There are three sources of food open to survivors which can be salvaged from the disaster and can be found in the wild. These are the ones that are provided by the rescue and relief agencies.

Remember, if the water supply is limited, the amount and type of food eaten must be strictly controlled. Eat less and avoid all dry, starchy food or salty meat. Go for foods high in carbohydrates.

Depending on the location and devastation, it may be possible to salvage food from your home, nearby shops, supermarkets, or just floating around in the wreckage. If you do find such food supplies, there are some safety points to bear in mind:

- Many other people will be doing the same thing. Be careful of gangs and looters.
- Never taste raw food to see if it is edible, unless you have just killed an animal.
- Do not eat fish that you find floating in floodwaters or stagnant pools.
- Discard food that has come into contact with the floodwaters, unless it is in a tin or safe packaging.
- Disregard any poultry, fish, or meat that has been exposed to heat over 40°F for any duration of time. This includes eggs that have been near heat, left in the sun, or covered in floodwater.
- Discard any food that has a bad odor, or looks bleached in color, or has an extremely wet texture.
- Do NOT discard tinned or well-packed food just because of the **sell by date**—check it before discarding.
- Gather any tins or sealed packs of food that look unopened and are airtight. Remove labels if they have been in contact with the floodwater and sterilize (see *Sterilization* section below).

We have already touched on the subject of stealing or looting, but when it comes to water, food, warmth, and shelter, we need to consider our needs and the needs of others, such as our children. Taking something that does not belong to you after a disaster is technically stealing, but who would scorn a mother for feeding her children, or taking clothes and blankets from a supermarket to provide them with warmth?

WARNING—After many disasters, especially in cities, both police and army are given orders to, shoot on sight, at any looter they see, even if your crime is minor. The fact that you simply took a bottle of milk for your child will rarely segregate you from punishment.

Any food, canned or packaged, can still be contaminated by flood or tsunami waters. Wash off all dirt and debris before opening. (source unknown – multi-usage)

Sterilization

Clean anything you take or find that has been in contact with the floodwaters or near a heat source for any length of time. The best and simplest way is to get a bucket of clean water, boil it and let it cool if you are not sure. Add about an egg cup of bleach to a normal sized bucket half filled with water (approximately two gallons). Brush off any access dirt, remove labels, and place in the bucket. Leave them for around five minutes, then remove and air dry. You should now be able to open the can or package with little chance of contamination.

In more remote areas, such as those people who suffered the tsunami in Ache, Indonesia, you may be forced to live off the land until the rescue services and aid agencies reach you. In almost every corner of the world, there is food to be found in the wild. In the sections below, I have listed some plants, fruit, insects, birds, and animals that are all edible.

Food Supply

For many of us, the way we buy and store food has changed over the past fifty years. Supermarkets are open 24/7, so there is little need to hold vast stocks that may become out-of-date. There has also been a change in food prices around the world, with many basic items, such as rice, having increased dramatically over the past few years. In short, food is becoming one of the most valuable commodities we have. In any situation, especially after a major disaster, food will be in short supply; in the long term, if you do not have food, you are not going to survive.

Due mainly to the convenience of supermarkets, most families only stock enough food to feed their family for a week. After a disaster, when your family runs out of food, you will have to fight with the hordes of hungry people who are looting the stores and roaming the streets looking for something to eat. After Hurricane Katrina and the earthquakes in Haiti and Chile, news reports showed people raiding and looting markets for food. After almost every single disaster, where the social order has collapsed, looting has taken place. Legally, the starving may not steal even bread, yet there is a moral ambiguity that stealing food to survive is accepted by most.

Manufactured Survival Food

There is a wide variety of both military and civilian manufactured food rations. If you were to find yourself on a life boat after an aircraft crash or ship sinking, you would most probably be expected to survive on boiled sweets. If it were a government emergency, they would first distribute what food was available locally from the supermarkets; once this was gone, you soon end up eating compressed emergency

Author's Note: At certain times of the year, there is an abundance of garden and farm food growing. Where I live in Spain, it is possible to walk just a few meters in any direction before finding something edible. We have oranges by the millions, apples, figs, almonds, and walnut trees dotted along the country pathways. As long as they are free from contamination, everything should be good to eat. Fruit trees, vegetables, and berries are delicious, but make sure they are cleaned and washed before being eaten.

Use rations that have been especially prepared for emergencies and that have a long shelf life. (BCB Int. Ltd.)

rations. These have no texture, little taste, and are simply a small square block that will provide you with enough food to sustain life. Some NGOs will supply Debren-type rations, which are one step up from emergency. The Debren ration comes in biscuit form and a 500 gram pack will provide 2,500 calories. The good thing is that they are nutritionally balanced and can be made into a porridge, which can be served to young children.

The military, on the other hand, has some great rations, normally known as MREs (Meal Ready to Eat). These rations contain precooked individual meals, which are both nutritious and tasty. In the main, a soldier will receive a complete one day ration pack. This will provide him or her with breakfast, lunch, and dinner, plus all the various sundries required, such as toilet paper. Some nations (France, Spain, and Italy) also include a small sachet of wine in the ration.

NGOs will supply a lot of food after any emergency, but again, this is aimed at sustaining life. The basic food supplied by NGOs varies from vegetable oil, rice, pasta, sugar, and salt. If you're lucky and have children, you might also receive milk powder and dried beans. Occasionally, a tinned meat or fish will be distributed in the larger family packs, but typically, the NGO food packs are very basic.

Preparing and Cooking Insects and Animals (Domestic and Wild)

You will be surprised by how much food can be found if you seriously look for it. Naturally, different parts of the world provide different foods, but the basics are all the same. For most races, eating animals and insects is totally alien, but in places like Asia, it is considered the norm. Dog meat has been used as a survival food in times of hardship and war; many explorers to the North Pole have eaten their Huskies.

Author's Note: Normally, I would not write this in a survival book, and many people might find it offensive to even think about eating pets such as cats, rabbits, dogs, mice, etc. Likewise, eating dogs is forbidden under law in some countries and is banned by Islamic and Jewish law. But let's put this into context: you and your family are in the aftermath of a disaster and there is NO food now or for the foreseeable future. Do you want to see your family die? Are you prepared to die? If the answer to this question is yes, then you should not have purchased this book in the first place.

To be more realistic, the chance that you will have to eat your pets, or anyone else's for that matter, is highly unlikely. But, in the event that you are forced to, treat it as you would any other animal food.

When looking for food, remember one important fact: if it walks, flies, crawls, swims, or just sits in the mud, it's edible (well, almost everything). The thing to do is not to eat the animal or insect in its natural form, but turn it into a form that is palatable. Likewise, never eat a lot of one single food, and always test new food from the wild in small quantity first to be sure that it's safe.

While they have a bad reputation, rats can provide good eating. Rats are common and are found all over the world. In parts of South America where they are a major infestation problem, they have been processed and canned for human consumption, being called, 'Star Foods' (rats spelled backwards). Despite what you hear, rats do not eat rotten food; however, they do carry germs and lice. Skin the rat and in particular, discard the rump end, intestines, and head.

Rabbits are to be found in most parts of the world, from the Arctic Circle to the jungles and deserts. They are fairly simple to catch and make delicious meals. However, there is very little fat on rabbits, and for this reason, other animals should be trapped to supplement your diet.

Whenever you are out hunting or foraging for edible plants, watch out for evidence of other small game—squirrels, rats, mice,

You can eat just about anything if you prepare it correctly, but best stick with things you recognize. (Barry Davies)

Eggs are one of man's oldest foods, and they still comes in the same packaging. (Barry Davies)

birds, water fowl, etc. They will reveal their presence by the nests, burrows or dens, as well as their tracks and runs, meal remains, droppings, territorial markings, and maybe calls, songs, or even smells.

Remember that birds' eggs are a tasty and safe food, so don't neglect them as a viable source. If you observe birds nesting, check the nest for eggs. All eggs are edible and provide a good balanced meal when eaten with stewed nettles. Beware of angry and protective birds, such as swans or seagulls, as they will attack you.

Most frogs are edible; however, most of the meat is on the legs. They are easy to catch: by tapping the water gently with a flat piece of wood, when the frog appears, tap it on the head. Frogs will reveal their whereabouts at night by croaking. Patience is needed at the outset, for if they are plentiful, they can always be heard somewhere other than the place you are!

Snakes are great to eat, and you can eat most of it. The problem lies in actually finding and catching the snake after a disaster. They are experts at camouflage and will shy away from humans. On sunny days, they can be caught out in the open and should be pinned with a forked stick. Slowly place a small forked stick behind their head and pin it to the ground. Sever the head from behind the stick, strip off the skin, split it down the middle, and remove the center gut. Roast or fry for best results. Special Forces soldiers have been known to eat snakes raw.

Author's Note: Most people are afraid of snakes—or at least the idea of snakes. In fact, our fears are very much exaggerated. Less than 10% of all snakes are dangerous, and almost all of those will do their best to get out of your way if they can. One tip when hunting for snakes, move very slowly, snakes react to sudden movement. **Remember not to touch the head, even when it has been removed from the body, as severed snake heads may still bite!**

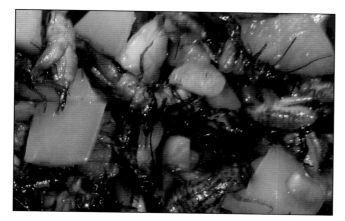

When you eat insects, always gather the one that can't run away. (Barry Davies)

Most snails found in Europe and America are an accept-able source of food. They are rich in nutrients, yet it is advisable not to eat more than twelve in a sitting. Some snails are dangerous to eat; these are normally brightly colored and easily identified. To prepare your snails, it is best if you starve them for a few days or leave them in a bucket of salt water which will purge their system. Boil for about twenty minutes, but make sure not to overcook them, as they will become hard!

Worms make good eating as well, but the thought puts many people off. The simplest way is to dry them in a 'Billy Can' (see page 232) by the fire, shaking the tin from time to time to stop them from burning. Once dry, they can be crushed to a powder providing a protein base for soups.

Wild and Domestic Plant Food

Obtaining food from domestic and wild plants is a surviv-al technique to be learned and practiced. While all domestic grown crops are edible, well under one half of all wild plants are edible—and most of them only in parts. Knowl-edge and skill, therefore, are needed to take advantage of nature's bounty.

In many parts of the world, there are vast areas of culti-vated land providing various fruits and vegetables through-out the year. Providing that they have not been contaminat-ed by floodwaters, these will offer you sustenance in the way of root vegetables or berries. Even where an area has been flooded, there may be fruit trees bearing apples or oranges. If you know what plants are grown in or near your

The edibility test is always the best answer if you don't recognize plant food. (Barry Davies)

location, you should be able to find enough food to keep yourself alive.

Food from the wild is a little different. While many people can still recognize a blackberry bush plus one or two other species, the majority of people do not know about the bounties of wild food. If you are not certain of a plant's identity, or need to find if any particular plant is edible, the best and most simple way is to carry out an edibility test. The edibility test may seem to be time-consuming and over-cautious, but it has served many survivors well in the past.

Warning the 'Edibility Test' does not work for wild mushrooms and fungis.

Edibility Test for Wild Food and Plants:

1. Never collect plants from polluted waters or areas. Always clean them thoroughly before attempting to eat or cook, and remove damaged or inferior parts.
2. Do not assume that every part of a plant is edible because you have found that one specific part is.
3. Do not waste time in testing any plant unless it is abundant. It is a waste of time and effort to test any plant if it is not easily and plentifully obtainable.
4. Test for the presence of any contact poison in the plant. Crush the leaf and rub some sap onto the skin of the inner wrist and wait fifteen minutes. If no itching, blistering, or burning occurs, then continue on to step five.
5. Hold a small portion in your mouth for five minutes. If no unpleasant reactions occur, chew the plant, again looking for unpleasant signs (extreme bitterness, burning or soapy taste). If there are no unpleasant signs, swallow the juice, but spit out the pulp. Allow another eight hours to pass.
6. If no ill effects develop (sickness, dizziness, sleepiness, stomach aches, or cramps), eat a slightly larger amount—a teaspoonful, for example—and watch for similar effects for another eight hours.

7. If no negative effects are revealed, eat about a handful of the plant. A final twenty-four hours without trouble indicates that the plant is safe and can be eaten in larger quantities.
8. Eat only healthy plants, avoiding all with rotting parts, mold, diseases or insect infestation.
9. Avoid any plants with milky sap (except dandelion, Goat's Beard, and coconut), or a bitter or burning taste or having caustic sap. Always boil leaves which have prickly hairs (e.g., stinging nettle).
10. Test only one plant at a time, on one person at a time, so that the cause of any ill effects can be pinpointed
11. Even palatable wild plants may prove detrimental to health if eaten in large quantities or over a long period. Whenever possible, make a salad or vegetable stew, combining leaves, berries, nuts, inner bark, and root-stocks. You will achieve a more balanced diet, as well as a tastier meal. This is one occasion when variety really is the spice of life!

The scope of this book does not allow for a detailed list of all the edible plants and I doubt if many people would take notice, but it is worth mentioning two of the very common plants that are found on our planet. If you remember these two, then it will act as a catalyst to prompt you to look for others.

Dandelion (Taraxacum Officinale)

The dandelion is perennial and widespread throughout the northern temperate regions. Leaves are shiny, bottle green, deeply toothed, fifteen centimeters, form rosette at plant base—inner leaves erect, outer leaves shorter, and spreading. Flowers are yellow, solitary on stems up to thirty centimeters, bloom March to August, with much milky sap. Young leaves may be eaten raw. Their bitter taste is alleviated if soaked for two hours in cold water. Developing shoots, before stems begin to grow, can be used like Brussels sprouts. Older leaves, with a rough center vein removed, are better if boiled. Cleaned roots can be boiled like potatoes, having a pleasant taste. Sun-dried roots, baked and crushed, provide an excellent coffee substitute.

The leaves and roots, available throughout the year, are a valuable food source.

Stinging Nettle (Urtica Diotica)

The stinging nettle is a perennial herb distributed throughout the temperate regions of the world. Stems grow up to 120 centimeters, carrying heart-shaped leaves three to eight centimeters long, toothed, and covered with fine hairs which produce a 'sting' when touched. Found in woods, forests, and any sheltered grassy place, they are often gathered together in large colonies. Young shoots are gathered in March and April. Before flowering, they can be eaten fresh, provided they are dipped in boiling water to remove formic acid from "stings." They are also known as a very good source of Vitamin C. Other leaves should be chopped and boiled to remove acid, but for no longer than six minutes to retain as much food value as possible. They can also be used as a ingredient for stew. Leaves, when dried and rubbed, make a very acceptable tea. Freshly pressed juice (one or two teaspoons per day) makes an excellent pick-me-up after an exhausting day.

List of Survival Foods

The common stinging nettle is a great source of food. (Barry Davies)

Food is stored in our homes, supermarkets, warehouses, and farms. It is estimated that there is enough food to keep the entire world going for at least three weeks (or even longer). The farm-to-table system we have adopted is now so sophisticated that little interrupts it; produce is bred, grown, or caught to a system. It is processed, shipped, and distributed. It is consumed and replaced. In fact, our world relies on this process. Can you image what would happen if a disaster was large enough to stop it?

Well, it did happen.

Although it was known as the Great Irish Famine (1846-1849), an estimated one to three million people in Great Britain and Ireland died. The Soviet Union suffered famine losses between six and ten million people between 1932 and 1933. More recently, between 1990 and 2003, the Iraqi people suffered as a result of famine; but the daddy of them all was China. In the three years between 1959 and 1962, an estimated minimum of twenty million people died as a result of famine.

Yet, the sources of wild animal food remain abundant; mammals, birds, reptiles, fish, crustaceans, and insects can all be eaten. Any of these can provide food that, pound for pound, have much higher food-value than most material derived from plants. They do not provide it willingly, however, and most have to be hunted, trapped, or caught. Without taking into account any religious or civil law on food consumption, here is a list of just a few things that can be eaten:

Worms	Goats
Grubs	Seals
Termites	Fish
Ants	Penguins
Cockroaches	Birds
Bees and Wasps	Camels
Snails and Slugs	Crocodiles and Alligators
Hedgehogs	Lizards
Rabbits	Kangaroos
Rats	Cattle
Snakes	Horses
Wild and domestic Cats	Monkeys and Apes
Wolves	Turtles and Tortoises
Wild and domestic Dogs	Frogs and Toads
Pigs	Crabs
Deer	Shrimp
Bears	Shellfish

CARRY AND COOK FOOD

In all my years of learning and teaching survival, there are two items I recommend for you to make. The first is a

'Billy Can.' A Billy Can will serve as a mug, mess-tin, food and water storage, and cooking pot. You will need to find a large catering-sized can, like those used in restaurants. Remove the open top completely and then pierce two holes opposite each other near the open end. Place a piece of strong wire through the holes to form a carrying handle. You now have a Billy Can. No self-respecting survivalist would be without one!

The second item is a 'Yukon Stove.' (Yes I know I have mentioned it before but it's really a great survival asset.) If you are in one location for more than twenty-four hours, you should certainly consider building this type of stove. It will provide a secure way of heating your safe shelter and help with the cooking. You could build it indoors on concrete, but it would be better constructed on an earth floor. The Yukon Stove normally takes about two hours for one person to construct, that is, providing most of the materials are at hand. I have always taken the time to construct a good Yukon Stove and it has made life extremely bearable, from all aspects.

The principle is simple: you need to form a tortoise-type shell made of rocks, mud, and stone. At one side, you must leave a hole for the intake of fuel and air, and with another at the top as a chimney. Two further refinements are very desirable. If you can find a flat metal tin box, build this into the wall of your stove to act as an oven. The second improvement is to use a large flat rock on the top of the stove which can act as a griddle for drying insects or even frying birds' eggs.

One of the great advantages of a Yukon Stove is that it can be left unattended while you are working at other activities, and you'll be able to return to a warm fire and hot meal. By covering the fuel/air intake with another stone, the rate of burning can be partly controlled. In wet weather, the oven enables fuel to be dried. Clothing can be laid over the outside of the stove and will dry

The Billy Can, simple but so useful. (Barry Davies)

without burning. You can warm yourself without risk of being burned.

Remember to provide effective ventilation
if you intend on using a stove or heater inside
your shelter. This means two openings: one at
the top of your shelter as a chimney, with
another close to ground level to admit fresh
air. If a group of people are sleeping in a heated, closed shelter, one of them should stay
awake on carbon monoxide guard duty, or
better still, carry a battery powered sensor in
your grab bag.

PROTEIN SOUP

Most people will turn their nose up at a big
fat maggot, a thick-shelled beetle with twenty
legs, or a handful of ants. The point is that this
is all protein, and all good for you. Even if it
looks too disgusting to put in your mouth—
trust me, your stomach will not mind.

When I ran my survival courses for Special
Forces Pilots at the NATO LRRPS School in
Southern Germany, I had many British, American, and
European students. My favorite part was getting them to eat
the unattractive creatures. The simplest way was to dry
them all out by slowly roasting them in a tin. Once cooked, I
would crush them all with a stick until they were a mass of
brown powder. I would then fill the tin with boiling water
and simmer for a few minutes. All the nasty bits, like the
wings and shell would float to the surface, which I would
skim off. What was left was Protein Soup. This simple soup
will keep you going for weeks, and you can reheat it. However, it is best not to reheat it more than once.

The Yukon Stove,
always a winner
when surviving. It
will keep you
warm, conserve
fuel, dry your
clothes, cook your
food, and can be
left unattended.
(Barry Davies)

Chapter 12

DISASTER FIRST AID AND EMERGENCY CARE

Threat to life.

While first aid is of primary concern immediately after a disaster, it is not within the scope of this book to cover more than the basics. The main focus must be on your own safety and physical care, followed by providing help for others. Just remember, many people will be dead or beyond help, and priority assistance should be directed towards those that have a chance of survival.

In all cases where a medical emergency has risen, all efforts should be made to contact professional medical assistance. The procedures described in this book are designed to deal with medical emergencies when professional help is unavailable and the risk of death or long-term disablement prevails. Additionally, extreme treatments should only be carried out when the patient's life is undeniably under the threat of death and without promise of immediate professional help. In all cases, moderation, common sense, and general consensus, including that of the patient when conscious, must influence the final decision.

In the event of a medical emergency, the patient will be deemed to be responsible for diagnosis and treatment. Where several medical people are available, the responsibility will rest with the most proficient, as listed below in order of proficiency:

- Doctor
- Nurse
- Paramedic
- First Aid-trained personnel
- Team leader (no experience)

IMMUNIZATION

Many diseases such as Typhoid, Paratyphoid, Yellow Fever, Typhus, Tetanus, Cholera, and Hepatitis can all be vaccinated against. It is essential to obtain as many vaccinations as possible, making sure immunization records are kept up-to-date. Prior to visiting any foreign country, you are advised to seek current medical advice and take extra immunizations and precautions. Make sure you carry a good supply of anti-malarial tablets where necessary.

The Threat to Life

It is not my intention to go into a long, drawn-out set of procedures for first aid, and I intend only to cover the basics for saving a life. In medical terms, there are five main threats to humans: the inability to breath, severe blood loss, heart malfunction, shock, and disease. The airway can be cleared, blood loss stemmed and replaced, wounds closed, shock prevented, and disease cured.

During and after a disaster, a medical emergency can happen at any time. If you are in an isolated or hostile area and without the means of immediate rescue, then you must rely on your own resources and experience—a good medical pack will also help a lot.

In addition to a medical pack, do not forget any current medication you or others may be taking. An estimated 27% of people need regular medication to sustain their health. In many cases, such as heart disease, it is vital. What do you do when your home, pharmacy, and nearest working medical facility can no longer support you? The answer is simple: if you are reliant on medication, pack at least one month's supply in your disaster grab bag. Remember other members of your family, especially the young and very old.

ASSESSMENT

The first priority is to determine the nature of the disaster and its immediate impact. For example, a tsunami will have created vast coastal flooding, while an earthquake will have destroyed many buildings; a terrorist bombing will cause instantaneous pandemonium. An initial assessment of the type of disaster will point out any immediate medical problems. The priority of the individual is basically down to two major factors; the number of people affected and the presence of continuing hazards.

Triage.

The first thing to do is a detailed assessment of yourself and your current predicament. Are you trapped or in immediate danger? If you are not in any immediate danger, are you free to assist and help others close by without further risk?

Triage (derived from the French for sort or sift) is the name given to the process of sorting casualties; the aim is to achieve the maximum good for

the maximum number of casualties. All disaster casualties are sorted, prioritized, and treated according to their individual needs. This is the basis for immediate first aid, resuscitation, and emergency transportation to a medical facility. Triage means matching the casualties' needs with available resources, in order to achieve the best outcome for the maximum number of casualties. It starts at the disaster site and continues along to the hospital.

To minimize further deaths and alleviate the suffering of all casualties, an effective assessment must be made and those most at risk identified. While triage categories may differ slightly between countries, the dead are normally marked as Black/White, while for survivors, the general categories are as follows:

- First priority is for those with life-threatening injuries in need of urgent medical care, requiring priority transport, with or without appropriate resuscitation. These are tagged RED.
- Second priority is for those with significant injuries, but in a stable condition and for whom treatment can wait. This category is also reserved for those that are not expected to live. These are tagged YELLOW.
- Third priority is for the walking wounded who can be treated locally. Psychological casualties are included in this category. These are tagged GREEN.

Disaster First Aid

While the above is the official method of dealing with mass casualties, your immediate individual priorities to first aid will not equate. Nonetheless, the ability to carry-out first aid in any shape or form has enormous value after a major disaster. This value is beyond measure where there may be no prospect of skilled assistance for several days. Even though your medical supplies may be inadequate or entirely absent, you will still have the skills to provide first aid for yourself and other survivors.

If you purchased this book, but skipped over this section as 'boring,' once again, I come back to the applications now available for most smart phones. There are even videos on 'how to' for just about every medical emergency. The problem is that with first aid, by the time you have looked it up and started the lifesaving procedure, the patient is already dead.

However, before we even consider providing any first aid or medical help, we should avail ourselves of a few do's and don'ts.

- Stay calm, no matter how serious an injury or how dangerous the situation. Panic will impair the ability to think and will lower effectiveness. Time will be wasted, and time can mean life.
- Avoid any unnecessary danger to yourself. This is not cowardice, as you will be no good to anyone if you needlessly suffer injury yourself.
- Think carefully, but quickly before you act.
- Do your best to reassure and comfort any casualty. If really serious, lie. Telling people the truth will sometimes push them over the edge.
- Find out if there are any other uninjured or active survivors who can help to deal with the situation. In particular, look for any survivor with medical qualifications or better experience than your own.
- When assessing individual casualties, use your own senses to the fullest: ASK, LOOK, LISTEN, SMELL, and then THINK and ACT!
- If conscious, ask the casualty to describe his symptoms and to tell you what he thinks happened and what he feels is wrong.
- Reassurance and rest play a vital part in the treatment since they can lower the rate of heartbeat and reduce the flow of blood around the body. Reassurance will also prevent the patient going into shock.

Self-Help

The first priority is to help yourself before you help others, as you may also be injured. It is also possible that you may become injured while you are on your own, and in this case, it is sensible to have a self-help routine:

- Try and rest. Lie down somewhere, but preferably not in the direction of blowing wind.
- Use direct pressure on your wound to control the bleeding. Apply a dressing, sterile, or improvised, if possible.

- If available, use a bandage to maintain pressure. Tie it firmly but not so tight as to restrict circulation.
- If possible, elevate the injury and support it. Pain will be less if you try and keep it as still as possible.
- Try and make sure that you can keep warm.

Check Breathing and Provide CPR

The first priority is to check that the patient is breathing and the airway is clear. If the patient is talking without any serious signs of forced breathing, the airway is generally clear.

If you are dealing with an unconscious casualty, listen with your ear close to the nose and mouth, as you should be able to hear and feel any breath. Also make sure to watch out for chest and abdominal movement at the same time. If there are no signs of breathing, take immediate action to ensure that the air passages are clear.

Supporting the neck with one hand, ease the head backwards with the other. Keeping the head back, lift the chin upwards. This action will open the air passage and bring the tongue forward to prevent it from being an obstruction. Check quickly inside the mouth to find and remove any other cause of blockage, i.e., dentures, vomit, or other materials. Once the air passage is open and clear, the casu-

CPR

alty may begin breathing again. If this happens, and his heart is beating, put him into the coma (or recovery) position. (This is illustrated later in this Section.) If there is a visible injury to the front or back of the head (which might indicate damage to the neck or spine), maintain the clear airway with the head back. Improvise some form of collar or head support to keep the head correctly positioned. If breathing does not re-commence, the casualty must be given help with respiration. This can best be done on a mouth-to-mouth basis. Procedure as follows:

Warning: If at all possible, use a vent aid which reduces the risk of the first aider coming into contact with patient's body fluids.

- Taking a deep breath, pinch the casualty's nose to prevent air loss. Open your own mouth wide and seal your own lips around their open mouth. Blow into their lungs, watching for expansion of the chest. When the maximum expansion is reached, raise your head clear and breathe out and in. Look now for the chest contraction; when this has happened, repeat the procedure four times. It may be more convenient to use mouth-to-nose

CPR

contact. In this case, the casualty's mouth must be kept shut to prevent the loss of air.

- Following the fourth assisted breath, it is important to check that the casualty's heart is beating. The oxygen having been taken up by the blood must be delivered to the body's vital organs. Feel for the carotid pulse in the neck.

- If there is no heartbeat, chest compression must be carried out. BE SURE that there is NO heartbeat before beginning chest compression. Far more harm than good will be done if attempted chest compression interferes with an existing heartbeat, however weak it may be.

- If the heart is beating, continue giving assisted breaths at between sixteen and eighteen a minute. When the casualty begins breathing for himself, continue giving assistance at his natural rate until breathing is normal. Then place him in the coma (recovery) position.

- Check that the casualty is lying on a firm surface. Kneeling alongside, locate the bottom of their breastbone. Measure the width of three fingers up and place the heel of one hand on the bone, laying the other hand on top. Keeping the elbows rigid, lean forward so that your arms are vertical and your weight is bearing down on the casualty's chest. Depress the breastbone by between four and five centimeters. Lean back to release the pressure, allowing the breastbone to return to its original position. Perform fifteen compressions at the rate of about eighty per minute. (Count, one back two back three back and so on, leaning forward on each number.)

- If you are successful, breathing and circulation will restart at the same time. The casualty needs both, so assisted breathing and chest compression must be carried out together. You should continue for at least fifteen minutes.

Warning—If you are the only survivor administrating first aid, and there are several other injured people waiting for your attention, think TRIAGE and make a decision on your priori-

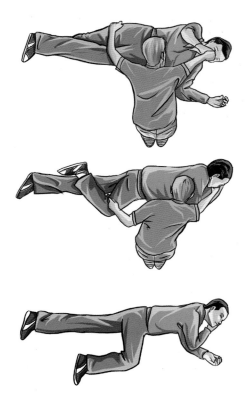

Recovery
position.

ties. There is no point in doing fifteen minutes of CPR on a dead man when the person next to him is bleeding to death.

Coma or Recovery Position

Generally, an unconscious survivor who is breathing, has a reasonable heartbeat, and is without other injuries demanding immediate attention should be put into the coma (recovery) position. This position, illustrated below, is the safest because it minimizes the risk of impeded breathing. The tilted-back head ensures open air passages. The face-down attitude allows any vomit or other liquid obstruction to drain from the mouth.

The spread of the limbs will maintain the body in its position. If fractures or other injuries prevent suitable placement of the limbs, use rolled clothing or other padded objects to prop the survivor in this position.

Tracheotomy (only to be performed by a qualified person)

If there are signs of respiratory failure and CPR is not possible due to lower face damage or an upper airway blockage, then a tracheotomy may need to be performed. When the trachea (windpipe) is blocked by an immovable object preventing the casualty from breathing, then a small hole is opened in the front of the neck and a tube inserted so that the air can reach the lungs.

The opening is made immediately under the chin by cutting a vertical slit through the center of the thyroid gland. Under ideal conditions two tubes are inserted: the first has a dressing-like seal and the second tube fits inside the first tube and can be removed or cleaned out if it became blocked with mucus. The main indications for a tracheotomy are:

- An obstruction of the larynx.
- Serious damage to the lower face and bottom jaw.

Where blockage of the windpipe has taken place and no other measures give relief, performing a tracheotomy should take place as soon as possible.

BLEEDING

Bleeding should be stopped as soon as possible; this is best done by direct pressure. Place a dressing over the

Author's Note: I have deliberately left out the images and precise instructions to perform a tracheotomy. For a medically qualified person, a tracheotomy is not a difficult operation and they will know exactly what to do.

During the First World War, many soldiers were left for dead. On one occasion, some German prisoners who were being escorted back behind the lines were resting by the side of the road. One of the prisoners (who had been a pre-war medical student) realized that one of the many corpses, lying in the nearby ditch, was actually moving. Pulling the man from the mud, the German rendered aid by cutting into this man's throat and inserting a piece of rubber tube. That man was my grandfather and he went on to live until he was eighty-seven. He would not have a bad word said about the German people.

Bleeding

wound and apply firm but gentle pressure with the hand. A sterile dressing is desirable. If one is not available, any piece of clean cloth can be used. If no dressing is ready for immediate use, cover the wound with your hand. If necessary, hold the edges of the wound together with gentle pressure. Any dressings used should be large enough to overlap the wound and cover the surrounding area. If blood comes through the first dressing, apply a second over the first, and if required, a third over the second. Keep even pressure applied by tying on a firm bandage. Take great care that the bandage is not so tight that, like a tourniquet, it restricts the flow of blood.

If the wound is large and no suitable dressings are available, bring the edges of the wound together and use the dressings to keep the wound closed. To arrest the flow of blood from a very large wound, make a pad of the dressing and press it into the wound where the bleeding is heaviest. The object of this treatment is to slow down or stop the loss of blood until the body's own defenses come into play.

Elevation

If there is no danger of any other injury being aggravated, an injured limb is best raised as high as is comfortable for the casualty. This reduces the bloodflow in the limb, helps the veins to drain the area and assists in reducing the blood loss through the wound.

Indirect Pressure

If a combination of these procedures is not successful, the use of appropriate pressure points must be considered. It is necessary to recognize the type of external bleeding, because pressure points can only be used to control arterial bleeding. Arteries carry the blood outwards from the heart, in pulses of pressure. At this stage, the blood has been oxygenated and filtered of its impurities. Arterial bleeding is revealed when bright red blood spurts out in time with heartbeat. Blood from the veins flows out steadily, with less pressure, and is darker red.

A place where an artery runs across a bone near the surface of the skin constitutes a pressure point. There are four pressure points readily available to control heavy arterial bleeding—one in each limb. Those in the arms are on the brachial arteries. These run down the center of the inner side of the upper arm.

Pressure points for the legs are on the femoral arteries, which run down the inside of the thigh. The pressure points can be found in the center of the groin, and can be compressed against the pelvis. This is easier to do if the casualty's knee is bent. When using pressure points to control bleeding, make full use of the opportunity to dress the wound more effectively. Pressure application:

- Locate the fingers or thumb over the pressure point and apply sufficient pressure to flatten the artery and arrest the flow of blood.
- Redress the wound.
- Maintain the pressure for at least ten minutes to allow time for blood-clotting to begin. DO NOT EXCEED FIFTEEN MINUTES or the tissues below the pressure point will begin to be damaged by the deprivation of arterial blood. It is essential to release the controlling pressure after FIFTEEN MINUTES.

Tourniquet

Applying a tourniquet is a dangerous procedure. However, if the damage to a limb is so severe it plainly requires amputation, or if part of the limb is missing and direct pressure will not stop the bleeding, you may need to apply a tourniquet. The tourniquet can be made from whatever cloth is at hand, but avoid any thin material that will cut into the flesh. Place it around the extremity, between the wound and the heart, five to ten centimeters above the wound site. Never place it directly over the wound or a fracture. Use a stick as a handle to tighten the tourniquet and tighten it only enough to stop blood flow. Clean and bandage the wound. The tourniquet must be slowly released every ten to fifteen minutes for a period of one to two minutes; however, you should continue to apply direct pressure at all times. It must be stressed that applying a tourniquet to prevent blood flow is a dangerous procedure and should only be attempted when all else has failed.

Foreign Bodies

Where a bomb has exploded, there will be some survivors injured by flying debris. Smaller fragments and projectiles like broken glass can be removed. Unless life threatening, larger foreign bodies should be left in place, as pulling at them may do further damage. Instead, control the bleeding by direct pressure, squeezing the wound in line with the foreign body. Next, form a padded ring which will fit neatly over the protruding object and secure it with a dressing.

Sucking Wounds to the Chest

If air is allowed to enter the lungs from puncture wounds to the chest or back, then a sucking wound will develop. Always check for sucking wounds if missiles of any form have penetrated deeply or a rib is protruding from the chest or back. The lung on the affected side will collapse and as the casualty breaths in, the sucked air will also impair the efficiency of the good lung if the condition goes untreated. The result is a lack of oxygen reaching the bloodstream that could cause asphyxia. Check for the following:

- Chest pain.
- The sound of air being sucked in from the chest.
- Difficulty in breathing.
- Bright blood bubbling from a chest wound.
- Blueness around the mouth.

If a sucking wound is suspected, immediately cover the area with your hand. Support the casualty in a lop-sided sitting position with the functioning lung uppermost. Cover the wound with a clean dressing and place a plastic sheet over the top so that the plastic overlaps the dressing and wound, making sure to tape it down to form an airtight seal. Leave one of the lower corners free so that air can escape when the casualty exhales. If a foreign body is present in the wound, do not remove, but pack with a ring as described above and fit an airtight seal.

Abdominal Wound

There is little that can be done for a serious penetration of the abdominal cavity, especially if the wound is caused by a missile. Lay the casualty down and raise their knees. This will minimize any muscle and skin stretching of the abdominal wall. Control any external bleeding, clean the entry wound, and apply a dressing. Check for signs of internal bleeding.

Butterfly Closures

In the absence of any skilled doctor or medic, it is possible to close some minor cuts. Small to medium straight edged cuts can be held together after cleaning with butterfly closures. These are similar in appliance to plasters, in as much that they have a sticky surface which adheres to the skin. The wound should be pinched together and the surrounding area needs to be completely dry before butterfly closures are applied.

INFECTION

Open wounds, including the presence of foreign bodies and lacerations, are all open to contamination and the development of infection. The amount of infection is directly related to the amount of time between wounding and treatment. The longer the delay, the greater the bacteria can multiply and start infection. Early treatment prevents the infection from becoming established, thus prompt and adequate treatment is most important in the fight against wound infection. Delays can lead to poor wound healing and even death. A course of suitable antibiotics will help control the infection. One or more of the following factors governs the main cause of wound infection:

- Delay in treatment.
- Inadequate cleaning of the wound.
- Foreign bodies left within the wound.
- Inadequate drainage.
- Non-sterile dressing.

FRACTURES

A major fracture may be very obvious with the bone sticking out of the flesh. If there are not visible signs, you should suspect a bone fracture if any or all of these signs are present:

- Difficulty in normal movement of any part of the body.
- Increased pain when movement is attempted.
- Swelling or bruising accompanied by tenderness in the area of the injury.
- Deformity or shortening of the injured part.
- Grating of bone heard during examination or attempted movement.
- Signs of shock.
- The survivor having heard or felt a bone break.

The only treatment available in a survival situation is immobilization of the fracture. Unless some other immediate danger threatens, splint the casualty before moving them. In any case, handle them with the greatest care to avoid further pain or additional injury. If there is a wound associated with the fracture, remove the clothing in the immediate area and treat the wound before fitting splints.

Splints can be improvised from sticks, branches, suitable pieces of wreckage, or equipment—even a tight roll of clothing or bedding. Pad the splint and fasten it so that it supports the joints above and below the fracture. A fractured leg can be partially immobilized by tying it to the good leg if nothing else is available. A fractured leg may be deformed, shortened, or twisted unnaturally. In such cases, realignment should be attempted before immobilization, if the casualty is prepared to allow it. Carefully and gently pull the end of the limb and reset or straighten it.

Fracture

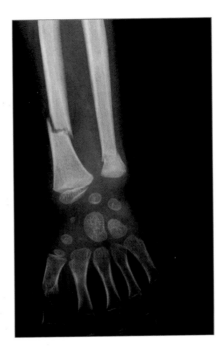

When all that is possible has been done, apply the splints. The only further help that can be given is to raise the injured part to cut down swelling and discomfort, and to treat any symptoms of shock. The casualty then needs rest.

Concussion / Skull Fracture

Terrorist bombings produce a lot of concussions and skull fractures. These are seen mainly in people who have been relatively close to the point of detonation. If a survivor is even briefly unconscious, if clear or blood-tinged fluid is coming from the ears or nose, or if the pupils of his eyes are unequal or unresponsive, then skull fracture or concussion should be suspected. If they are unconscious, their breathing and pulse should be monitored. If their breathing and pulse are normal, they should be placed in the coma position. If they are conscious, place them in a reclining position with head and shoulders supported in either case, keeping them warm and handle gently. Seek knowledgeable medical assistance as soon as possible. Symptoms of skull fractures include:

- Obvious injuries to the head.
- There may be blood or a clear, watery cerebrospinal fluid emitted from the ear or nose.
- The eyes may be bloodshot, turning to black (bruising) later.
- The pupils of the eyes may be unequally dilated.
- The person may lapse into unconsciousness.

Crush Injuries

In the majority of crush injures, some form of weight has fallen on the victim or the victim has been forced against an immovable object. In the first instance, the fallen object may still be covering the victim and will have to be removed prior to any treatment. In the latter case, it should also be fairly obvious how the crush injury occurred, i.e., the chest impacted with the steering wheel when the car was involved in an accident.

The removal of any weighted object from the body of a casualty should be done with care. Test the weight before attempting to lift the object as you may cause further damage to the victim—get help if available.

Once the object or casualty has been moved, check for breathing and circulation. Next, examine the casualty. The crush impact area should be correlated to the position of the impact object, i.e., if the driver of a car has hit an immovable object stopping the car suddenly, his chest may have impacted with the steering wheel. Check for broken ribs and internal organ damage such as to the heart and lungs.

Broken Ribs

A direct blow or an object falling on the chest normally causes rib fractures. Depending on the amount of force and the angle of the blow, rib fractures can be complicated by a sucking wound or breathing can be impeded. General signs of a rib fracture include:

- Sharp pain at the site of the fracture.
- Difficulty in breathing.
- Open chest wound.
- Bruising under the skin.

Treatment should be based on restoration of breathing and immobilizing the fracture. Lay the casualty down in a relaxed and sitting position with the head and shoulders supported and the body leaning towards the injured side. Place a pad over any exposed wound and hold this in place by placing the casualty's arm (injured side) in a sling. If a rib bone is exposed through the chest wall, then there is a strong possibility that the lung may also be damaged.

BURNS

The immediate aim when treating any burns is to lessen the ill-effects of the excessive heat. Do this by gently immersing the injured part in cold water or slowly pouring cold water over it. Continue with this treatment for up to twenty minutes or longer if the pain is not relieved. Cooling in this way will stop further damage, relieve pain, and reduce the possibilities of swelling or shock. Offer reassurance to the survivor.

A burn opens the way for infection to enter the body, which means that a dressing should be applied. A sterile, non-fluffy burn dressing is best, but any suitable piece of clean material will do. Dressings and bandages can be made fairly sterile by boiling or steaming them in a lidded container. Scorching of material will also kill most germs.

A solution of tannic acid will assist in the healing of burns. Tree bark boiled for as long as possible will provide this as well. Oak bark is the best source, but chestnut or hemlocks are also good alternatives, as any bark will yield some tannic acid. As the water boils away, replace it with more, adding extra bark if possible. A strong tea solution will provide the same assistance. Do not use either solution until cold.

If any restricting clothing or other item is being worn near the burned area, remove it before any swelling develops. Do not touch the burn, nor use any form of adhesive dressing. If any blisters form, do not break or drain them. They are a natural protective cover for

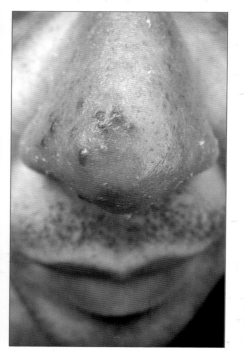

Burns

the injury and should themselves, be protected. If burns or scalds are severe, lay the survivor in a comfortable position as soon as possible. If he is unconscious, place him in the coma position. Remember these points:

- Cool the burned area by immersion in cold clean water or fresh snow.
- Protect hands and feet from further infection with a sealed polythene bag.
- Do not use adhesive or fluffy dressing.
- Do not break blisters or remove loose skin.
- Do not apply ointment, oils, or fats to the burn.

MEDICAL PACK

To be honest, I cringe every time I see a commercial medical pack. They offer little of value, other than the odd bandage and sticky plaster. As with the Disaster Grab Bag, whether or not you live in a disaster prone area, your home should contain a decent medical box. By this I don't mean a container packed with leftover medication; I mean a medical kit that will serve you and your family throughout your

Always have a good medical kit handy. (BCB Int. Ltd.)

daily lives. Here is a list of what I think you should put in a medical pack. Obviously, the contents will change slightly depending on your location. Additionally, if you or anyone in your home has some medical training you should adjust the items accordingly.

- **Large Wound Dressings:** Include at least four large and four medium wound dressings, plus four large burn dressings in your medical kit. As any soldier will tell you, always have if ready for immediate use.

- **Vent Aid:** Put at least two vent aids in your medical pack. When treating family, you are most probably safe when doing CPR, but if you are treating a stranger, use a vent aid.

- **Sharps:** A pair of good scissors, and a dozen or so mixed size safety pins. Two surgical blades take up little space and are best left in their protective sterile wrapping. In use, they can be held between the fingers or a handle can be fashioned from a small stick. Do not discard used surgical blades, sterilize by boiling and re-wrap.

- **Pain Control:** Aspirin will relieve mild pain, headaches, and reduce a fever. Carry a strip of about a dozen soluble aspirin tablets. Dihydrocodeine (similar to military DF118) also offers excellent pain control, but use only as prescribed.

- **Plasters:** Carry various sizes and shapes of waterproof plasters. Larger plasters are best as they can always be cut down if necessary. Keep your plasters together in a waterproof sachet.

- **Suture Plasters:** If you are unable to administer stitches, butterfly sutures will prove successful in closing small wounds.

- **Mosquito Repellent:** The chances of contracting malaria and other mosquito-carried diseases can be reduced if the correct precautions are taken. Anti-malarial tablets, as prescribed by a doctor and need to be taken; but it is just as important to deter the insects from biting you in the first place. Therefore, it is recommended that you include a mosquito/insect repellent in your kit.

- **Antihistamine Cream:** Antihistamine cream will soothe the severe itching and irritation that insect bites or allergies can cause. Antihistamine tablets can be carried as an alternative, but beware as some can cause drowsiness.

- **All-Purpose Antiseptic:** Potassium Permanganate crystals are easy to carry and provide an all-round sterilizing agent, antiseptic, and anti-fungal agent. A tube of general purpose antiseptic cream is also very handy.

- **Salt:** Salt is essential when traveling in tropical climates. Carry a small amount to make sure that the salt balance in the body is maintained. Try to reserve this resource for medical uses only and refrain from using it for culinary purposes.

- **Electrolyte Drinks:** Most survivors are guaranteed to suffer from dehydration. This can be occur in both hot and cold climates and is mostly attributed to diarrhea. While replacing water loss is the priority, body salts and minerals can also be replaced by adding an electrolyte drink.

- **Rescue Strop:** While this may seem like an odd thing to include in a medical pack during a disaster it could come in extremely handy, and almost all in the military carry them in Afghanistan to help rescue wounded soldiers. It's basically a webbing tape with a loop that fits over the shoulders and allows you to pull someone clear of danger. Ideally it should be about three and one half meters (ten and one half feet) and made of three centimeters (one and one half inch) of webbing tape.

- **Spare Medication:** If someone in your home is reliant on daily medication, you should include enough of the required medication to last for at least a week, preferably a month.

Chapter 13

MODERN SURVIVAL EQUIPMENT

This image shows an SAS
Disaster Grab Bag;
everything
I ever needed to survive
anywhere in the world.
(BCB Int. Ltd.)

The development of survival equipment has changed very little since WWII. There have been many advances, primarily in communications; both military and civilian communication devices will operate in just about every place we are likely to need help. These communications simply negate the need for carrying a large amount of survival equipment. Telling people where you are, using GPS accuracy, and guiding them into your location (signaling) really makes it so much easier for the rescue services and cuts down the amount of time we are in peril.

Almost all these functions can be found in the smart phone. True, there are times when a smart phone will not work and you need more conventional survival equipment, so to be on the safe side, I have made a list of both the old and newer items.

Once made, your Disaster Grab Bag is best kept in a good strong rucksack and every item within it should be assessed for its usage. This will mean that sometimes you will need to make difficult choices on what to include and what to leave out. Ultimately, each item must increase your chances of survival until help reaches you.

A selection of items which could potentially be included in a Disaster Grab Bag is listed below. The notes will help you to decide on their usefulness in different situations, i.e., do you live in an area prone to forest fires, or a location close to an earthquake fault? The final choice will be dependent upon your personal preferences, your skills, and the location and type of expected disaster.

DISASTER GRAB BAG

Throughout this book, I have talked about a Disaster Grab Bag; the bag that contains all the immediate things of use, during and after a disaster. Naturally, the contents will depend on your location and the type of disaster you are most likely to face.

I have seen many lists that provide for a Disaster Grab Bag, and while a few are suitable, most are rubbish, and so is the quality of the items included. The quality of the items selected for your Disaster Grab Bag is as important as selecting the items themselves. The last thing you need after a disaster is a bag full of junk!

Millions of people live in or close to a natural disaster zone and some 700 million die each year, and around 500 people die as a result of war or civil unrest. When the time comes and you need to run from a disaster, what will you be holding? With a Disaster Grab Bag, you will have everything you need to give you and your family the very best chance of survival—it's that simple.

Moreover, despite the millions of deaths that could have been prevented over the years if people had prepared a Disaster Grab Bag, in truth, few people will ever bother to prepare one. When they are swimming in the mire of a tsunami, or watching as their children suffer from injuries they cannot treat, it will be too late. To put it into context, you would not leave home without your wallet; it's normal, you may need it. The only difference is that you need your wallet most days and it becomes habit and part of your daily routine. You may never need a Disaster Grab Bag, that is, until the disaster is upon you.

If you think you can put off making a Disaster Grab Bag until during or after a major disaster, you are sadly mistaken. At best, you will finish up with a plastic grocery bag with a large bottle of water, a knife from the kitchen, some soup or beans, and a roll of sticky plaster. At worst, your home could be gone, your village gone, and help will not reach you for at least a week. Think about it seriously, if you live in an area prone to disaster, predictable or unexpected, make a Disaster Grab Bag!

Now I live in Spain. The question is, 'do I have a survival bag?' The answer is yes. There is no perceived threat to me, my family, or my home, other than forest fires. For this, I have a small rucksack which contains all the important documents: house deeds, insurance policies, passports, and cash. Both my wife and I have a spare suitcase which

Author's Note: When I was a soldier in the British SAS, I always carried a military survival kit. It was part of my belt equipment and it NEVER left my side during operations around the world. Those days, the survival kit was designed more for 'Escape & Evasion' than disaster survival, but the principle is still the same. I never had to use my survival kit, despite having been in many serious situations, as none were grave enough for me to open the pack; but the survival kit stayed with me for over eighteen years.

contains clean clothing and toiletries which is kept close to the safe. We always park our cars in such a way that we can easily drive away without having to turn or reverse, one at the rear entrance and one at the front. That's another thing I learned in the SAS: never park with the front of the car facing inward; always reverse into a parking spot. That way, your escape is quick and clean.

After I had built the house, I constructed a wall around it, the nearest point being ten meters away. This is my shield. I have also made sure that I have at least two escape routes that are clear of high vegetation or trees. I built my home with my labor, laying every block with care and love. I will not relinquish it without a fight. We are prepared with water points at each corner of the garden, a 36,000 liter underground reserve tank with high pressure pump, which is battery operated; there are no exposed combustible materials close to the house. Luckily for me and Mary, while I have seen many forest fires close by and the destruction of many homes, nothing has come close to us.

Making a Disaster Grab Bag

With a good Disaster Grab Bag, you will possess the resources to begin to make good use of your survival skills and techniques. Most important of all, your Survival Kit will be the catalyst which stimulates thought and provides the will to start building your defenses against the enemies of survival.

The personal Disaster Grab Bag is of the utmost importance. It should be carried on your person at any time when the possibility of a forthcoming survival situation exists. Pilots and some special forces are issued with escape and survival equipment, but it is easy for anyone to construct a basic Disaster Grab Bag. However, the choice of its contents is still crucial. That choice may vary according to the type and location of operation.

You may well be forced to compromise in your choice— between what you feel you need and the limitation on what can be carried. Your decision on the items to be included in the Grab Bag can only be made after all the items have been carefully considered. You must assess every item's usefulness, its adaptability, and its weight or bulk. This assessment has to be made, keeping in mind the strong possibility

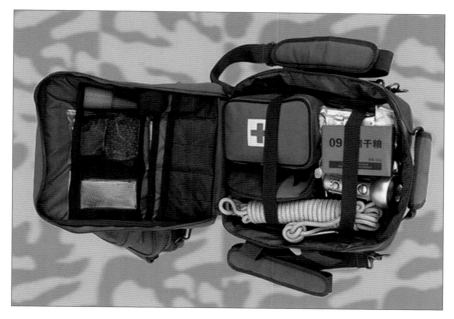

that the kit may be your only initial resource. You must select items on the criteria that together, they are small enough for you to carry at all relevant times, and that each will increase your chances of surviving or escaping. They will be the catalysts to essential action and will be the keys to open the store of natural resources, because they will be the tools with which your survival skills and techniques can be stimulated and utilized.

Another piece of advice, **'buy cheap, buy twice.'** The problem is that after a major disaster, you don't get a second chance. The Disaster Grab Bag you make may be all that stands between you and death. It represents the last hope you may have of surviving whatever perilous situation in which you may find yourself. Select survival equipment like your life depended upon it, because it just might.

Bear in mind that many Grab Bag contents are perishable or have expiration dates. Grab Bags require regular maintenance. Food, water, pyrotechnics, batteries, and medicines are among the items which always have a limited life. I always carried an escape kit as an SAS soldier, and I have had a Disaster Grab Bag ready in my home for over twenty years. Each January, I not only replace the perisha-

Think about what is useful for your Grab Bag and don't duplicate items. Lots of food is NOT a priority. Don't forget medication and baby food, if required. (Barry Davies)

bles but also review the items to see if something better has come on the market.

Finally, we must also take into account that the world has evolved and that we can now communicate far more efficiently, better than ever before. Society in most parts of the world has come to understand the need for swift responses to an emergency. Even in remote places, news of a disaster travels swiftly and the needed response by the rescue services and NGOs is rapid. A single phone call, text, or email is enough to get help.

Listed below is a selection of possible components of a Disaster Grab Bag. Together, this list is designed to aid anyone caught up in a disaster. In addition, I have added several other items required by those operating in a war zone.

Disaster Grab Bag (Contents List)

1 x Rucksack 30 liter. Pack everything inside.

1 x Spare mobile phone and battery if you have one.

1 x Disaster Survival Instructions.

1 x Cooker with plus 2 packs of fuel.

1 x Flint & steel fire lighter. Will light at least 2500 fires, wet or dry.

2 x Tinder cards. Will help start a fire with your flint & steel.

1 x Waterproof matches. Will light in heavy wind; will not go out even when placed in water.

4 x Candles with lantern. Beats batteries every time.

1 x Liter collapsible water container for water storage.

2 x Packs of water purification tablets (will treat 200 liters of water).

2 x Salt sachets for cooking and rehydration.

1 x Mess tin (cooking for 4 people).

4 x Spoons.

4 x Debren-type ration (5 year shelf life). Boring, but will sustain life.

1 x Bulk dried food, 850 grams (suitable for all religions), 4 people for 3 days with a 4 year shelf life.

1 x Mayday compact signaling mirror (with instructions). Best way to attract attention.

1 x Howler whistle, for use in the dark or fog.

1 x Solar / Dynamo radio and torch to listen to emergency reports and advice; also, a light and battery charger for your mobile phone.

4 x Printed bags (printed with survival instructions). Cheap but effective sleeping bag, will protect you from the worst elements.

1 x Parachute cord or similar (15 meters). A million uses.

1 x Small medical pack with instructions (treat small cuts and wounds).

2 x Sanitizing gel.

2 x Packs toilet paper (4 people for 3 days).

1 x Snap-Seal waterproof bag (for your private documents).

Mobile Phone

When I wrote my last survival book, I think I mentioned that a phone could be used as a signaling device at night, and that was the limit of its use. Today, the first survival tool I would recommend is a cell phone. Why? Because the world has grown up and there are now some 4.8 billon phone connects (July 2010) and a series of interlinking networks to support them. Besides, it is the quickest and easiest way of communication and getting help. A smart phone is best if you can afford it; BlackBerry, iPhone, or a Samsung Galaxy are all good examples. Why a smart phone? Simply because they also provide a host of other functions that can be extremely useful even when there is no network. GPS navigation / flash for signaling / light to guide your way in the darkness / instructions on how to survive / first aid manual and a whole host of other useful applications.

Your mobile phone will serve you well before, during, and after any disaster. (BlackBerry)

Mobile Phone Applications

Prior to, during, and more realistically after a major emergency or disaster, the networks will switch off the circuit switch / voice call functionality. They do this because with the amount of mobile phones now in circulation, and the amount of people wishing to make a call, the system would simply be overwhelmed by general public usage. However, many of the authorities, government agencies, and emergency services will retain a full voice service. The network

Begin chest compressions. If the victim is not breathing, place the heel of your hand in the middle of his chest. Put your other hand on top of the first with your fingers interlaced. Compress the chest at least 2 inches (4-5 cm). Allow the chest to completely recoil before the next compression. Compress the chest at a rate of at least 100 pushes per minute. Perform 30 compressions at this rate (should take you about 18 seconds).

There are many applications that would be beneficial after a disaster – CPR for example. (Barry Davies)

license to operate will contain certain clauses that allow the government to do this.

While a voice call may not be possible, both text and broadband internet will likely remain accessible by the public, as this operates on a different system. This means you can still text (the most common form of communication) and use the internet for email or to download information.

Although network disruption is common during a major disaster, it will soon become a thing of the past as new research is being developed that should start appearing around the start of 2012. This mesh network enables ordinary mobile phones to make and receive calls without the need for phone towers, Wi-Fi, or satellites.

Whereas there is very little you can do about the network disruption, you can at least make sure your battery is fully charged; better still, carry a spare battery with you when making long journeys in remote areas. Even when the network has been switched off, in order to allow the emergency services to operate more efficiently, there are still a lot of functionality with a mobile phone.

Pre-Disaster

Your mobile phone may be the first warning that you'll have of any pending disaster. Ideally, if you live in a disaster-prone area or are traveling to one, it would be beneficial to make sure you have a list of phone numbers in your contact list; these should include all family, close friends, local emergency services, etc. Remember, immediately after any major disaster, the networks will be limited, so if you are going to make a phone call for help or to assure a loved one, do it DIRECTLY.

Look after your Mobile Phone

The mobile phone is evolving at a rapid pace, as is network coverage. Nevertheless, it becomes a useless piece of technology if the battery is dead. A fully charged battery removed from the mobile will last for up to six months, in some cases up to a year. If your battery is getting low while in use, you might want to try pressing the keys *3370#; this sometimes releases the battery reserve, but does not work on every phone. Take care of your cell phone and treat it with respect, keeping it fully charged whenever possible. If you are venturing into the outback or a remote area, consider taking a solar charger with you. Better yet, invest in a wind-up mobile phone charger. That way, you will always have power, sun or not.

Make sure you program in the number 112, as this is the define mobile phone standard emergency number, so it will work on GSM phones even in North America where GSM systems redirect emergency calls to 911, or Australia where emergency calls are redirected to 000. It is one of

Any navigation application will help during a major disaster when streets and buildings have been reduced to debris. (Barry Davies)

Author's Note: A full list of mobile phone applications is found in Annex B at the end of this book.

two numbers (the other being the region's own emergency number) that can be dialed on most GSM phones, even if the phone is locked or has no SIM card. Once you dial 112, the mobile will search any existing network to establish the emergency number for you.

If you are lucky enough to have a spare smart phone for your Disaster Grab Bag, then download as many useful applications as possible, as these will work even without a network signal. Always remember: even with no network, you may still be capable of receiving Wi-Fi on your smart phone. This will give you access to many social network applications. These functions include a flashlight and compass, plus you can download emergency and medical applications which will help guide you.

Other Survival Items

Matches

A dozen or more kitchen matches that have been completely immersed in melted candle wax will be both waterproof and wind resistant. They should be carried in a waterproof container (an empty vitamin pill container is excellent).

Survival matches made to light and burn under any conditions, even underwater. (BCB Int. Ltd.)

Survival matches are now commercially available, which are windproof, waterproof, or both. These can be bought from most leading camping and outdoor pursuit shops, or found in ration packs. These better quality matches are packed in airtight containers, each match being handmade and coated with protective varnish, and burn for about twelve seconds when lit. They will not go out even if completely immersed in water or exposed to the strongest winds.

Flint and Steel Fire Lighter

This is a rugged and dependable item of equipment, which will provide thousands of opportunities to light fires

in all kinds of weather. It is best carried as part of a 'fire set,' which also incorporates other basic essentials for lighting fires in hostile conditions. It is a simple device whereby a hardened piece of steel with jagged teeth is drawn over a flint containing a high percentage of magnesium. This produces a large amount of hot sparks which, when fed into dry fire starter (tinder), will start a fire.

A good flint and steel fire lighter will light around 2000 fires wet or dry. Every fighter pilot has one in his emergency kit. (BCB Int. Ltd.)

Tampon or Fire Tinder

The secret of lighting a fire is down to the spark supply and the tinder. Over the years, I have experimented with many types of tinder and by far the best is the cotton wool in a tampon. It is now standard issue in most RAF pilot survival kits. Do not forget to blacken your cotton wool first with old charcoal, as it will accept the spark better; otherwise, invest in a few commercialized fire tinders.

Candle

A four-inch candle weighs less than one ounce, yet will burn for up to three hours if it is protected from the wind. The best choice is a candle made from 100% Stearin (solid-

Fire tinder is designed to aid when starting a fire under adverse conditions; you can also use cotton wool or old wound dressing. (BCB Int. Ltd.)

ified, edible animal fats). This will light in any temperature, serve as emergency food, and lubricate items as diverse as a zipper and the hand-held socket of a bow-drill fire maker. It is practically indestructible, being immune to dropping or soaking in water. Besides providing light, it will, if burning in a tin, make a heater for a small, snug shelter.

Survival Bag

One of the most frequent dangers to be faced in a survival situation is the involuntary loss of critical amounts of body heat. This loss occurs through convection, conduction, or radiation.

Several large black polythene bags used for garden fertilizer make an excellent survival bag. Once inside, the body is protected from wind and rain. Conductive heat loss can be minimized by placing the bag on insulating materials (bracken, straw, grass, etc.). The bag can also play a role in obtaining water, and as part of a shelter.

Printed survival bag. In the mayhem of a disaster it is easy to forget what to do next. This simple plastic sack will help keep you warm and is printed with basic survival tips as a reminder. (BCB Int. Ltd.)

Water Purification Tablets

These provide a quick and convenient way of sterilizing water. Each tablet will purify one liter of water in about ten minutes. The tablets will kill bacteria—but they do not remove any dirt present in the water. The treated water will taste of chlorine. Make sure to aim for carrying about fifty tablets in your kit.

Swiss Army Knife or Gerber

The Swiss Army knife, which incorporates extra blades, scissors, can and bottle openers, screwdrivers, and a saw among its many implements, is ideal. It is strongly recommended that a small pocket knife should be carried as a

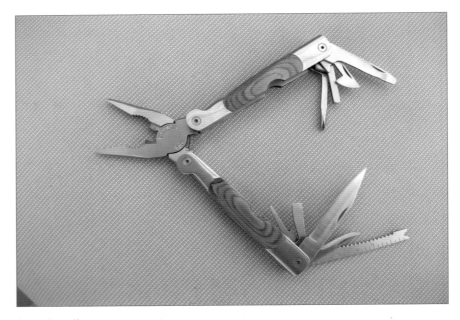

A good quality multi-tool will go much further than a knife. (BCB Int. Ltd.)

matter of course. Gerber and other manufacturers produce a great range of multi-tools which are extremely handy. When purchasing items, always buy good quality so you know it will last.

Parachute Cord or Strong String

Many a farmer will tell you that he never goes out without a quantity of string in his pocket. The same principle should apply to survivors, except you would be better off using a parachute cord. This extremely strong cord with a breaking strain of about 250 kilograms, is braided over strands of thinner cord, which can be pulled out and used for thread or fishing. Carry at least fifteen meters in length.

Heliograph

There are various types of heliographs on the market; most of them require a two-handed operation. In the past

Author's Note: Don't go buying a large survival knife like the type Rambo used. They are mainly useless, and after a disaster you are unlikely to see many bears or wild boar to kill and you might end up hurting yourself!

Heliograph designed for one-handed use and when used correctly, can flash a rescue helicopter some 20 miles away with great accuracy. (BCB Int. Ltd.)

few years, however, a new one-handed signaling mirror has entered the market and is very effective. The accuracy of these new heliographs is very high, but one should take time to practice the use before venturing into the wild. A heliograph is one of the best ways of attracting a helicopter.

Author's Note: Hiromitsu Shinkawa is a sixty-year-old man who was washed out to sea as the tsunami water receded after the earthquake in March 2011. He was at sea for forty-eight hours, clinging to what had been the roof of his house. By the time he was rescued, he had drifted some ten miles out at sea. He was quoted as saying, "No helicopters or boats that came nearby noticed me. I thought that day was going to be the last day of my life." A heliograph would have made a large difference.

An air marker balloon is a professional rescue beacon generally used in forests or jungle areas as it will rise above the trees. (BCB Int. Ltd.)

Fluorescent Tape and Light Sticks

Fluorescent tape comes in a variety of colors and is an extremely good item after any disaster. It will allow you to make items so other people will take notice; danger areas from falling debris, gas and electricity leaks or breakages, corrosive fuel, etc. It can also be used to mark a safe route in the dark, smoke, or fog. Cyalume light sticks can be used in the same way.

Air Marker Balloon

The air marker balloon is an advanced signaling device which was primarily designed for both military and Special Forces operating in forest or jungle areas. Its primary function is to indicate a location for a parachute drop or to request a rescue. When inflated it will rise to seventy-five meters above the ground (250 feet) and is held in place by a strong tether. The system is simple to use and can be operated by a single person, the main element being to inflate the balloon with the 136 liter of helium gas which comes as part of the kit. Once aloft, it provides a clear signal for any pilot to see and hone in on. Two chemical light disks can be attached to both sides of the balloon giving an excellent signal at night, especially if the pilot is wearing night vision goggles.

Smoke Grenade

One of the best devices you can have to signal distress is a smoke grenade. The military use these all the time to

Smoke grenades are a great way of attracting attention but make sure it's coloured smoke as disasters can produce lots of fires. (U.S. Military)

mark their position or to signal for a helicopter pickup. The main advantage of a smoke grenade is that it can be seen from both the ground and the air and will almost guarantee getting someone's attention.

While it is possible to make smoke from a wide variety of household materials, the system referenced below on the website link is good because it will allow you to make and store your smoke bomb safely prior to any disaster as part of your disaster equipment. After a disaster, plain white smoke can sometimes be mistaken for normal fire; therefore it is best to construct a colored smoke grenade. http://chemistry.about.com/od/chemistryhowtoguide/a/coloredsmoke.htm

Flare Set

In a survival situation, signal flares attract attention better than most other methods. A standard flare kit protectively houses up to nine different colored flares and a launch pistol. Great care should be taken when firing the flares, making sure to point the flare skywards before firing.

CONCLUSION

While I have always had a fascination with survival, its appliance to a disaster had not really crossed my mind very much. In researching and writing this book, however, my eyes have been opened. The sheer brute force of Mother Nature is awesome to say the least, and during the past few months while writing this book, hundreds of thousands of people have died from natural disasters. War, terrorism and civil unrest have come in at a close second.

This has been the focus of my writing; not to deliver a great volume on the subject of disasters, but simply to help you stay alive. YOU are the one that will make things happen if you are ever trapped by a disaster; even if you just think about this book, and it acts as a catalyst to get you thinking, it would all have been worth it.

Finally remember, we rarely arrive in a disaster zone without nothing. You will have the clothes you stand up in are wearing, a little money in your pocket, and yes, your cell phone. You are almost safe, so go into survival mode. However, do not go crazy. Work with Mother Nature, not against her. The animals have no tools or survival aids; they eat when there is food: do likewise. Do not build a fire if the weather is warm, do not carry water when surrounded by rivers or lakes, and do not go looting when there is fruit on the trees and vegetables in the ground.

APPENDIX A

GENERAL DISASTER SURVIVAL ADVICE

It's is a sad fact that the majority of people will not be prepared for any type of disaster. Today, we rely so heavily on others to help us during a crisis that we have forgotten how to help ourselves. Given the number of people currently on the planet and the way we live in towns and cities, it is most likely that you will find yourself with others. You will have left it to the last minute to make preparation; be without the means to protect yourself or the transport to move to safer place.

But if you are alive, then you will become a survivor. However, it takes much more than knowledge and skills to build shelters, get food, make fires, and travel without the aid of modern navigational devices to survive successfully. It takes what Americans do best; leadership, confidence, guts, and determination.

Yet, while it is always easy to say 'be prepared,' sadly in this modern world, we are seldom prepared. Despite the many warning signs of pending disasters, we still leave it to the last minute to be prepared, and in the end, it's usually too late. We wait to see what the television announcer tells

Authors Note: A Malaysian scout I worked with in the jungles of Asia once told me a story which still holds true to this day. One day, as we moved through the jungle, we came face to face with a large cat which bared its teeth and made a very angry hissing sound. The Malaysian scout simple shouted at the animal and it turned and ran off. I was impressed, until the scout told me 'it was not afraid, it was simple being cautious—that is how most animals survive!' Wild birds and animals steer clear of humans; it's not that they don't trust us; although many have good reason to, it's just that they are cautious, and withdrawal or fight is the simplest form of survival.

us to do, or listen to the disaster taking place just a few miles away. You need to act and think fast—let the animal instinct in you take over. When you see or hear something out of the ordinary, take caution; not because there is a direct threat, but because your senses tell you to.

Below is a list of the actions that will commonly apply to most disasters. If you do nothing more, please read and remember these actions. When a disaster is about to happen, do not wait for news of its arrival by the media—it will be too late. Get comfortable, wear suitable clothing, and be prepared to stay in the same clothes for several days. Most disasters will force you to move, so think about where you are going, and if with others, how you will all make the journey. You will almost be forced to live rough for a few days, and you may face several dangers. From my personal experience, I have highlighted the best tips and advice that I can provide.

Heed Early Warnings

With the exception of earthquakes, few natural or man-made disasters happen without some sort of warning; and while the warning time can vary from a minutes to several days, in most cases, there is enough time to make a decision. When you have decided that a move is necessary and practicable, it is better to implement your decision sooner rather than later. You will be stronger, your resources will be intact, and your resilience and mental ability will be at their best.

Make sure to always travel within your own or the groups capabilities. If there are some member of your group that is fitter and more active, use these as trial finders to lead your group through the best route. This is important if you have elderly people or infants with you. Trail finders will use more energy but should select a route that is easy, passable, and above all else, safe.

Always have a regular rendezvous point, somewhere prominent that everyone can remember, and a long term objective which everyone knows about just in case your party get split up. Even when the going is easy, always keep within the limits of the slowest person, unless circumstances force you to move quicker. Think responsibly and remember: it may be the case that you cannot save everyone, so do your best to save as many as possible. Do not sacrifice others in senseless rescue attempts unless you are confident you can do it.

Keeping Warm

We are all used to living in a temperature-controlled environment, in our homes, in the car or at work. When a disaster is imminent, dress for the occasion and be prepared to face the elements. The type of clothing and how you wear it will determine your body temperature. Using several thin layers will keep you far warmer than one thick layer, as they trap the warm air produced by the body functioning. Additionally, by adding or removing a layer, one is able to control the body's heat. If you are exerting yourself by walking at a swift pace, be aware that you will sweat and that the sweat will not only make your clothing wet, thereby exposing you more to the cold, but it will also degrade the fibers of the fabric. Therefore, when doing strenuous exercise, remove some of your under layers, replacing them once you have stopped. That way you will always have a dry layer next to your skin.

- Your underclothes (those next to your skin), should be made of a thin, cotton material— something like a loose fitting thermal cotton vest. This layer will absorb perspiration, thereby removing excess moisture from the skin. It is important that this layer is changed frequently and kept as clean as possible.
- The next layer ideally should be a garment that can be fastened at the neck and wrists, thereby trapping the warm air. For example, a thick wool shirt or zip-up collar type- sweater.
- A third layer should consist of a fleece-type jacket that can easily be removed when the body begins to overheat.
- Finally, choose an outer garment that is wind and, if possible, waterproof. This could be made from tightly woven cotton, polycotton, fiber-pile material, or nylon. It should be fitted with a good hood, protecting as much of the head and face as possible. Garments made from such materials as Gore-tex are excellent, as they allow trapped vapor to permeate through the fabric and reduce overheating.

Unexpected Overnight Camp

When forced to move, you will almost certainly find your-self in need of an overnight place to make shelter. In most cases, you will find a suitable building but in areas where the devastation has been catastrophic; however, it may be necessary to spend a night outdoors. Such a situation will test all your skills of improvisation and former camping experience. In reality, you should have about your person some form of minimal survival kit; however, you may have only what you stand-up in. If you are alone, you must formu-late your own actions. If in a group, you must rely on the judgment of the group leader or senior person.   T h e leader of any survivor group should have enough experi-ence to improvise a basic shelter from the materials in the area. Just as importantly, they should be able to keep the hopes of the group high, yet realistic. The chances of surviv-al for a party that has given up hope will be a lot less than those with a sense of optimism.

Emergency Shelter

When no buildings are available, make for any forested areas, as this location will provide many opportunities to make a shelter. Fallen logs can be used to make an espe-cially simple type. Move two fallen logs so that they are close to each other and dig a trough between them. Cover the area over the top of the logs with branches, foliage, or

A realistic shelter after any disaster can be made from anything that comes to hand, especially if it is on safe ground, warm, and dry.

Authors Note: With all emergency shelter sites, check for the possibility of dangers. Shelters by water, especially if they are in the lowlands, may be susceptible to sudden flooding. Coastal sites may be in danger from high tides or storms. An area of fallen trees in a forest may signify that the area has a shallow soil. In high winds, trees could blow over and crush you; however, one which has already fallen will not prove a danger and may even provide you with the convenient beginnings of a shelter. Be aware of the possibility of rock-falls and mudslides, so always check for visible evidence of previous rock or mudslides in the area.

bark. Building a shell-like frame and covering it with bark shingles forms a good shelter.

There are several forms of emergency shelter shown previously in this book, but the common lean-to type of shelter is the one most commonly built, as it is the simplest to construct. The only important thing to remember is to build it so that the roof slopes down into the prevailing wind. The frame itself could be covered by any material that is available: plastic sheeting, foliage, a ground sheet, wreckage panels from destroyed homes, etc. Turf blocks or a firm, dried mud layer on top of foliage provides an excellent cover as it is both water-proof and wind-proof and will not blow away. Once the roof has been established, the sides can also be filled-in, using a similar mud and foliage or turf construction. With a little time and innovation, a simple lean-too can be turned into a comfortable dwelling as indicted in the photograph.

Carbon Monoxide Poisoning

While it is man's nature to make any dwelling warm and comfortable by having some form of heating, always make sure your shelter has good ventilation. Carbon monoxide poisoning can easily happen if you burn a fire or a stove in an unventilated place, such as a tent or temporary shelter. Some types of gas are colorless and odorless, and usually once you realize that you are being poisoned, you may lack the energy to escape. It is best to be aware of the dangers and make sure that you have adequate ventilation and that your flame burns blue instead of yellow. The symptoms of carbon monoxide poisoning are headaches, lethargy, confusion, nausea, and vomiting, followed by distressed breathing and loss of consciousness. Get the casualty into the fresh air as quickly as possible, put out the offending stove or fire, and ventilate the shelter.

Food

If you have time before the disaster strikes, always drink as much water as you can and eat some food before you leave your home—it maybe some time before your next meal. If you did not make a 'Disaster Grab Bag,' fill your pockets with anything that you can eat or drink, but do not burden yourself or delay too long before you move.

Author's Note: For many years while I was senior survival instructor at the International Long Range Patrol School (ILRRPS) in Southern Germany, I would have many American and European military pilots on my courses. The one thing I would teach them about food was the availability of rodents. For many years I would buy from South America a tinned food from a company called 'Star' which is RATS backwards—and yes, it was rat meat, and I would feed this to the students. Just as a matter of interest, you prepare any rodent just as you would a rabbit, but discard the guts and head. Not that I would advise eating rodents unless absolutely necessary, but they will be plentiful after most disasters.

A quarter of all mammals belong to a species of rodent or Myomorpha. They are found all over the world except in Antarctica and the high Arctic, and are found in every kind of habitat. Most of them are small, ground-dwelling animals, with the common house mouse and brown rat being typical. In general, they are seed-eating vegetarians, although many species such as the brown rat have developed much broader tastes. Others have specialized; the root and bamboo rats, for example, are burrowing animals that feed mainly on the roots of plants by gnawing them off beneath the surface. Rodents eat any kind of food that people eat. They also contaminate ten times as much food as they eat, with urine, droppings, and hair. They can carry at least ten different kinds of diseases, including bubonic plague, murine typhus, spirochetal jaundice, Leptospirosis, rabies, ratbite fever, and bacterial food poisoning. However, throughout man's history, they have been a source of food, especially during times of great disasters or famine. For although the rodent is dirty, the inner flesh is edible and nourishing.

How to Move in the Dark

At times it may be necessary to move in the dark, especially when a member of your party has been seriously injured and requires immediate medical attention, or if you notice that danger approaches. Of course, it is better to stay put, but if moving in darkness is the only option in your situation, you need to know the safest ways of doing this. Move only as far as you need to get out of immediate danger or to make contact with medical help. To venture further in darkness when it is not necessary is to risk further injury. Although being in complete darkness can be frightening, stay calm and take stock of the situation. Check that you have no other source of lighting on you. If you are moving with other people, make sure that everyone stays in touching distance with the next person. If you have a rope or lifeline, rope everyone together.

Unless a life really depends on it, do not try crossing a river or flood waters in darkness, as it is extremely dangerous and if you must, use one of the techniques described in river crossing below. While it is a good idea to follow a stream of river on the flat, never follow water down a steep mountainside, as it will inevitably have a waterfall somewhere; and even if it's a small one, it will be enough to injure you in the dark.

Using the Senses

You may find that your senses become heightened in the dark, and this is a good thing, for you can use them to your advantage. However, be aware that heightened senses means that even familiar noises may sound much closer and louder and to some maybe un-nerving. Stay calm, and keep a dialogue going with yourself or each other if necessary. Try to gain quality 'night vision.'

The best way to achieve night vision is by waiting until the eyes have become accustomed to the darkness, and maintaining it by shutting out any bright light source, such as a torch or car-headlight. If you must look at a bright light once you have your night vision, always cover one eye to protect it. Remember though, that low light conditions can cause the eye to be deceived, especially by distance. It is vital to use all the body senses when walking at night.

Authors Note: When I first joined the army, I was told by one of the instructors that if I kept my mouth open during darkness, it would increase my sound reception. Whether this is true or not, I have always done it, and find that it does work. Likewise, during the many night-time operations I carried out during my time with the SAS made me realize that mans' primeval senses have not been completely eradicated. Many an occasion when danger was imminent, the senses reached out into the darkness and often tingle the brain with a warning. Over the years I have learned to accept and become cautious when these odd feeling arise, warning my when danger is pending. One thing that I have learned is not to be afraid of the dark, because animals will avoid you, and other humans will be equally as unsure as you are.

Memory

If you intend on traveling at night, have a good look at the terrain over which you will travel while it is still light out. Prior to the onset of darkness, you should have a good idea of the surrounding countryside. If your memory is good, it may aid you in finding a route out in the dark. Distance can be confusing, as you will be forced to move slower, so try if possible to locate features that you can identify. If you have no idea of your exact location, always move cautiously downhill. Finding a stream or river will normally lead you to the safety of a road or track; however, you should avoid walking to close to the edge in darkness.

Navigation by Night

Navigation by the stars has been used for centuries, and is still employed in map making. Learning about the stars is beneficial in itself, but this knowledge comes into its own in survival navigation. Bright stars that seem to be grouped together in a pattern are called constellations. The shapes of these constellations and their relationships to each other do not alter. Because of the earth's rotation, the whole of the night sky appears to revolve around one central point, and using this knowledge can help you to find directions.

In the Northern Hemisphere, a faint star, called Polaris, the Pole, or the North Star, marks the central point. Because of its position, it always appears to remain in the same place, located above the North Pole. As long as Polaris can be seen, the direction of True North can be found.

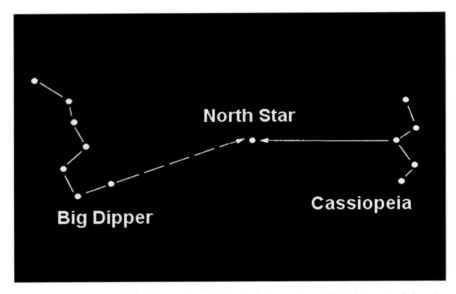

North Star

Cassiopeia

Big Dipper

To find Polaris, first locate the constellation known as 'The Plough' or 'The Big Dipper.' The two stars furthest from the 'handle' always point towards Polaris. Take the distance between the two stars and then follow the line straight for about six times the distance. At this point, you will see the Pole Star.

If you are unsure which way to look or wish to confirm that you have found Polaris, look for another constellation called Cassiopeia. The five stars that make up this constellation are patterned in the shape of a slightly squashed 'W.' It is positioned almost opposite the Plough, and Polaris can be found midway between them. As long as the sky is clear, the Plough, Cassiopeia, and Polaris remain visible in the sky all night when seen from any country north of 40 degrees N. latitude.

Crossing Water

After some disasters, such as a tsunami or heavy flooding, you may be required to cross deep and treacherous waters. While small or narrow rivers and streams are easily crossed by jumping or wading if shallow enough, larger stretches of water demand much more respect. Of course, it is best to avoid the situation in the first place by careful route planning and sticking to higher ground, but this is not always possible. Even when confronted with a major water obstacle, it may be possible to follow the water's edge and circumvent the problem.

Never attempt to cross a rain-swollen river, as they are deep, very fast, and highly dangerous. During periods of heavy rain, the water flow in rivers can fluctuate rapidly and conversely, once the rain has stopped, the water level may drop quickly too. Bearing this in mind, you should decide whether it is best to wait for the water level to drop or whether it is viable to find another place to cross safely. Crossing a strong flowing or deep water is no light decision and should only be considered as an emergency procedure, a last resort when any other decision would compromise health or safety further.

Crossing without a rope should not normally be attempted; however, if it is certain that a crossing can be safely undertaken and if the water level is relatively low, then there are certain methods by which this may be achieved. While a group of people offers support and stability, always use the strongest swimmer to go first. If you find yourself in a situation where you must cross water alone, follow the procedures below.

Crossing Alone

If under normal circumstances, a water crossing is deemed possible, choose the widest, slowest point, avoiding bends, as the speed of the current will increase when wading from the inside of the bend to the outside, as will the depth of water. Wade through rather than jumping from stone to stone. Even a simple slip can result in an immobilizing sprain or other injury—and perhaps loss of equipment. If you have a rope, the crossing should be secured to the bank and used as a safety-line. Use a solid stick as an extra point of contact and to probe the water bed.

Crossing without a Rope

If the water is slow but deep, consider swimming across. Securing your rucksack in a tightly tied bin-liner will form an excellent floatation aid. Weak swimmers can take off their trousers, wet them before knotting the legs ends,

gripping the waistband, and swing the trousers over the head in an arc-like motion. This will trap air in the trouser legs and provide a good floatation aid.

If you are in a group, then three people standing side by side together, arms linked around each other's shoulders, with the weakest swimmer in the middle is a good method. Move across the water with the strongest member against the flow of the current. Moving slowly and supporting each other if one should stumble or fall. Take care when entering and leaving the water, especially if the banks are steep; hold onto the bank and help the weakest person out first.

Elderly and infirm people should be given full support on both sides; likewise, very young children should be carried 'piggyback style.'

Water Crossing Techniques with a Rope

One of the most common ways to cross water is to secure a safety line between two banks. This requires the rope to be taken to the opposite bank by the first person, who should also be the strongest swimmer. When making their way across, either wading or swimming, they should adopt one of the methods described about. They should also be secured to the safety-line so that they can be pulled back if they get into difficulty. Once across and the line is secured, each person should use a Karabina, or rope loop to clip onto the line before crossing. The last person across should unclip the safety-line and attach it to their body before crossing, in order that they may be pulled across if necessary.

Once you have crossed the water, you are likely to be cold with your morale a little on the low side. Change into spare dry clothing, if you don't have any, seek the nearest shelter and get yourself warm and dry.

- Plan your route to avoid having to cross water.
- Always look for a bridge or safe crossing first.
- Cross only if absolutely necessary.
- Choose the widest and shallowest stretch.
- **Never,** unless life threatening attempt to cross a river in flood.
- If alone use a buoyancy aid.
- Use a safety line if available.

Disease

After any major disaster, specially flooding, disease spreads quickly. You should not attempt to enter or walk across an area of land that you know to be contaminated. You may not be putting yourself at risk, but the damage of transmitting the disease from one place to another, and thus, infecting others is very high. In rural areas, dead animals, cats, dogs, cattle, pigs etc., will almost certainly be dead after major flooding. Their bloated bodies will quickly contaminate the waters. Likewise, in urban areas, refuse, rats, sewers, and dead animals will pollute the area; even when the waters have receded, the disease remains. Flies and other insects will feed and transmit the disease rapidly. As we have seen recently in Thailand, the largest risk from contaminated water comes in the form of digestive disorders or the infection of cuts to the hands and legs. While normal medical aid should take priority, if these are not available there are several herbal alternatives which I have used successfully over the years.

Digestive disorders

An excellent cure for diarrhea is rushed charcoal and an herbal tea. Simple wood charcoal from last night's fire crushed and put in hot water is a great remedy for unset stomach. Remember to keep your fluid intake high when

The great thing about the Dandelion is that everyone recognizes it, and it is a great survival food and herbal medicine.

suffering from diarrhea. In addition, you might also try these other simple remedies.

Dandelion (Taraxacum officinale) leaves, washed and eaten raw, or cooked like spinach, make an excellent aid to digestion. Try to include some in your survival diet as a preventative.

Dog rose (Rose conino) petals and/or hip are a very good stomach settler. Before eating any of the vitamin-C-rich hips, remove the hairy seeds inside them.

Antiseptic

Open cuts and wounds are very vulnerable to contamination from dirt or flood waters. To prevent wounds from becoming infected, they can be washed with an infusion made with these herbal medicines:

Greater plantain (Plantago major) leaves and stems. In an emergency, chew the leaf of this plant to a pulp and use it directly on the wound.

Selfheal (Prunella vulgoris) flowering stems. This plant too can be chewed, for a quickly prepared pulp.

Dried burdock (Arctium lappo) root, made into an infusion. This is ideal to prepare for long journeys. The leaves can also be infused but are less potent.

Birch (Betula pen dub) leaves when infused make an all-purpose disinfectant.

Signaling

One of the best ways to get yourself rescued is to make contact with the rescue services; but to do this, you must make yourself visible. Signaling is a means of communication which can take the form of shape, sound, silhouette, and sight. Sound can encompass anything from shouting, and whistling, to using a mobile phon. Sight can mean using a signaling mirror to making a smoking fire. Whichever signaling method you choose will depend on what equipment is available and the conditions you find yourself in. For example, a direct link via a mobile phone, survival radio, or satellite phone will produce rapid rescue results; by contrast, the light from a signal fire will only be seen one the search aircraft are flying over your location, and after a major disaster there can be lost of small fires.

Signal Fires

A signal fire needs to be ready and lit at a moment's notice; therefore, all the tinder and wood must be dry. The fire is constructed so that the tinder is in the middle, ready for lighting. The aim is that once the tinder is lit, all the other fuel should light easily and burn without too much effort on your part. This type of fire needs to be protected from water; therefore, you should try to shelter any signal fire. If you are able, build three of these fires in a triangle, thirty meters apart. Make sure that the ground around the fire is adequately cleared of vegetation so that the fire will not spread beyond its boundaries once lit. Using any oil or petrol that you may have can speed up ignition.

Your rescue may come at any time, night or day. When the moment arrives, remember that you'll need to produce the contrast. Produce white smoke by burning green or damp vegetation added to a very hot fire. Burning oil or rubber (old vehicle tires) will produce black smoke. At night, a large bright fire gives the clearest signal. To work properly, the signal fire must stand out from its background. In any event, the most important thing is to make sure that your signal fire is going to light quickly and burn fiercely, thus increasing your chances of being seen and therefore rescued.

Signal Contrast

As I have mentioned, some disasters create many small fires, which makes it difficult for the rescue services to associate your fire from the others. Disrupting the normal pattern of the terrain creates contrast. Do this by introducing regular shapes that do not naturally occur: circles, squares, letters or straight lines. A large circle, with minimum diameter of three meters can be made using stones or some contrasting material. On sand, use rocks, sticks, cacti, or seaweed. Choose the things which make the best contrast against the background surface. If air marker panels are available, use these first and construct improvised signals secondly. If you require specific help is indicated by these internationally recognized signals:

It is possible to make a distress signal even when swimming in the water, simply form a larger group and make it easier for the rescue helicopter or boats to see you.

I	Have seriously injured
Δ	Safe to land here
SOS	Save Our Souls

If any possible rescuers are seen or heard, use any available clothing or material, such as flags, and keep waving. If you have foil survival blanket and the sun is shining, use this as a giant mirror. Do anything that will catch a searcher's eye.

Human Signal

We always think of surviving on dry land, but after many disasters, you may find yourself surrounded by water. The vast bland uniformity of the wide flood waters make searching extremely difficult. If search aircrafts have no identifying signal on which they can fix a position, their efforts will resort to a visual observation. Added to this, when the water is deep, only the head and shoulders are visible. One method for any number of survivors is to band together as this will provide a much better chance of being spotted. A flotation circle or conga line will form an excellent human marker.

APPENDIX B

LIST OF USEFUL WEBSITES FOR DISASTERS, WEATHER, WAR

If you find yourself in a pending disaster, be it Mother Nature or man-made, you could do worse than check out the appropriate websites below to see what happening and stay up-to-date with events. Those selected cover mainly America and the United Kingdom, but there is a whole host out there that you can Google to cover just about any disaster on the planet.

http://www.fema.gov/
http://www.dhs.gov/index.shtm
https://www.cia.gov/library/reports/archived-reports-1/
 Ann_Rpt_2003/swtandhs.html
http://www.homeoffice.gov.uk/counter-terrorism/current-
 threat-level/
https://www.mi5.gov.uk/
http://www.weather.gov/
http://nowcoast.noaa.gov/
http://wwwghcc.msfc.nasa.gov/GOES/
http://stormadvisory.org/map/atlantic/
http://www.weather.com/newscenter/hurricanecentral/
 update/index.html
http://globaldisasterwatch.blogspot.com
http://www.accuweather.com/
http://ibiseye.com/#
http://www.myfoxhurricane.com/
http://www.wunderground.com/
http://www.stormpulse.com/

APPENDIX C

LIST OF USEFUL MOBILE PHONE AND IPAD APPLICATIONS

While I have tried several of the applications below, many I have not, —so you try them at your own risk. Additionally, I have tried to select those applications which are free—free is good. If you intend to download and use any of these applications, please do so before you venture off on your travels. Google Latitude is possibly one of the best free phone applications around and it works on just about any modern platform, added to which it's free (thank you, Google). There are lots more out there and new applications are being built every day, so stay tuned. Finally, you may never need any of the applications, but for those that do:

BlackBerry

Google Latitude
TrackMe
DisasterAlert, Cost: $29.99
Mobile First Aid & CPR Guide, Cost: $2.99
Mobile Paramedic, Cost: $9.99
One Touch Flashlight, uses the video lite which is very bright (great app)
BAKLight turns your blackberry into a torch (free)

iPad and iPhone

Google Latitude
SAS Survival Guide by Lofty Wiseman is highly recommended. It will cost you around $6.00, but you can get a free Lite version.
Ship Captain's Medical Guide by Double Dog Studios

SOS iEmergency
AccuWeather Free for iPad
MyFoxHurricane

Android

Google Latitude

Red Cross S.O.S: This is a real must for anyone with an
Android phone or pad; really brilliant (free)

U.S. Army Survival Guide: Puts the entire U.S. Army Survival Guide on your phone, and it works offline.

FlashDroid turns your phone screen into a torch (free)

Windows Mobile

Google Latitude.

Linterna is a Windows Mobile tool which sets the brightness
to maximum with a white paper so it can be used as a
torch (free).

Pocket LiTE is a quick and easy torch app for your Windows
Mobile device with SOS function.

DEFINITIONS

Aftershocks—Smaller earthquakes following the main earthquake.

Al Qaeda—A global militant group founded by Osama Bin Laden.

Ammonium nitrate/fuel oil (ANFO)—A mixture of fertilizer and diesel oil to make explosives.

Body waves—Deismic waves that propagate from earthquake focus to the surface; classified as primary (P) and secondary (S) waves.

Carbon Monoxide Poisoning—A toxic gas that is colorless, odorless, tasteless and non-irritating, making it very difficult to detect.

Disaster—Defined as an occurrence that causes great distress or destruction.

Elastic Rebound Model—States that the sudden release of stored strain in rocks results from movement along a fault.

Epicenter—Location on earth's surface that lies directly above the focus of an earthquake.

Euskadi Ta Askatasuna (ETA)—Armed separatist organization of the Basque region.

Explosive Ordnance Disposal (EOD)—Men and women of our armed forces who deal with explosive devices.

Federal Emergency Management Agency (FEMA)—A department of U.S. Homeland Security, this is one of the best places to seek advice on any disaster.

Focus—Zone within earth where rock displacement produces an earthquake.

Fujita Scale.—This scale is an indicator of the damage we can expect, depending on the speed of the tornado.

Improvised Explosive Device (IED)—A type of home-made bomb widely used by terrorist.

Irish Republican Army (IRA)—Was a republican revolutionary military organization.

Lithosphere—Rigid outer layer of earth, including the crust and upper mantle.

Major Supply Routes (MSR)—Roads travelled by military convoys.

Modified Mercalli Intensity Scale—Measures the intensity of an earthquake.

Moment Magnitude Scale (MMS)—A method of measuring earthquakes' intensity.

National Oceanic and Atmosphere Administration (NOAA)— A federal agency focused on the condition of the oceans and the atmosphere.

Non-Government Organization (NGO)—A legally constituted organization that can work independently of government to supply those in need with advice, medical assistance, water, food, and shelter.

Post-Traumatic Stress Disorder (PTSD)—A severe nervousness disorder as a result of exposure to the sights of war or disaster.

Richter Scale—Measures the magnitude of an earthquake

Search and Rescue (SAR)—Organizations that use all possible means to locate people who are lost or caught up in a disaster. Also used to rescue downed pilots and retrieve Special Forces working behind the lines.

Secondary Effects—Non-tectonic surface processes that are directly related to earthquake shaking.

Seismic Gap Theory—States that strong earthquakes are unlikely in regions where weak earthquakes are common and the longer the quiescent period between earthquakes, the stronger the earthquake will be when it finally does break loose.

Seismograph—Instrument that records earthquake waves, helps locate the epicenter and focus of an earthquake.

Special Air Service (SAS)—United Kingdom's Elite Special Forces.

Subduction Zone—A long, narrow zone where one lithospheric plate descends beneath another.

Surface Waves—Seismic waves that travel along the outer layer of the earth; classified as Love and Rayleigh waves.

Theory of Plate Tectonics—States that the lithosphere is divided into a number of relatively rigid plates that collide with, separate from, and translate past one another at their boundaries; this disruption commonly results in earthquakes.

Tsunami—A natural phenomenon consisting of a series of waves generated when water in a lake or the sea is rapidly displaced on a massive scale. The effects of a tsunami can range from unnoticeable to devastation.

Unmanned Combat Air Vehicle (UCAV)—An unmanned aircraft capable of delivering weapons.

Volcanic Explosivity Index (VEI)—A measurement of volcano activity developed jointly by the U.S. Geological Survey and the University of Hawaii.

Index